Progress in IS

More information about this series at http://www.springer.com/series/10440

Marko Nöhren

Enterprise Software Sourcing Performance

The Impact Logic of On-Demand, On-Premises, and In-House Software on Dynamic Fit and Process-Level Performance Outcomes in Client Organizations

Marko Nöhren
University of Mannheim
Mannheim, Germany

This book is based on a doctoral thesis successfully defended at the Business School of the University of Mannheim

ISSN 2196-8705   ISSN 2196-8713   (electronic)
Progress in IS
ISBN 978-3-319-23924-8   ISBN 978-3-319-23926-2   (eBook)
DOI 10.1007/978-3-319-23926-2

Library of Congress Control Number: 2015955262

Springer Cham Heidelberg New York Dordrecht London
© Springer International Publishing Switzerland 2016

Printed on acid-free paper

Springer International Publishing AG Switzerland is part of Springer Science+Business Media (www.springer.com)

To my family

Acknowledgments

The process of developing and writing this book has been an enriching experience. I would like to thank all those people who have supported my work and personally accompanied me during my time as a research assistant at the University of Mannheim.

First and foremost, I would like to thank my academic advisor Prof. Dr. Armin Heinzl. I very much appreciate the freedom of research he gave me. He always encouraged me to develop my own ideas, while at the same time offering insightful comments and pragmatic advice.

I would like to express very special thanks to Prof. Dr. Michael Rosemann, who invited me to a research stay at Queensland University of Technology in Brisbane, Australia. He taught me how to think "out of the box" and to pursue innovative ideas in academic research. It was a great pleasure to work with Michael and I am grateful that we kept in touch ever since.

As a part of my empirical study, I had the opportunity to conduct interviews with CIOs, CEOs, and IT managers in multiple companies. I very much appreciate the insightful conversations. I am very thankful for the time and effort that the participants invested to support my research and me.

This study was partially supported by the research project "ProdIT—Productivity of IT-based Services" as part of the "Strategic Partnership—Productivity of Services," led by the Fraunhofer IAO. I thank all project members from the Center for European Economic Research and Pierre Audoin Consultants for valuable discussions.

I had the pleasure to spend 3 years as a research assistant at the Department of General Management and Information Systems at the University of Mannheim, Business School. I would like to thank the team and especially my former colleagues Tommi Kramer, Kai Spohrer, Alexander Scheerer, Saskia Bick, Christoph Schmidt, Erik Hemmer, Sebastian Stuckenberg, Thomas Kude, Jens Förderer, Lars Klimpke, Miroslaw Lazic, Sven Scheibmayr, Aliona von der Trenck, and Tillmann Neben for a great and unforgettable experience. A special thank goes to Niklas Schwarzer, who supported me as a working student. I also thank all the students, who supported the ProdIT project.

Furthermore, I would like to thank Professor Dr. Irene Bertschek and Prof. Dr. Christian Becker for serving as members of my dissertation committee. The German Federal Ministry of Education and Research (BMBF) and the German Academic Exchange Service (DAAD) supported this research.

Mannheim, July 2015   Marko Nöhren

List of Abbreviations

AMCIS	Americas Conference on Information Systems
BEA	Bescheinigungen elektronisch annehmen
BWW	Bunge Wand Weber
CEO	Chief executive officer
CIO	Chief information officer
CMS	Campus management system
COO	Chief operations officer
CRM	Customer relationship management
ECIS	European Conference on Information Systems
ELENA	Elektronisches Entgeldnachweis-Verfahren
EMEA	Europe, the Middle East and Africa
ERP	Enterprise resource planning
HTML	Hypertext markup language
ICIS	International Conference on Information Systems
IH	In-house
IT	Information technology
KBV	Knowledge-based view of the firm
MIDS	Management information and decision support
N.A.	Not applicable
OD	On-demand
OP	On-premises
PACIS	Pacific Asia Conference on Information Systems
PCS	Procurement system
POS	Point-of-sale
RBV	Resource-based view of the firm
RDT	Resource-dependence theory
RIT	Representational view on information technology
RQ	Research question
SCM	Supply chain management

SEPA	Single Euro Payments Area
SET	Strategic-economical-technological
TCE	Transaction cost economics
WHS	Warehousing system

Contents

List of Figures

List of Tables

Chapter 1
Introduction

1.1 Problem Statement

Today, organizational business processes depend more than ever on information technology (IT) and are significantly influenced by their efficiency, their effectiveness, and their reliability (Bertschek et al. 2014). As a consequence, the global IT market is growing by more than 8 % annually (Bartels et al. 2010). On this market, the corporate software sector is one of the fastest growing segments (Bartels et al. 2010; Lo et al. 2009). With an overall turnover of approximately US$400 billion, the corporate software market holds a share of more than 16 % of the global IT purchases (Bartels et al. 2010). In this market segment, process-centric enterprise software—such as enterprise resource planning (ERP) systems and individual components for customer relationship (CRM) or supply chain management (SCM)—constitutes one of the largest and most severe IT investments (Agarwal and Sambamurthy 2002; Luo and Strong 2004; Shang and Seddon 2002; Sia and Soh 2007; Strong and Volkoff 2010). Following the latest market data, the global ERP market shows an annual growth of 2.2 % and reached in 2012 an overall turnover of US$25.8 billion with SAP (25 %), Oracle (13 %), Sage (6 %), Infor (6 %), and Microsoft (5 %) as biggest players (Forbes 2013).

Process-centric enterprise software has shifted from a substantial operational to a strategic success factor for companies (Chen et al. 2010; Wang et al. 2008a). Sophisticated enterprise systems contribute to generating superior business processes, to maximize an organization's performance, to increase user satisfaction, and to support the company's growth. However, despite a growing market and an increasing strategic value of such systems, large and small organizations around the globe face the same fundamental dilemmas: scarce financial resources (e.g. Bartels et al. 2010; Bélissent et al. 2010), alignment and performance issues in enterprise software's post-implementation phase (e.g. Maurer et al. 2012; Sia and Soh 2007; Strong and Volkoff 2010; Swanson and Ramiller 2004) as well as an increasing complexity of software sourcing (e.g. Nöhren et al. 2014; Schwarz et al. 2009).

© Springer International Publishing Switzerland 2016
M. Nöhren, *Enterprise Software Sourcing Performance*, Progress in IS,
DOI 10.1007/978-3-319-23926-2_1

Scarce financial resources Since the time of economic downturn in 2009 and a very slow recovery from this financial crisis, IT decision makers have been more and more confronted with cost pressures and lower monetary resources (Bélissent et al. 2010; Luftman et al. 2013; Matzke et al. 2009). Business value of IT is tremendously important but a highly controversial subject for researchers and practitioners (e.g. Bélissent et al. 2010; Dehning and Richardson 2002; Melville et al. 2004). In the light of increasing financial pressures, the question raised: Is IT—and especially large-scale enterprise systems—boon or bane? Consequently, boosting IT productivity is the name of the game and is increasingly understood as one essence of a company's competitiveness and profitability (Bélissent et al. 2010).

Alignment and performance issues in post-implementation phase Along with investing more and more money in enterprise software (Bartels et al. 2010), growing financial pressures in the aftermath of the economic downturn determined an increasing focus on IT's efficiency and effectiveness as well as on justifying IT's impact on business performance (Bélissent et al. 2010; Lo et al. 2009; Luftman and Ben-Zvi 2010). It is not surprising that IT managers are confronted with the challenge of enhancing IT's contribution to business productivity by improving alignment between IT and business (Luftman and Ben-Zvi 2010; Luftman et al. 2013; Tallon 2007). Increasing the fit of IT with business processes has been among the highest management priorities for more than 20 years now (Chan and Reich 2007; Luftman et al. 2013). Despite theoretical and practical necessity to understand the phenomenon of alignment between an organization and its process-centric enterprise software, it has rarely been studied and little is known about its impact on business performance (Sia and Soh 2007; Strong and Volkoff 2010).

Increasing complexity of software sourcing Across the years, the global enterprise software market has been subject to several tremendous changes. First, companies are increasingly shifting from in-house software—developed by a corporate's IT department or by a subcontracted software house—to packaged applications (Sawyer 2000). Packaged applications are standardized software artefacts developed by specialised companies based on industry best-practices and sold via market mechanisms to a large consumer base (Nöhren et al. 2014; Sawyer 2000; Sia and Soh 2007). The inherent standardization of such systems puts pressures on its alignment with business processes and impacts performance of organizational units (Grant 2003; Shang and Seddon 2002; Sia and Soh 2007; Strong and Volkoff 2010). Second, the appearance of on-demand software ("software-as-a-service") changed the packaged enterprise system's landscape (Bélissent et al. 2010; Merz et al. 2011; Winkler et al. 2011). The "as-a-service"-model differs from traditional on-premises delivery in which software is operated and deployed on company's own computing infrastructures (Winkler et al. 2011). In an on-demand setting, IT resources are transformed into a continuously provided service—like banking or telecommunications—delivered to client organizations via the Internet (Bolton 1998; Susarla et al. 2010; Yang and Tate 2012). This leads to fundamental differences in software management, software operation, and control over future developments (e.g. Choudhary 2007a; Currie et al. 2004; Koehler et al. 2010; Lehmann and Buxmann 2009; Stuckenberg et al. 2011; Xin and Levina 2008; Yang and Tate 2012).

In summary, enterprise systems are crucial for companies' daily operations and emerged to key strategic success factors for corporate's business processes (Cotteleer and Bendoly 2006). Today, companies can choose among three types of software sourcing. Whereas packaged applications (on-premises and on-demand) are on the rise and responsible for approximately 45 % of global software purchases, custom-built applications still account for around 20 % of the market (Bartels et al. 2010). As the Internet becomes ubiquitous, faster, and increasingly accessible, applications in the cloud diffuse on the global software market (Hsieh and Huang 2012; Niemann 2013). While process-centric enterprise systems were traditionally sourced in an on-premises or an in-house setting, ERP-as-a-service is on the rise (Koslowski and Strüker 2011; Niemann 2013). It has emerged to a fundamental opportunity for small and medium-sized companies to access leading process-centric software systems while avoiding high IT infrastructure costs, support costs, or large software license fees (Lacity et al. 2009, 2013). However, it is expected that despite the fact that on-demand services cut clients' costs and speed up their access to upgrades, such systems are less customizable, which influences integrability and performance (Lacity and Willcocks 2013; Niemann 2013; Nöhren et al. 2014). As a consequence, enterprise systems frequently fail to deliver the expected value during post-implementation phase (Grant 2003; Shang and Seddon 2002; Sia and Soh 2007; Strong and Volkoff 2010; Swanson and Ramiller 2004).

1.2   Research Objectives

Despite an increasing importance and a long tradition of IT value research (e.g. Barua et al. 1995; Brynjolfsson 1993; Dehning and Richardson 2002; DeLone and McLean 1992, 2003; Melville et al. 2004; Soh and Markus 1995), there is still uncertainty in view of the outcomes of IT in general as well as enterprise system's contribution to performance of business processes and organizations. Previous research in the field of process-centric enterprise software outcomes frequently investigated performance of specific types of software artefacts such as ERP systems (e.g. Cotteleer and Bendoly 2006; Grant 2003; Houdeshel and Watson 1987; Ranganathan and Brown 2006; Shang and Seddon 2002). These studies provide definitions of the inherent characteristics of the software artefact contributing to value and how this value can be measured. For instance, in an early study on software performance by Houdeshel and Watson (1987), a single case study to assess success of an internally developed IT system was conducted. In their study, in-house sourcing led to multiple benefits such as an improved communication among internal and external stakeholders and improved information quality.

Drawing upon a review of vendor-reported success stories combined with IT manager interviews, Shang and Seddon (2002) developed a list of 21 indicators to assess performance of packaged ERP systems. These indicators were grouped into operational, managerial, strategic, IT infrastructure, and organizational benefits. Ranganathan and Brown (2006) analysed the impact of ERP implementation on abnormal returns. In particular the effects of application's functional and physical scope as well as vendors reputation has been investigated. There are three key shortcomings of studies related to this area. First, the underlying software sourcing mode was not explicitly taken into account. It is not differentiated between in-house, on-premises, and on-demand applications. Second, most studies investigated impacts on an organizational level. Limited research is done on a business process level. Third, a direct link between enterprise software and performance is attributed. The mediating role of software alignment is underinvestigated.

Due to significant differences between in-house, on-premises, and on-demand enterprise systems with respect to deployment and control on future developments (e.g. Choudhary 2007a; Currie et al. 2004; Koehler et al. 2010; Lehmann and Buxmann 2009; Stuckenberg et al. 2011; Xin and Levina 2008; Yang and Tate 2012) an impact of sourcing modes on alignment and performance can be attributed and will further be elaborated in this study. Research on software sourcing emphasizes the role of particular sourcing arrangements (e.g. Abokhodair et al. 2012; Banker and Kemerer 1992; Hahn et al. 2013; Keil and Tiwana 2006; Malladi and Krishnan 2012a, b; Nidumolu 1995; Schwarz et al. 2009; Zhang and Seidmann 2010). Studies in this area analyses what are the influences on the decision for a specific software sourcing mode and what are the impacts on the outcomes of this decision. For instance, Schwarz et al. (2009) conducted a conjoint analysis aiming at understanding factors influencing IT manager's decision to source software either in an application service provisioning mode or to develop customized systems in a domestic or an offshore outsourcing setting. Drawing upon specific characteristics of the on-demand and the on-premises licencing model, Zhang and Seidmann (2010) discussed the optimal software delivery mode from a monopolistic vendor's perspective. In their two-period conceptual model the key impact factors are quality uncertainty and network effects. In addition, Choudhary (2007a) developed a conceptual mathematical model to compare software quality in "as-a-service"-settings with those in on-premises modes. Taking a vendor's perspective, the author compared intentions to invest in product quality. The key shortcoming of findings in this area is that studies are either conceptual in nature or focus on not more than one or two types of sourcing arrangements. No study has been found about the directly incorporated in-house, on-premises, and on-demand sourcing simultaneously. Consequently, the complexity of software sourcing was not treated in previous research.

In light of an increasing importance of managing IT and business alignment (Luftman et al. 2013) a strong body of research emphasizes the role of software alignment and fit as central mediator between enterprise software implemented within an organization and its business process performance outcomes (e.g. Cao 2010; Maurer et al. 2012; Sia and Soh 2007; Soh and Sia 2004; Strong and Volkoff

2010). These studies focuses on what constitutes fit and alignment of applications, how it is achieved and how fits and misfits emerge across organizational subunits. However, three key shortcomings of scholars related to this area of research can be identified. First, most of these studies are conceptual in nature. Second, their main focus is on packaged applications in general. No distinction between on-demand and on-premises sourcing is made. In addition, the alignment of in-house applications is not discussed so far. Third, studies in this area do not explicitly discuss the need for software and organizations to coevolve over time. The important role of this dynamic behaviour of software and business processes is discussed in the presented study.

This work aims at closing the research gaps identified above by studying the relationship between software sourcing modes and software sourcing value (see Fig. 1.1). It contributes to literature in two ways. First, the impact of in-house, on-premises, and on-demand software on software sourcing value is investigated by posing the following two research questions:

| Research question 1 | How do software sourcing modes impact software alignment? |
| Research question 2 | How do software sourcing modes impact performance outcomes? |

Second, this study's intention is to contribute to the discussion of how software alignment impacts business process performance and whether fits or misfits between organizations and enterprise systems are harmful or beneficial for companies (Chan and Reich 2007; Maurer et al. 2012). Thereby, it adds to conflicting research on the effects of software alignment (Chan and Reich 2007; Maurer et al. 2012; Sia and Soh 2007; Strong and Volkoff 2010) by posing a third research question:

| Research question 3 | How is software alignment related to performance outcomes? |

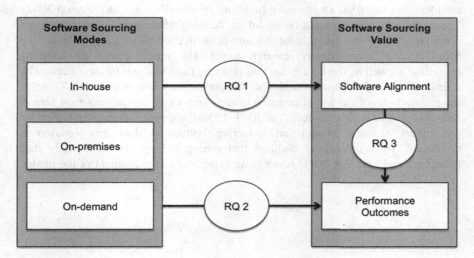

Fig. 1.1 Research framework

1.3 Research Design

The selection of an appropriate research design is a fundamental step in each research endeavour (Heinrich et al. 2011). In answering the research questions outlined above, an exploratory qualitative field study was conducted (Guillemette and Paré 2012). The exploratory nature of this research method was particularly valuable for two reasons: First, as outlined above, research on software sourcing modes and software sourcing value in terms of alignment and performance is in an early stage. As a consequence, the field either lacks strong conceptualizations of related constructs or does not provide quantitative measurement models for structural equitation modelling. Second, by combining various streams of research that existed highly independent from each other (see Chap. 2), this study taps into a novel area of investigation. Conducting an exploratory qualitative field study allows for not merely testing proposed relationships based on reference theories (Yin 2009) but also to include emergent findings from data interpretation in theory building (Eisenhardt 1989; Ravishankar et al. 2011).

A theory is a system of lawlike statements on the relationship between constructs for a certain excerpt of reality (Bacharach 1989; Heinrich et al. 2011). It can either be derived from an existing body of research (deductive) or is developed from data (inductive) (Gregor 2006; Heinrich et al. 2011). The inductive approach starts with a theorist's general wonderment (Shepherd and Sutcliffe 2011). Thereby, no *a priori* selected reference theory limits the interpretation of raw data (Venters and Whitley 2012). The first step of theory building in this study is an inductive analysis of raw data in terms of previous literature (Winkler 2009) in order to define software sourcing modes and to derive a generic model of how software contributes to performance. In a deductive approach, a *"theorist discovers a problem in the literature (. . .) and then sets out to create a solution to that problem"* (Shepherd and Sutcliffe 2011: 361). Guided by the inductive literature approach, reference theories are identified based on a systematic literature review (Webster and Watson 2002). These theories are particularly useful in defining relationships among related concepts. A combination of inductive and deductive literature analysis leads to a formulation of a preliminary research model. This model guides the sampling procedure as well as the data collection process. Data analysis process starts with a deductive top-down interpretation of the preliminary research model. Thereby, the propositions of the initial research model *"helps to focus attention on certain data and to ignore other data"* (Yin 2009: 130). Following a deductive test of the preliminary research model, an inductive bottom-up data interpretation is conducted. New theoretical findings that emerged from the field study data (Shepherd and Sutcliffe 2011) result in an extension and refinement of the model.

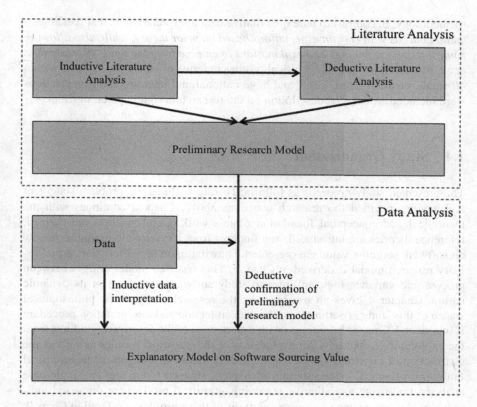

Fig. 1.2 Research design

Figure 1.2 illustrates the combination of deductive and inductive theorizing in this study.

Each scientific work needs to outline its philosophical stance in terms of its inherent ontological and epistemological viewpoints (Chalmers 1999; Creswell 2009). The aim of this study is to open the "black box" between software sourcing modes and its outcomes. In doing so, the study at hand bridges between realism and constructivism (Guba and Lincoln 1994; Kirsch 2004; Madill et al. 2000). A deeper discussion on the philosophical stance is provided in Chap. 4.

In answering the research questions introduced above and evaluating the pre-liminary research model, an exploratory qualitative field study (Guillemette and Paré 2012) is conducted. This methodology is closely linked to traditional case study research (Eisenhardt and Graebner 2007; e.g. Eisenhardt 1989; Yin 2009). However, whereas traditional case study research frequently focus on investigating the deeper structure of a phenomenon by analysing a small number of cases in-depth (Yin 2009), the exploratory field study design bridges between qualitative and quantitative research by including a larger number of such empirical profiles across multiple situations (Guillemette and Paré 2012). The key advantage of this methodology, in contrast to pure quantitative data interpretation, is that it enables a *"data analysis with certain expectations based on prior theory, while also allowing some unexpected findings and explanations to emerge from the data"* (Ravishankar et al. 2011: 41). In sum, 44 empirical profiles in terms of enterprise systems within 40 small, medium-sized, large, and huge national and international organizations were included. A detailed description on the research design is given in Chap. 4.

1.4   Study Organization

The presented study proceeds as follows: Having outlined the problem statement and having specified the research questions above, Chap. 2 continues with the theoretical and conceptual foundation of this work. Core concepts are defined, reference theories are introduced, and findings from a systematic literature review on software sourcing value are presented. Drawing upon this discussion, a preliminary research model is derived in Chap. 3. This research model bridges between process and variance logic in order to study software alignment in its dynamic nature. Chapter 4 gives an overview on the research design. The philosophical stance of this study is outlined and the data collection and interpretation procedure is introduced. Chapter 5 continues with a discussion of the descriptive findings from the exploratory field study. An explanation of the empirical profiles as well as the distribution of construct values is provided. A deeper discussion of the empirical findings is presented in the subsequent chapters. Chapter 6 provides the single-case analysis. Following a qualitative reasoning, empirical profiles are discussed individually. An aggregated cross-case synthesis of these profiles is offered in Chap. 7. The preliminary research model is tested and refined. New propositions emerged from an inductive data interpretation. The large number of empirical profiles within this study allows for a statistical test of propositions. Chapter 8 presents the final explanatory research model and concludes with the theoretical and practical implications of this study as well as a discussion of its limitations and required future research. Finally, a closing statement is given in Chap. 9. Figure 1.3 gives an overview on the study organization.

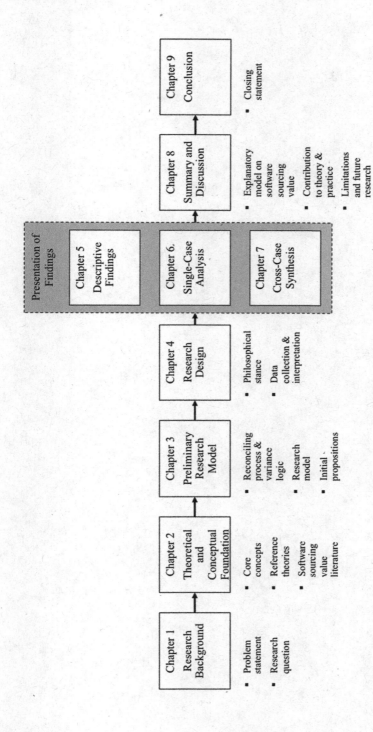

Fig. 1.3 Study organization

Chapter 2
Theoretical and Conceptual Foundation

This chapter outlines the theoretical and conceptual foundation of the presented study. The investigation starts with a definition of the core concepts in Sect. 2.1. Drawing upon representational view of IT, which serves as central theoretical lens for this study, a novel definition of software sourcing modes is presented. IT alignment and its relationship with representational view of IT is discussed. Section 2.2 continues with a systematic literature review on software sourcing value. Software sourcing value is classified into an intermediate outcome in terms of software alignment and dependent concepts in terms of business process and sourcing performance. Section 2.3 gives a summary of the theoretical and conceptual foundation which serves as basis for the development of a preliminary research model in Chap. 3. The chapter design is given in Fig. 2.1.

2.1 Definition of Core Concepts

The presented study builds on the representational view of IT (Wand and Weber 1990). This section starts with a discussion of this theoretical perspective. Representational view of IT is applied to define the core concepts under study. In particular, a novel interpretation of software sourcing modes and the related in-house, on-premises, and on-demand settings is given. This section continues with a definition of IT alignment in general and shows its relationship to representational view of IT. A deeper discussion of the alignment between software and business processes is given in Sect. 2.2.

© Springer International Publishing Switzerland 2016
M. Nöhren, *Enterprise Software Sourcing Performance*, Progress in IS,
DOI 10.1007/978-3-319-23926-2_2

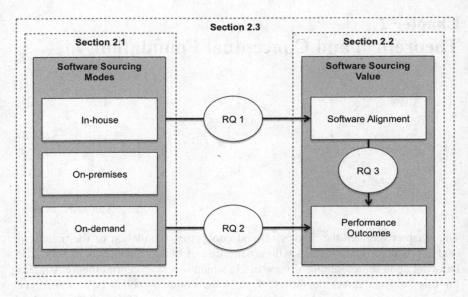

Fig. 2.1 Chapter design

2.1.1   Representational View of Information Technology

The representational view of IT (RIT) draws upon system's ontology. Ontology is a philosophical domain dealing with models of reality in terms of assumptions about how the world is made up and what the nature of things is (Guba and Lincoln 1994; Soh and Sia 2004). It defines how to describe the structure of the world in general (Wand and Weber 2002).

In information systems research, the Bunge-Wand-Weber (BWW) ontology has been applied to define the IT artefact (Soh and Sia 2004; Strong and Volkoff 2010). Instead of focusing on the way IT is managed, used, and implemented in organizations, and how these factors impact quality, performance, and adoption, BWW ontology views *"information systems as independent artefacts that bear certain relationships to the real-world system they are intended to model"* (Wand and Weber 1990: 61). In this view, information systems are seen as a representation of an organization and its reality (Wand and Weber 1990). Thereby, BWW seeks to understand what constitutes proper information systems by focusing on the properties an IT artefact needs to possess in order to fit with the requirements of a firm (Wand and Weber 1990). It is distinguished between physical, deep and surface structure elements of IT systems (see Fig. 2.2) (Wand and Weber 1990):

- **Surface structure** refers to the frontend of an IT system (Sia and Soh 2002). It is seen as a gateway where users interact with a particular IT artefact. Consequently, it describes how IT systems appear to their users (Wand and Weber 1995). Surface structure elements *"manifest the nature of the interface between*

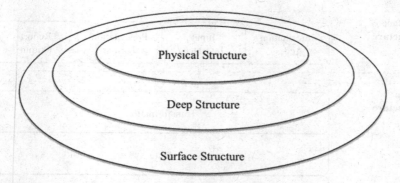

Fig. 2.2 Representational view on IT artefacts

the information system and its users and organizational environment." (Wand and Weber 1990: 61). It describes how real-world meanings are delivered by the system (Sia and Soh 2007).

- **Deep structure** refers to the core of the real-world system that an IT artefact is designed to model (Sia and Soh 2007; Strong and Volkoff 2010). It *"manifests the meaning of the real-world system the information system is intended to model"* (Wand and Weber 1995: 206). An IT artefact is made up of things that can either be real or conceptual in nature (Sia and Soh 2007). These things have intrinsic properties attached and exist at a certain state, which is changed through transformation (Sia and Soh 2002, 2007).
- **Physical structure** refers to the technology used to implement an IT system (Wand and Weber 1990, 1995). It explains *"ways in which deep and surface structures are mapped onto underlying physical technology"* (Strong and Volkoff 2010: 750). Examples of physical structures are networks, printers, or mass-storage devices (Strong and Volkoff 2010; Wand and Weber 1990).

Drawing upon the distinction between physical, deep, and surface structure elements, the software artefact was recently defined from a RIT perspective (Sia and Soh 2007; Strong and Volkoff 2010). This definition of software serves as a basis for a novel theory-guided interpretation of in-house, on-premises, and on-demand sourcing modes, which is presented afterwards.

2.1.2 Software Sourcing Modes

Software sourcing encompasses two distinct components that needs to be defined. From a RIT perspective, **software** is seen as a set of deep and surface structures mapped onto physical IT infrastructures (Sia and Soh 2007; Strong and Volkoff 2010). The structural elements of software artefacts are given in Fig. 2.3 (Sia and Soh 2007).

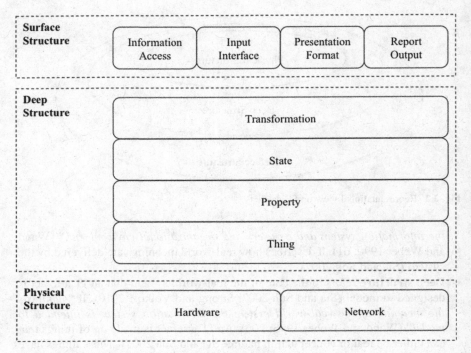

Fig. 2.3 Representational view on software artefacts

Starting with the deep structure, software artefacts are made of *things* (Sia and Soh 2007). Such things are the most elementary units in RIT (Sia and Soh 2007; Wand and Weber 1990). If a thing is connected with other things, a system is formed (Wand and Weber 1990). Inventory items, customer orders, or supplier accounts are examples for things related to software artefacts (Sia and Soh 2007).

All things must have certain *properties* attached (Sia and Soh 2007). These properties are functions that map things into value (Sia and Soh 2007; Wand and Weber 1990, 1995). Examples of software properties are inventory numbers, sales amounts, or unit prices stored within the system (Sia and Soh 2007).

The *state* of a thing refers to the vector of all property values of the thing (Wand and Weber 1990). Accordingly, a state is a set of conditions a thing might take, such as a status of a production order (Sia and Soh 2007).

A *transformation* of a thing is a change in its state (Wand and Weber 1990). Each transformation has a certain space—a set of possible changes that can occur in a thing—and a transformation law—rules that define which changes are legal—attached (Sia and Soh 2007; Wand and Weber 1990). Examples for software transformations are rules for production planning and execution, or the calculation of cost (Sia and Soh 2007).

While deep structures describe the core of a software artefact, surface structure refers to the user interface of an application (Sia and Soh 2007; Wand and Weber

1995). Each software artefact possesses a certain *input interface*, a particular *data representation format*, specific rules for *information access*, and a defined *report output* (Sia and Soh 2007). Examples of software surface structures are input parameters, content of production reports, and formats of order documents (Sia and Soh 2007).

Physical structures refer to the underlying technology linked to the software artefact (Strong and Volkoff 2010; Wand and Weber 1990). Despite the fact that these structures are not directly part of a particular software artefact, they are essential to implement, operate, and use an application (Strong and Volkoff 2010). Physical structures refer to the *hardware* on which an application is installed and to the *network* infrastructures that link systems and users with each other.

Having specified the software artefact, this section continues with a definition of software sourcing taking a RIT perspective. In general, **sourcing** refers to the procurement of goods and services from internal and external entities. It can be defined as turning over parts of a corporate's IT function to a third party vendor, who in exchange provides and manage IT assets and services for monetary returns over an agreed period of time (Apte et al. 1997; Kern 1997). Such a corporate's IT function includes three subfunctions that can be outsourced (Dibbern and Heinzl 2009; Heinzl 1993):

- **System development function** (e.g. development of own applications, adaptation of standard software)
- **System operation function** (e.g. maintenance of existing applications, implementation of updates)
- **Management function** (e.g. planning, coordination, and controlling of systems)

Organizational acquisition arrangements for these three subfunctions can be categorized according to the two dimensions *ownership* and *location* (Murray et al. 2009; Tanriverdi et al. 2007). The first one refers to the degree of vertical IT resource integration (Anderson and Parker 2002). It is differentiated between insourcing (hierarchical governance) as well as pure and hybrid outsourcing approaches (market governance) such as selective outsourcing, bi-sourcing, joint ventures, or strategic alliance sourcing (e.g. Currie and Willcocks 1998; Du et al. 2009; Kim and Park 2010; Lacity and Willcocks 1998; Lee et al. 2004). Insourcing defines an acquisition strategy where IT resources and all related operational and management activities are held within an organization's hierarchy (e.g. Cha et al. 2009; Kern et al. 2002a, b; Kishore et al. 2004). Contrary to this, outsourcing refers to an acquisition strategy where IT resources, IT tasks, and IT activities are contracted out to an external provider (e.g. Kern et al. 2002a, b; Kern 1997).

Location refers to the global position of IT subfunctions (Heinzl 1993). It can be differentiated between onshoring, nearshoring, and offshoring of system development, system operation, and management (Davis et al. 2006; Heinzl 1993; Nöhren et al. 2013). The global location of IT subfunctions is significant in understanding performance of globally executed software development and maintenance projects (e.g. Dibbern et al. 2008; Schwarz et al. 2009) and in analysing the role of global

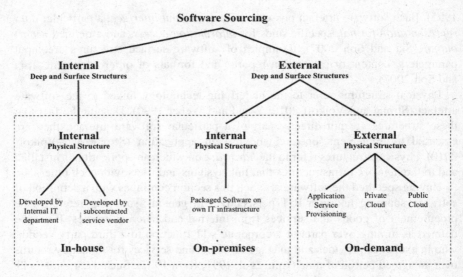

Fig. 2.4 Representational view on software sourcing modes

network structures in delivering outsourced tasks and activities (e.g. Ang and Inkpen 2008; Nöhren and Heinzl 2012). In this study, software sourcing modes are defined taking an ownership perspective. The global location of software vendors is not further investigated.

Looking at literature in the area of software sourcing, no strong definition of the phenomenon exists (e.g. Banker and Kemerer 1992; Choudhary 2007a; Kern et al. 2002a, b; Schwarz et al. 2009; Walden 2005; Wang 2002). However, *"(...) as software becomes an ever-increasing proportion of information technology, it is necessary to update IT outsourcing theory to consider the different types of ownership that software allows"* (Walden 2005: 699). Drawing on RIT, different software sourcing arrangements are classified according to their ownership on physical, deep, and surface structures and are categorized into in-house, on-premises, and on-demand modes (see Fig. 2.4).

The in-house mode encompasses applications where physical, deep, and surface structures of the software artefact are held within a firm's hierarchy. In this sourcing arrangement, an application is custom-developed for a specific firm (Schwarz et al. 2009). The development is either performed by an internal IT department or a subcontracted software vendor under control of the client (e.g. Nidumolu 1995; Schwarz et al. 2009; Wang 2002). The enterprise system is installed on a corporate's IT infrastructure representing an internal deployment. In contrast to this, the ownership on deep and surface structures of packaged applications is held by a software vendor. The design of these structures is impacted by requirements of a large customer base resulting in inherent software structures determined by industry's best practices (Maurer et al. 2012; Sia and Soh 2007; Strong and Volkoff 2010). Packaged systems differ with respect to their physical structures in terms of their deployment. They can be classified into a subscription-based on-demand model and perceptual-licensing for on-premises applications (Choudhary 2007a; Winkler et al. 2011). Whereas on-premises applications are installed on a firm's own IT infrastructure (internal physical structures), on-demand applications are hosted with a software vendor (external physical structures) and are accessed via Internet (Winkler et al. 2011). As a result, we see a decreasing extent of ownership on physical, deep, and surface structures from in-house through on-premises to on-demand sourcing.

2.1.3 Information Technology Alignment

As outlined above, RIT sees the IT and software artefact as a representation of a real-world system in terms of an organization (Strong and Volkoff 2010; Wand and Weber 1990). If real-world things, properties, states, and transformations (deep structure) are insufficiently represented by the artefact, or if a system's interface (surface structure) differs from the way people access, input, or retrieve information in reality, misalignments occur (Sia and Soh 2007). In this perspective, the degree of alignment can be seen as the extent of IT representing organizational reality. The presented study is rooted into previous research on IT alignment. A deeper definition of software alignment from a RIT perspective is given in the next section.

Alignment has been conceptualized and defined in various ways. It can be viewed as a "(...) *state in which the goals and activities of a business are in harmony with the information systems that support them*" (McKeen and Smith 2006: 93). For more than two decades, alignment of IT and business has been among the top five management concerns (Chan and Reich 2007; Luftman and Ben-Zvi 2010; Luftman et al. 2013). IT and business leaders see alignment as a key enabler of efficiency and effectiveness and therefore focus on initiatives that enhance the maturity of alignment between IT and business (Luftman et al. 2013). Against this background, numerous studies have been conducted, investigating positive outcomes of alignment such as an increased competitive advantage (e.g. Floyd and Woolridge 1990; Kearns and Lederer 2003) as well as organizational and business process performance (e.g. Bergeron et al. 2004; Byrd et al. 2006; Choe 2003; Tallon 2007). Other studies focused on antecedences of alignment such as shared decision making between IT and business units (Kearns and Lederer 2003) as well as the role of these units' shared understanding (Preston and Karahanna 2008; Reich and Benbasat 2000). Furthermore, three alignment cultures in organizations were identified (Ravishankar et al. 2011) and how alignment and related capabilities evolve over time (Sabherwal et al. 2001) was studied.

Alignment research varies with respect to the level of analysis. Chan and Reich (2007) distinguish between studies on organizational level (e.g. Kearns and Lederer 2003), system and project level (Floyd and Woolridge 1990; Grant 2003; Tallon 2007), as well as individual level (Tan and Gallupe 2006) such as the task-technology-fit model (Goodhue and Thompson 1995). The presented study defines software sourcing from an outsourcing perspective. In particular, software sourcing is seen as outsourcing of parts of a corporate's IT function on a system's level.

According to a literature review by Chan and Reich (2007), prior research on IT alignment can be classified into five dimensions. First, on an **informal structure dimension**, the distinct nature between informal and formal organizational set-ups were compared (Chan and Reich 2007). It had been discovered that the informal structure serves as a key antecedence for achieving IT alignment. For instance, Chan (2002) found that a fit between IT and business strategies had resulted in higher levels of performance. It was claimed that this was rather a result of informal organizational structures in terms of trust, commitment, or friendship between business and IT managers than a consequence of formal and instituted organizational procedures (Chan 2002).

The second dimension focuses on **cultural alignment** by studying the cultural fit between IT and business (e.g. Chan and Reich 2007; Ravishankar et al. 2011). For instance, by focusing on the implementation of a knowledge management system within a case company, Ravishankar et al. (2011) investigated the impact of organizational cultures and subcultures on realizing strategic IT alignment. Two important findings were derived. First, three organizational cultures—referred to enhancing, countercultural, and chameleon subculture—shaping the effects of top-down versus bottom-up system implementation were identified. Second, it was suggested, that the same system could result in alignment in one organizational unit whereas it leads to misalignment in another department (Ravishankar et al. 2011).

Third, on a **social dimension**, IT alignment refers to "the state in which business and IT executives understand and are committed to the business and IT mission, objectives, and plans" (Reich and Benbasat 2000: 81). Studies in this field investigated the role of shared understanding, shared knowledge, and communication processes among people involved in IT planning (e.g. Preston and Karahanna 2008; Reich and Benbasat 2000). Research focused frequently on the formal relationship between business and IT managers. To give an example, by taking a resource-based view of the firm perspective (see Sect. 2.2.1), Kearns and Lederer (2003) studied how social exchange between CEO and CIO resulted in higher levels of strategic IT alignment. In particular, the effect of reciprocal structures, where CEOs participate in IT planning and CIOs participate in business planning was studied. It turned out that this social alignment resulted in significant higher levels of strategic alignment (Kearns and Lederer 2003).

Particular attention had been paid to structural and strategic alignment (Chan and Reich 2007). Previous studies found a positive impact of both dimensions on process as well as organizational performance (Bergeron et al. 2001; Powell 1992; Tallon 2007). **Strategic alignment** describes the extent to which a certain business plan is in line with a corporate's IT plan and how IT strategy supports business strategy (Chan and Reich 2007; Henderson and Venkatraman 1993; Kearns and Lederer 2003). **Structural alignment** refers to the fit between structures and processes of a business unit and those of the IT system (e.g. Aier and Winter 2009; Chan 2002; Henderson and Venkatraman 1993). The presented study combines the strategic and structural dimension of IT alignment. As it will be shown in this work, dynamic fit, which serves as measure of software alignment, is related to the structural dimension of IT alignment (Maurer et al. 2012; Nöhren et al. 2014; Strong and Volkoff 2010). The process by which dynamic fit is generated is transferred into strategic alignment pattern referred to as gestalt and non-gestalts in Chap. 3 (Mintzberg 1987; Sabherwal and Robey 1995; Venkatraman 1989). These alignment patterns are related to the strategic dimension of IT alignment.

2.2   Literature Review

Having defined software sourcing modes and IT alignment from a RIT perspective, this section continues with a systematic literature review in order to define software sourcing value and concepts related to performance outcomes and software alignment. The analysis is organized as follows: Sect. 2.2.1 starts with a definition of additional theoretical lenses that were identified by the literature review. These reference theories were found to be valuable in defining the dynamic fit process (Sect. 2.2.5) and in building a preliminary research model in Chap. 3. Section 2.2.2 defines IT value in general and presents previous process models on how IT artefacts contribute to performance of organizations and business processes. These process models are synthesized into a more generic model on IT value generation that outlines the relationship between software alignment and performance outcomes. Section 2.2.3 continues with a definition of performance outcomes. Drawing upon the literature review, two dependent concepts in terms of business process and sourcing performance have been identified. Earlier contribution to software alignment is discussed in Sect. 2.2.4. The concept of dynamic fit is developed based on three previously published notions of software fit. Due to the fact that the developed dynamic fit concept is non-deterministic and dynamic in nature, the process by which dynamic fit is generated and related concepts are outlined in Sect. 2.2.5.

The literature review followed the guidelines by Kitchenham et al. (2009) as well as Webster and Watson (2002). After the research questions were clarified in the first chapter of this study, the search process including a definition of keywords and relevant sources of knowledge was designed. As shown in Appendix A, a combination of two types of keywords was used. Whereas the first type focused on the IT artefact under study, the second row included keywords related to performance outcomes. As indicated by Webster and Watson (2002), major contribution to a specific research topic is most likely to be found in highest ranked publication outlets of a discipline. Therefore, this literature review focused on the top eight IS journals as defined by the Association for Information System's senior scholars' basket of journals.[1] In addition, the leading German-based international journal on

---

[1] http://ais.site-ym.com/?page=SeniorScholarBasket

management information systems as well as the top five international conferences as shown in Appendix A were included in this review.

The usage of very general keywords led to more than 8000 search results. Consequently, a second search, in which keywords were limited to abstracts only was conducted. Thereby, the total number of search results was reduced to less than 400 papers. Those papers' abstracts, introductions, discussions, and conclusions were read (Dibbern et al. 2004) in order to determine whether the study was helpful in answering the research questions (Kitchenham et al. 2009). Remaining papers had been combined with a forward and backward search as recommended by Webster and Watson (2002).

2.2.1   Theoretical Lenses in Software and Sourcing Research

Having outlined RIT as central theoretical lens of this investigation, this section continues with a definition of additional reference theories identified by the literature review. Looking at research on software sourcing, a variety of reference theories were applied to explain performance outcomes. An overview of those theoretical lenses as well as their respective elucidations of software sourcing value is given in Table 2.1.

2.2.1.1   Organizational Structure Theories

Institutional theory and RIT frequently served as reference theories for studying the fit between organizations and its IT systems (e.g. Chiasson and Green 2007; Nöhren et al. 2014; Sia and Soh 2007; Soh and Sia 2004; Strong and Volkoff 2010). These theoretical lenses are particularly helpful in defining structures related to the organization and those related to a certain IT artefact under investigation as well as in understanding external and internal contingencies shaping those structures (Scott 1987; Sia and Soh 2007; Strong and Volkoff 2010; Wand and Weber 1990).

Institutional theory (Scott 1987) is related to the nature of organizational structures. The core concept of this theory is the institution, which is seen as an organized and established procedure (Berente and Yoo 2012). Institutional theory attends to the deeper and more robust aspects of social structures. In particular, institutional theory focuses on how structures, norms, and rules are shaped by a social and an organizational context and how they become established over time (Berente and Yoo 2012; Jones and Karsten 2008). This context is primarily driven by an organization's internal and external environment and a firm's interaction with it (Lu and Ramamurthy 2010; Sia and Soh 2007). Institutional theory argues that longevity and survival of an organization can only be achieved when a firm remains consistent with changing internal and external environmental conditions over time (Scott 1987; Vessey and Ward 2013).

Table 2.1 Theoretical lenses on software sourcing

Paradigm	Reference theory	Key contribution to software sourcing	References in software sourcing literature
Organizational structure theories	Representational view of IT (RIT)	Identification of inherent characteristics of software resulting from deep and surface structures; explanation of software-business process fit	Nöhren et al. (2014), Sia and Soh (2007), Strong and Volkoff (2010)
	Institutional theory	Role of external and internal contingencies defining environmental, business process and software structure change	Sia and Soh (2007), Soh and Sia (2004), Xin and Levina (2008)
Organizational resource theories	Resource-based view of the firm (RBV)	Identification of inherent characteristics of business processes	Benlian et al. (2009), Schwarz et al. (2009)
	Resource-dependence theory (RDT)	Identification of relational characteristics in software sourcing relationships	Schwarz et al. (2009)
	Knowledge-based view of the firm (KBV)	Identification of inherent characteristics of business processes	Schwarz et al. (2009), Winkler and Brown (2014)
Organizational governance theories	Transaction cost economics (TCE)	Identification of inherent characteristics of software artefacts	E.g. Schwarz et al. (2009), Susarla et al. (2009), Winkler and Benlian (2012), Winkler and Brown (2014)
	Agency theory	Understanding risks and costs in sourcing settings; particularly relevant for customized software development	Winkler and Brown (2014)

2.2.1.2   Organizational Resource Theories

Organizational resource theories, including resource-based view of the firm, resource-dependence theory, and knowledge-based view of the firm see companies as collection of resources, which are central to firm strategies (Dibbern et al. 2004; Winkler 2009). **Resource-based view of the firm** (RBV) is a widely acknowledged theoretical lens on describing, explaining, and predicting organizational relationships (Barney et al. 2011). RBV defines a corporate resource as *"an asset or input to production (tangible or intangible) that an organization owns, controls, or has access to"* (Helfat and Peteraf 2003: 999). Such human, physical, and organizational resources are mandatory to fulfil a company's task and result in a sustained competitive advantage if they are valuable, rare, and imperfectly mobile (Barney 1991; Dibbern et al. 2004; Mata et al. 1995; Nöhren and Heinzl 2012). A resource is valuable if it enables a firm to conceive or implement a strategy, which improves its efficiency and effectiveness (Barney 1991). It is seen as rare, if it is not possessed by a large number of competitors (Barney 1991). Imperfect mobility or non-tradability means that a resource cannot be imitated by competitors or substituted by any another resource (Barney 1991; Wade and Hulland 2004).

RBV had widely been used to study the value of IT (e.g. Bharadwaj 2000; Melville et al. 2004; Mithas et al. 2011). According to Mata et al. (1995) three attributes of IT can be a source of sustained competitive advantage. First, building superior IT assets is typically very cost intensive (see also Soh and Markus 1995). Corporate's *access to capital* serves as a source of competitive advantage. Second, a *proprietary technology* protected by patents or other security mechanisms can prevent a valuable IT resource from being copied (see also Teece 1986). Third, *managerial IT skills* in terms of management's ability to build and exploit IT applications that support business units are imperfectly mobile in nature. Such skills are developed over long periods of time. In contrast to this, *technical IT skills*, which refers to the know-how needed to execute IT-related tasks such as building, maintaining, or implementing IT applications, are rather a source of temporary competitive advantage (Mata et al. 1995). In a later study, Bharadwaj (2000) defined IT as a set of IT infrastructure resources, human IT resources, and intangible IT-enabled resources such as know-how and corporate culture. *Human resources* encompass technical and managerial IT skills. *IT infrastructure resources* are physical assets such as computers, communication technologies, platforms, and databases. Finally, *IT-enabled intangibles* are organizational resources like knowledge assets, synergies, and a firm's customer orientation (Bharadwaj 2000).

Whereas RBV focuses on internal resources, **resource dependency theory** (RDT) takes an outside perspective. In particular, RDT argues that organizations are not able to produce and provide all resources needed internally (Pfeffer and Salancik 1978; Schwarz et al. 2009). To varying degrees, all firms depend on some resources of their external environments and must actively engage in managing their ecosystems as well as their resource flow (Borman 2006; Dibbern et al. 2004; Pfeffer and Salancik 1978; Sia et al. 2008). By outsourcing parts of the IT function, firms increase their dependency on their vendors (Sia et al. 2008). This is particularly true in the context of sourcing packaged applications by outsourcing deep and surface structure of an IT artefact. To avoid a strategic vulnerability resulting from resource dependency, sourcing options need to be carefully evaluated (Kern et al. 2002a, b). Due to the fact that RDT rather focuses on how to manage an ongoing outsourcing relationship, how to increase power over a strategic resource from external environment, and explain why firms procure packaged applications instead of building their own systems (Schwarz et al. 2009), this theoretical lens is not further investigated in this study.

Finally, **knowledge-based view of the firm** (KBV), as third perspective on corporate resources, can be seen as a spin-off of RBV (Barney et al. 2011). It centres knowledge as the most significant resource of the firm and claims that, due to the fact that knowledge-intensive resources are difficult to imitate (imperfect mobility) and are heterogeneously distributed among firms (rare), such resources are key factors of sustained competitive advantage and performance (Dibbern et al. 2008; Grant 1996; Herath and Kishore 2009). Competitive advantage results from a firm's ability to create, store, and apply knowledge (Jayatilaka et al. 2003; Kishore et al. 2004). Rather than focusing on physical, organizational, and human resources, KBV emphasized on the knowledge required for development and deployment of enterprise systems (Jayatilaka et al. 2003). KBV is often seen as complementary to transaction cost economics (see below) in explaining why firms engage in activities, which generate superior and valuable internal knowledge but appears to be inefficient from an economic point of view (e.g. sourcing of services internally while a hazard-free external market exists) (Reitzig and Wagner 2010).

2.2.1.3 Organizational Governance Theories

Transaction cost economics (TCE) is a widely used theory of the firm. Developed by Williamson (1973, 1979) and drawing upon Coase (1937), it argues that firms exist because using markets would be too costly. Firms boundary decisions are framed as "make-or-buy"-problems (Reitzig and Wagner 2010). TCE analyses the relative advantage of using an internal (hierarchy) or external (market) governance mode by focusing on costs of transactions (Sia et al. 2008). The key assumption is that firms aim at minimizing transaction costs when selecting a particular governance mode. These costs depend on asset specificity, uncertainty, and transaction frequency of an activity (Sia et al. 2008). *Asset specificity* refers to the degree to which an application can be redeployed to another context (Wang 2002). It *"takes a variety of forms—physical assets, human assets, site specificity, dedicated assets, brand name capital, and temporal specificity—to which individuated governance structure responses accrue"* (Williamson 1998: 36). If *asset specificity* is high, contractual partners have to provide specific investments in an outsourcing process that have little or no value to them (Wang 2002). *Uncertainty* refers to the risk of unforeseen contingencies that—for instance—result in renegotiations or opportunistic behaviour of vendors (Sia et al. 2008; Wang 2002). Finally, *frequency* is related to how often a transaction occurs (Wang 2002). Activities that are highly asset specific, that involve a high level of uncertainty, and that occur regularly are rather performed by an internal governance mode than by outsourcing (Gilley et al. 2004). It was found that out of these three components, asset specificity had the most consistent explanatory power in a wide range of empirical studies (Dibbern et al. 2008).

Agency theory is closely linked to the uncertainty construct of TCE (Bahli and Rivard 2003). It describes a situation in which a principal (client) engages with an agent (vendor) to perform a service (Hustad and Olsen 2011). Uncertainty arises from asymmetric information between the contractual parties (Dibbern et al. 2004). Conflicting goals, incomplete information, and different risk perceptions between principals and agents demand for appropriate accountability schemes to generate the expected value from the relationship (Winkler and Brown 2014). Consequently, principals have to set initiatives (e.g. in terms of contracts) to ensure that the agents behave in the expected way and to reduce the risk of moral hazard (Dibbern et al. 2004; Gefen et al. 2008). Due to the fact that the key focus of agency theory is on an optimal contractual arrangement between principal and agent in order to reduce costs and risks (Dibbern et al. 2004) than on analysing performance in sourcing of IT artefacts, agency theory was not further investigated. Agency theory is seen as particularly useful in studying customized software development tasks on a project level (e.g. Gefen et al. 2008).

2.2.2 The Value of Information Technology

Following a brief description of reference theories identified by the literature review on software sourcing, this section continues with a deeper discussion of the IT value term. Value refers to *"the importance, worth, or usefulness of something"* (Oxford Dictionaries 2014c). Ever since Nobel Prize winner Robert Solows famous quote in 1987 *"we see the computer age everywhere except in the productivity statistics"* (Brynjolfsson and Hitt 1998: 51), a huge body of research emerged, concerned with analysing and measuring IT's value for businesses, processes, organizations, and economies (e.g. Bharadwaj et al. 1999; Brynjolfsson and Hitt 1998; Chan 2000). It was found that *"firms derive business value from IT through its impacts on intermediate business processes. Such intermediate processes include the range of operational processes that comprise a firm's value chain and the management processes of information processing, control, coordination and communication."* (Mooney et al. 1996: 69). This *"IT value often lies in the cross-functional integration of business processes and the penetration of IT into the core of organizational functioning."* (Willcocks et al. 2002: 51).

Despite a vast number of studies on the value of IT, the debate on how IT contributes to performance still persists (Melville et al. 2004). The link between IT and productivity of a firm has widely been discussed but remained fuzzy and is little understood (Brynjolfsson 1993). Previous research can be classified with respect to three dimensions based on the questions of "where", "what", and "how" revolving around IT value. One of the major discussions revolves around the question of "where" to analyse and find the value of IT. Previous studies investigated IT outcomes on different organizational levels. With respect to this **level of analysis**, IT value research can be classified into three streams. The first stream is concerned with measuring value on a corporate level. Studies on this level analysed the impact of aggregated IT spendings, internally provided IT and non-IT capital, as well as IT strategy on market share and return on assets (Barua et al. 1995; Bharadwaj et al. 1999; Dehning and Richardson 2002). Most of these studies are econometrical in nature. A second stream of research focuses on individual level impacts. Analysis in this field emphasized the importance of IT design and IT management on users behaviour as critical factors for achieving desired organizational goals (e.g. Au et al. 2008; DeLone and McLean 1992, 2003; van der Heijden 2004a; Soh and Markus 1995). These studies were frequently linked to research in the field of social psychology. Finally, a third stream of research is on a process level assessing IT's value within corporate's IT functions and business units. It stresses the significance of IT resources in realizing and improving business process performance (Dohmen et al. 2010; Melville et al. 2004; Tallon et al. 2000).

The second dimension refers to the **IT anchoring** and the question of "how" IT influences outcomes. With respect to the relationship between predictor and dependent variable, previous research can be classified into criterion-free and criterion-specific definitions of IT value. The first one describes the IT artefact or its components as antecedence for achieving performance outcomes. In this perspective, IT drives efficiency and effectiveness of firms, processes, and individuals. For instance, Bharadwaj (2000) analysed the impact of superior IT capabilities that encompassed human IT resources, IT infrastructure resources, and IT-enabled intangibles on firm performance. Melville et al. (2004) found that human and technological IT resources enable business processes and impact their performance. The criterion-specific perspective defines IT as input to production. Performance is seen as a transformation of these inputs into desired organizational outputs. The IT artefact, the IT function, or its components are parts of the performance definition. For instance, Dehning and Richardson (2002) stressed how IT-related inputs such as IT spending and IT capital are related to certain levels of outputs. Barua et al. (1995) analysed how factors such as IT and non-IT capital as well as IT and non-IT purchases impact process (e.g. new product development and inventory turnover) and organizational performance outcomes (e.g. market share and return on assets). Banker et al. (1990) conducted a field experiment analysing performance gains of subsidiaries that used a particular business application in comparison to those where the application was not deployed.

Finally, the third question is concerned with "what" **IT impact** actually is. A huge body of research focused on the outcomes of IT in general as well as the performance of specific systems. Thereby, the notion of outcome is used in a vague and inconsistent way (e.g. DeLone and McLean 1992; Dibbern et al. 2004; Schryen 2010). Some studies defined outcome in terms of performance assessing the output from an economic point of view by including measures such as market value, operational efficiency, productivity, and profitability of IT (e.g. Brynjolfsson and Hitt 2000; Dehning and Richardson 2002; Heinrich et al. 2011; Kohli and Devaraj 2003; Melville et al. 2004). Other studies relied on the notion of success which describes the effectiveness of a system in terms of its actual and perceived contribution to operational, strategic, economic, or technological benefits (e.g. DeLone and McLean 1992, 2003; Grover et al. 1996; Lee et al. 2004). A deeper discussion of the dependent variable is given in Sect. 2.3. The position of this study is shaded black in Fig. 2.5.

Having classified the three dimensions of IT value research, this section continues with a discussion of four previously published process models on IT value. These models are synthesised into a more generic model which reveals the relationship between alignment and performance outcomes.

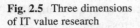

Fig. 2.5 Three dimensions
of IT value research

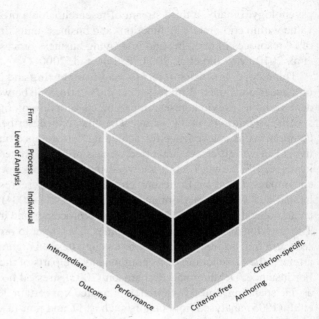

2.2.2.1 The Soh-Markus-Model on IT Investments

One of the earliest models on returns from IT spending is the business value model
by Soh and Markus (1995). Based on a review of five previously proposed IT
outcome models, the authors introduced a novel process model to capture the value
of IT. This model relies on the criterion-specific definition of outcomes. Soh and
Markus (1995) argued that *IT expenditures* lead to *organizational performance* in
three consecutive processes (see Fig. 2.6). Within the first process, referred to as "IT
conversion process", *IT expenditures* are seen as necessary conditions to build *IT
asset*. *IT assets* in terms of superior applications, infrastructures, skills, or knowledge arise when IT spending is transformed in an efficient and effective way. IT
management such as project management and the formulation of an adequate IT
strategy impacts this conversion process. Therefore, the "IT conversion process"
takes place within the IT function of an organization (Soh and Markus 1995).

Following the first process, the "IT use process" within the business units begins.
If a company had been able to transform *IT expenditures* into *IT assets*, these assets
form the basis to derive certain *IT impacts*. These impacts in terms of new product
developments, redesigned work pattern, or improved decision-making, can be
found on an organizational and on a business process level. However, like *IT
expenditures*, *IT assets* are merely necessary conditions to realize *IT impacts*.
Within the second process, actual and appropriate usage of the IT system by its
key stakeholder within the business units was defined as condition to realize
desirable impacts. Finally, the third process, following the "IT use process"

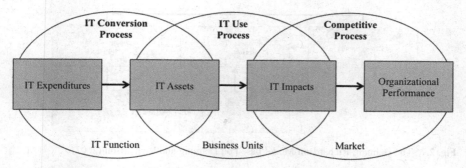

Fig. 2.6 The Soh-Markus-Model on IT investments based on Soh and Markus (1995)

describes the transformation of *IT impacts* into *organizational performance*. Thereby, it is differentiated between the notion of *IT impacts* referred to as value directly linked to a particular IT artefact and *organizational performance* as the indirect outcome of *IT assets*. *IT impacts* were described as necessary condition for *organizational performance* in terms of firm productivity or financial and stakeholder value. *Organizational performance* is realized on a market and is therefore mainly impacted by environmental factors such as the competitive position of a firm or its competitive dynamics. Due to the fact that the IT value generation process starts with certain IT spending, the Soh-Markus-model can be referred to as an investment-based IT value model (Soh and Markus 1995).

2.2.2.2   The Dehning-Richardson-Model on IT Investments

A second investment-based IT value model was introduced by Dehning and Richardson (2002). A systematic literature review was conducted and previous findings for the criterion-specific dimension of IT value were synthesized. It was found that foregoing research conceptualized IT-related investments with respect to (1) *strategy*, (2) *management*, and (3) *financial spending*. With respect to *IT strategy*, it was found that earlier studies assessed the impact of different types of IT deployment (e.g. ERP systems), time of IT sourcing (e.g. first-mover advantages), or the facilitation of new business strategies. Researchers investigating *IT management* emphasized the role IT and related capabilities hold within an organization. Finally, studies on *IT spending* measured investments in terms of total IT expenditures, costs of IT training, and staff costs (Dehning and Richardson 2002). By including IT strategy, IT management, and IT spending in the definition of IT inputs, the pure focus on financial expenditures like in the Soh-Markus-model (Soh and Markus 1995) was extended (see Fig. 2.7).

Key focus of this study was on exploring opportunities to capture returns of IT. A conceptual framework for measuring outcomes of IT investments on different levels was introduced (see Fig. 2.6). In particular, Dehning and Richardson (2002) derived a set of variables to capture outcomes of *IT spending*, *IT management*, and

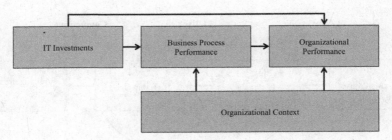

Fig. 2.7 The Dehning-Richardson-Model based on Dehning and Richardson (2002)

IT strategy on business process and organizational level. Process level concepts were related to measures such as inventory turnover, quality, and efficiency. It was found that IT investments result in direct and indirect effects on business processes performance. Direct effects referred to impacts such as reduction of inventory costs as output of transforming *IT spending*, *IT management*, and *IT strategy* inputs. Indirect effects are "collateral benefits" of IT investments, such as an improved quality of managers' decision-making following an ERP investment, which in return results in new opportunities for business processes. On an organizational level, Dehning and Richardson (2002) identified several market (e.g. event study, market value) and accounting measures (e.g. return on assets, market share). In addition, the crucial role of organizational contingencies such as industry sector, firm size, or competition shaping business process and organizational performance was exposed (Dehning and Richardson 2002).

2.2.2.3   The DeLone-McLean-Model on IT Systems

One of the most famous and most widely cited models in IT value research is the so-called DeLone-McLean-model of IT success (see Fig. 2.8). In this model, IT is seen as antecedence for achieving desirable outcomes. Drawing upon a review of 180 articles in the area of IT success, a process model to capture the complex nature of IT impacts on a system's level was developed. In particular, two central challenges in assessing IT outcomes were faced. The first one was the search of the dependent variable. Six IT value concepts were identified and included within the model. The second one was the question of how these concepts are interrelated with each other. A process model as shown in Fig. 2.8 was derived (DeLone and McLean 1992).

DeLone and McLean (1992) pointed out that due to the fact that IT value is typically defined in an elusive and vague way, almost every study relied on its own measures. In order to provide a more comprehensive picture, six identified IT outcome concepts in terms of *system quality*, *information quality*, *use*, *user satisfaction*, *individual impact*, and *organizational impact* were included within the model. The two concepts of *system quality* and *information quality* were directly attributed to the IT artefact and served as measures for *IT system performance*.

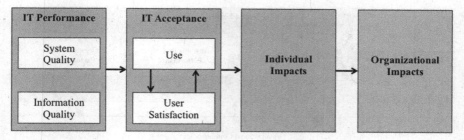

Fig. 2.8 The DeLone-McLean-Model based on DeLone and McLean (1992)

System quality describes the technical dimension of IT including measures such as ease of use, reliability, and response time. *Information quality* refers to the semantic dimension of IT compromising variables like information understandability, output accuracy, and usefulness of information. *IT system performance* is seen as necessary condition for *IT acceptance* in terms of *user satisfaction* and *use*. Whereas *user satisfaction* describes enjoyment and happiness of stakeholders such as managers and employees, *use of a system* is measured in terms of actual usage (use versus non-use), motivation to use the system, and frequency of usage. IT acceptance is seen as necessary condition for *individual impacts*. It refers to how IT contributes to performance of users (e.g. time for task completion) and managers (e.g. time and quality of decisions). *Individual impacts* serve as precondition for desirable *organizational impacts* expressing IT's contribution to innovation, market share, and profits (DeLone and McLean 1992).

The proposed process model was later transferred into a variance model, which was refined and tested empirically by DeLone and McLean (2003). Most essentially, the authors found that beside IT performance in terms of *information quality* and *system quality*, specific characteristics of a system's provider—such as assurance, empathy, and responsiveness—defines *service quality*. *Service quality* served as a third antecedence of acceptance of the IT system (DeLone and McLean 2003).

2.2.2.4   The Melville-Kraemer-Gurbaxani-Model on IT Resources

The latest IT value model was proposed by Melville et al. (2004). Drawing upon an extensive review of previous literature, the authors took resource-based view of the firm (see Sect. 2.2.1) as theoretical lens to describe how IT results in outcomes. In their integrative process model, IT is seen as antecedence for performance. The value generation process starts within an organization referred to as *focal firm*. Within a *focal firm*, IT business value can be realized from a combination of multiple *IT* and related *complementary organizational resources*. *IT resources* are categorized into *technological* and *human resources*. The former one compromises IT infrastructures and business applications within a company. The latter one combines employees' technical (e.g. programming and systems integration) and managerial skills (e.g. collaboration with internal and external units or project

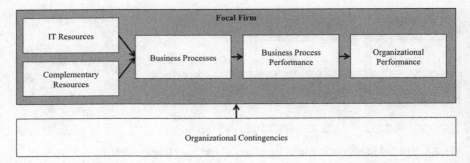

Fig. 2.9 The Melville-Kraemer-Gurbaxani-Model based on Melville et al. (2004)

planning). *Complementary organizational resources* refer to non-IT resources that provide synergies between IT and other firm resources (Melville et al. 2004). As defined by Barney, such resources are classified into physical (e.g. distributed locations and firm's global reach), human (e.g. skills and expertise), and organizational resources (e.g. advanced processes and corporate's structures) (Barney 1991; Nöhren and Heinzl 2012).

According to Melville et al. (2004), the combination of *IT* and *complementary organizational resources* impacts and enables *business processes* as shown in Fig. 2.9. *Business processes* are defined on an abstract level as value generating activities such as sales, manufacturing, and distribution, responsible for transforming sets of inputs into particular outputs. These *business processes* influence performance on two levels. It is differentiated between *business process* and *organizational performance*. The first one refers to measures of operational efficiency of business processes such as quality, inventory turnover, or cycle time. Performance on business process level is described as necessary condition for *organizational performance* in terms of profitability, market value, and competitive advantage (Melville et al. 2004).

In addition, Melville et al. (2004) emphasize on the importance of external *organizational contingencies* shaping the value generation process within a *focal firm*. It is differentiated between factors from the competitive micro environment such as certain industry characteristics and resources of trading partners as well as factors of the macro environment including characteristics on a country level (Melville et al. 2004).

2.2.2.5 Summary and Synthesis of Information Technology Value Models

To sum up, all the four afore-mentioned value models discussed above are concerned with justifying returns of IT in terms of IT-related financial and non-financial investments (Dehning and Richardson 2002; Soh and Markus 1995), IT resources (Melville et al. 2004), or IT systems in general (DeLone and

McLean 1992). None of these models expose the distinct role of a particular IT artefact such as process-centric enterprise systems. However, these four models are particularly valuable in understanding the questions of "where" to find the impact of IT, "how" the relationship between IT artefact (predictor) and its outcome (dependent) variable can be understood, and "what" categories serve as a measure of IT value on an abstract level. Three key contributions can be derived:

First, with respect to the "how"-question and the relationship between predictor and dependent variable, it was found that IT can be seen as an input (Dehning and Richardson 2002; Soh and Markus 1995) or as an antecedence (DeLone and McLean 1992, 2003; Melville et al. 2004) in an IT value generation process. In general, both IT anchorings are useful in IT value research. A criterion-specific perspective is particularly beneficial in measuring transformations of IT-related inputs in desirable outputs (e.g. Bharadwaj 2000; Nöhren and Heinzl 2012). The key conclusion of these studies is an assessment of performance of an internally executed transformation process. However, due to the fact that IT-related inputs are frequently seen as a bundle of variables (e.g. Alpar et al. 2001; Nöhren and Heinzl 2012), their individual impact on a dependent variable cannot be derived by taking a criterion-specific point of view. In contrast to this, a criterion-free anchoring evaluates the impact of a particular IT resource (e.g. Dibbern et al. 2008; Goo et al. 2008) on a particular dependent variable. As outlined above, this research focuses on process-centric enterprise systems and their impact on alignment and performance as dependent constructs. Consequently, enterprise systems are seen as antecedence in the value generation process, which makes a criterion-free anchoring appropriate.

Second, with respect to the level of analysis and the related "where"-question, it was found that IT outcomes could be captured on three levels within a firm. On an individual level, the value of IT artefacts for individual users can be assessed (e.g. DeLone and McLean 1992, 2003; Soh and Markus 1995). This level is particularly helpful when focusing on user-centric IT such as social software and collaboration systems where the outcome is primarily generated on a user level (e.g. Chai et al. 2011; Parameswaran and Whinston 2007; Suh et al. 2011). In contrast to this, the impact of process-centric enterprise software is best understood on a process level. Melville et al. (2004) found that IT's business contribution occurs in a successive manner. First, in combination with a set of complementary organizational resources, IT artefacts enable business processes (Melville et al. 2004). This is particularly true for process-centric systems such as ERP or CRM. These business processes result in business process performance first, before emerging to organizational level outcomes (Dehning and Richardson 2002; Melville et al. 2004).

Third, on a very abstract level, IT value models expose "what" IT value is. In particular, three key findings can be derived. First, IT generates an *intermediate outcome* that is directly attributed to a certain IT artefact under study. DeLone and McLean (1992, 2003) found that IT systems performance—reflected by the requirements of a firm—results in acceptance in terms of user satisfaction and actual usage in a first stage. In addition, Soh and Markus (1995) found that IT expenditures lead to the creation of IT assets in terms of useful, well-designed, or flexible applications. These *intermediate outcomes* contribute to performance outcomes. However, superior *intermediate outcomes* do not inevitably result in higher performance on business process or organizational level. Several internal and external contingencies shape IT's value generation process (Melville et al. 2004; Soh and Markus 1995). The lower the organizational level of measuring IT's contribution, the closer the link to a particular IT artefact under investigation and the less severe is the role of internal and external contingencies. Second, *intermediate outcomes* are frequently observed by the means of "fit". For instance, Soh and Markus speak of useful and well designed application in their notion of IT assets and highlight that IT must be "*(. . .) designed in such a way that it fits the firm's task effectively (. . .)*" (Soh and Markus 1995: 30). In addition, DeLone and McLean (1992, 2003) measure the *intermediate outcome* of software systems in terms of systems quality and information quality and how these components fit with user and organizational requirements. Third, when looking at IT's contribution to process and organizational performance, all four models discussed above point out that appropriate measures needs to be designed in close relationship to those potential values that can be realized by this particular IT artefact. Melville et al. defined business process performance as "*(. . .) a range of measures associated with operational efficiency enhancement within specific business processes, such as quality improvement of design processes and enhanced cycle time within inventory management processes*" (Melville et al. 2004: 296). According to Dehning and Richardson, "*business process performance measures include gross margin, inventory turnover, customer service, quality, efficiency, and other cost, profit margin, and turnover ratios.*" (Dehning and Richardson 2002: 9). Organizational performance can broadly spoken be operationalized in terms of a set of market-related measures such as return of investments, profitability, or market share (Dehning and Richardson 2002; DeLone and McLean 1992; Melville et al. 2004; Soh and Markus 1995). Drawing upon these findings, a more generic model of IT value as presented in Fig. 2.10 can be derived.

It can be deduced that each IT artefact such as enterprise software generates a certain *intermediate outcome*. This outcome is directly related to the artefact under investigation and can be measured in terms of its fit with the requirements of a firm. *Intermediate outcomes* impact *business performance outcomes* in terms of business process and organizational performance in two consecutive steps. The link between outcome and IT system becomes fuzzier from *intermediate outcomes* through *business process performance* to *organizational performance* due to an increasing influence of external and internal macro and micro environmental contingencies shaping value generation process. Previous studies frequently showed that firms might see internal process improvements from IT, but that the same gains do not emerge to a firm level (Mittal and Nault 2009). Consequently, this study focuses on *intermediate outcomes* in terms of software fit and its impact on *business process performance*. Organizational level outcomes were not investigated. The next subsection gives a definition of the performance outcome concepts applied in this study.

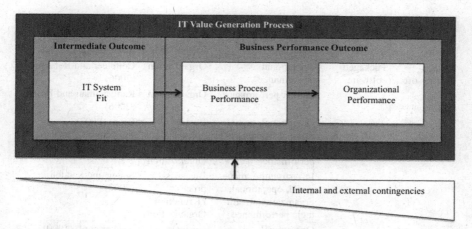

Fig. 2.10   A generic model on IT value generation process

2.2.3   Previous Contribution on Software and Sourcing Performance

Based on the generic model of IT value generation, this section continues with a discussion of literature related to software and sourcing performance. Previous findings are classified with respect to their research stream into studies on process-centric software performance (Sect. 2.2.3.1), software sourcing performance (Sect. 2.2.3.2), and IT outsourcing performance (Sect. 2.2.3.3). Findings are summarized in Sect. 2.2.3.4 and dependent concepts of this study are introduced. Table 2.2 gives an overview of previous contribution on software and sourcing performance.

2.2.3.1   Studies on Process-Centric Software Performance

Studies on process-centric software performance typically investigated performance of specific types of enterprise systems. Two studies that focused on performance outcomes of packaged ERP systems on an **organizational level** were identified. Cotteleer and Bendoly (2006) conducted a multimethod approach including interviews and reviews of several internal documents in order to assess the contribution of ERP implementation on operational performance within a case company. It was found that the investigated enterprise system contributes to *near-term operational performance improvements* (such as lead-time) and *long-term improvements* (such as learning effects) (Cotteleer and Bendoly 2006). In another study on ERP implementation, Ranganathan and Brown (2006) analysed enterprise system's impact on *abnormal returns*. In particular the effects of application's *functional* and *physical scope* as well as *vendor's reputation* were investigated. *Functional scope* refers to the types of ERP modules implemented. In particular it

Table 2.2 Previous contribution on software and sourcing performance

Research stream	Focus of investigation	Performance concepts	Impact level	Sources
Process-centric software performance	Packaged software	Operational performance	Organization	Cotteleer and Bendoly (2006)
		Market performance	Organization	Ranganathan and Brown (2006)
		Operational, organizational, strategic, technological performance	Business process IT function Organization	Grant (2003)
		Infrastructure, managerial, operational, organizational, strategic performance	Business process IT function Organization	Shang and Seddon (2002)
		Operational efficiency	Business process	Banker et al. (1990)
	In-house software	Financial performance, usage	Business process	Houdeshel and Watson (1987)
Software sourcing performance	On-demand software performance	IT-enabled innovation	Organization	Malladi and Krishnan (2012a, b)
		Net benefits	Organization	Walther et al. (2012)
		System quality and system effectiveness	Business process	Hsieh and Huang (2012)
		Orientation towards innovation	IT function	Malladi and Krishnan (2012a, b)
		Perceived performance, satisfaction	IT function	Susarla et al. (2003)
		Performance outcomes	IT function	Susarla et al. (2009)
	On-demand, on-premises software performance	Software quality	IT function	Choudhary (2007a, b)
		Profit (vendor)	IT function	Zhang and Seidmann (2010)
	In-house software performance	Effectiveness of functionalities	Organization	Banker and Kemerer (1992)
		Operational efficiency, responsiveness, flexibility	Business process	Nidumolu (1995)
		Outsourcing success (overlap with SET satisfaction)	IT function	Wang (2002)
IT outsourcing performance	Sourcing success	Overall satisfaction	Business process IT function Organization	E.g. Koh et al. (2004), Nöhren and Heinzl (2012), Saunders et al. (1997)
		SET satisfaction	Business process IT function Organization	E.g. Goo et al. (2008), Grover et al. (1996), Lee and Kim (1999), Lee et al. (2004), Saunders et al. (1997)

(continued)

Table 2.2 (continued)

Research stream	Focus of investigation	Performance concepts	Impact level	Sources
		Extended SET satisfaction	Business process IT function Organization	Lacity and Willcocks (2001)
	Project performance	Cost, duration, quality	IT function	Gopal et al. (2002)
		Contract performance	IT function	Domberger et al. (2000)
		(Extra) Costs	IT function	Dibbern et al. (2008)
		Project performance	IT function	Nidumolu (1995)
	Process performance	Perceived business process improvements	Business process	Downing et al. (2003)
	Firm performance	Abnormal returns	Organization	Agarwal et al. (2006), Gewald and Gellrich (2007)
		Long-term business impact	Organization	Mojsilović et al. (2007)
		Financial metrics	Organization	Wang et al. (2008a)

was differentiated between enterprise support modules (e.g. human resources) and value-chain modules (e.g. sales and distribution). *Physical scope* refers to number of sites (regional or international) an ERP system was implemented. It was found that both, functional and physical scope positively impact abnormal returns (Ranganathan and Brown 2006).

Two studies combined **IT function, process and organizational level** measures with each other. Both studies provide categorizations of items measuring firm performance, business process performance, and IT function performance. In an investigation of strategic alignment Grant (2003) conducted an in-depth exploratory single case study to examine the success of the introduction of an ERP system within a case company. In particular, the implementation of a global financial accounting and reporting system was investigated. This study measured ERP success in terms of its *strategic, organizational, operational*, and *technological impact. Strategic impact* (organizational level) refers to the support of long-term initiatives such as *strategic alliances* and *market opportunities. Organizational impact* (organizational level) describes enterprise-wide benefits like *coordination between and across business units. Operational impacts* (business process level) are efficiency gains in terms of *improved quality* and *improved decision support capabilities*. At last, *technological impact* (IT function level) was defined by the inherent characteristics of an application such as *standardized IT operations* and *improved processing power* (Grant 2003). Drawing upon a review of vendor-reported success stories combined with interviews with IT managers, Shang and Seddon (2002) developed a list of 21 indicators to assess performance of packaged ERP software on process and organizational level. These indicators are grouped into five dimensions, *operational, managerial, strategic, IT infrastructure*, and *organizational benefits*. *Operational benefits* (business process level) such as *cost reduction and productivity improvements* refer to software's impact on day-to-day activities. On a *managerial dimension* (business process level), measures such as *better resource management* and *improved decision making and planning* assess application's contribution to support activities of line managers. On a *strategic dimension* (organizational level), Shang and Seddon identified indicators for an enterprise system's impact on competitive advantages like *support for business growth* and *building external linkages*. *IT infrastructure benefits* (IT function level) refer to reusable and shareable IT infrastructures for multiple business applications. Finally, *organizational benefits* (organizational level) describe companywide improvements such as *empowerment* and *changing work pattern* (Shang and Seddon 2002).

Two early studies on software performance evaluated the impact on a **process level**. Houdeshel and Watson (1987) conducted a single case study to assess benefits and success of an internally developed management information and decision support system (MIDS). In their study, the in-house application led to multiple paybacks such as an improved communication among internal and external stakeholders and improved information quality. The success of the system was measured in terms of a *cost-benefit analysis, frequency of use*, and *user satisfaction* (Houdeshel and Watson 1987). Banker et al. (1990) conducted a study on *operational efficiency* of a point-of-sale and order-coordination technology (POS) within an American fast food company. By applying data envelopment analysis and non-parametric hypotheses testing, the authors benchmarked the efficiency of restaurants that had implemented the POS system with those that had not. It was found that the packaged software contributed to the efficiency of the sites. In their study, *operational efficiency* was defined as the effects of IT investments on a business process level (Banker et al. 1990).

To sum up, in the light of a set of internal and external contingencies shaping software's value contribution performance outcome (e.g. Dehning and Richardson 2002; Melville et al. 2004; Soh and Markus 1995), a thorough performance outcome measure needs to focus on a process level (Melville et al. 2004). Against this background, studies on organizational level impact of process-centric software (Cotteleer and Bendoly 2006; Ranganathan and Brown 2006) are not further investigated. Banker et al. (1990) as well as Houdeshel and Watson (1987) relied on a broad definition of business process performance in terms of operational efficiency, financial performance, and usage. These concepts were not specified in greater detail by the authors. Consequently, these studies are dropped from further consideration. The most comprehensive conceptualization of process-centric software performance was found by Grant (2003) as well as Shang and Seddon (2002). The authors defined a set of indicators for measuring perceived business process performance from an operational and managerial perspective.

2.2.3.2   Studies on Software Sourcing Performance

Most studies related to software sourcing performance focus on **on-demand software**. Among them, two papers were identified considering organizational level impacts. In a study on IT-enabled innovation, Malladi and Krishnan (2012a, b) analysed the impact of on-demand software adoption on *innovation* moderated by firm's past *outsourcing experience*, *internal IT architecture flexibility*, and *process management maturity*. The dependent variable was coded as binary variable specifying whether an organization has patented any IT architectures, products, services, or processes within the past year. A positive relationship between on-demand software usage and innovation was found (Malladi and Krishnan 2012a, b). In order to develop an updated DeLone-McLean IS success model, Walther et al. (2012) conducted literature review to identify success factors and value propositions in software-as-a-service research. Based upon an investigation of 36 papers, the authors classified most salient on-demand outcomes based on their number of usage in previous research. Ten variables such as *cost savings*, *cost flexibility*, and *mobility* had been identified as appropriate for measuring *net benefits* of software-as-a-service (Walther et al. 2012).

Three papers were identified studying impacts of on-demand software related to a corporate's IT function. Malladi and Krishnan (2012a, b) investigated the impact of cloud computing on *CIO's strategic focus*, which was defined as direction towards innovation and new product development capabilities. A positive relationship moderated by *process management maturity* and *internal coordination IT capabilities* was found (Malladi and Krishnan 2012a, b). In a study on application service provisioning, Susarla et al. (2003) tested factors impacting client's satisfaction with its service vendor. Drawing upon expectation disconfirmation theory, the influence of *perceived performance* was found to be highly significant in the derived path model. *Perceived performance* was defined as five-item construct including measures related to vendor performance (*better maintenance support*, *ability to implement IT solutions rapidly*, and *access to best technology*) and application performance (*ability to integrate information from various functional applications* and *low implementation and service costs*) (Susarla et al. 2003). In a later study on application service provisioning, Susarla et al. (2009) investigated the impact of contracting mechanisms on performance outcomes based on transaction cost economics. In particular, it was found that those contracts, that are not aligned with transaction attributes resulted in budget overruns and achieved lower performance (Susarla et al. 2009).

In conceptualizing *user satisfaction* with on-demand CRM, Hsieh and Huang (2012) differentiated between *system quality* and *process performance*. The former one refers to *perceived usefulness* and *ease of use* of an application. *Process performance* was proposed to be a measure of *system effectiveness* in terms of an assessment of the communication, marketing, and relationship performance of the CRM process. The authors emphasized the mediating role of *intention to use* in realizing *process performance outcomes* (Hsieh and Huang 2012).

Three studies were found that simultaneously address **on-premises and on-demand software** at the level of the IT function. Those studies were conceptual-mathematical in nature. In two studies by Choudhary (2007a, b) a model to compare software quality in a software-as-a-service setting with those in an on-premises mode was developed and refined. Taking a vendor's perspective, its intention to invest in product quality was mathematically deduced. In the proposed two-period model, *software quality* is seen as a function of time. Investments in software development and improvement were found to be more likely in on-demand settings. This should result in a higher quality of software-as-a-service compared to on-premises applications (Choudhary 2007a, b). A third mathematical model was introduced by Zhang and Seidmann (2010). Drawing upon specific characteristics of on-demand and on-premises licencing in terms of *uncertainty about quality and compatibility of future updates*, *network externalities*, and *provider's ability to commit to future prices*, the optimal mode to offer software from a monopolistic vendor's perspective was discussed. In a two-period conceptual model, optimal licensing strategy is mainly impacted by quality uncertainty and network effects (Zhang and Seidmann 2010).

In-house software was observed on three levels. On an organizational level, Banker and Kemerer (1992) introduced a non-empirical mathematical principal-agent model for performance evaluation of customized external software development projects. Taking a client's perspective, four measures for project outcomes, *short-term costs* (initial development cost), *long-term costs* (maintenance costs), *short-term benefits* (timeliness of software development), and *long-term benefits* (effectiveness) were derived (Banker and Kemerer 1992). On a business process level, Nidumolu (1995) studied the effects of vertical (coordination initiated by project managers) and horizontal coordination mechanisms (mutual communication between users and IT staff) on *project performance* in customized software development settings. In this study, *project performance* was measured in terms of *process* and *product performance*. The former one describes how well the software development process was conducted in terms of *learning*, *control*, and *quality of interactions*. The latter one refers to the performance of the delivered system by using measures for *operational efficiency* (e.g. *reliability of software*, *cost of operations*), *responsiveness* (e.g. *ease of software use*, *ability to customize outputs to various user needs*), and *flexibility* (e.g. *cost of adapting software to changes in business*, *cost of maintaining software over lifetime*) (Nidumolu 1995). Finally, performance of a corporate's IT function was studied by Wang (2002). Drawing upon transaction cost economics, a multiple regression analysis was conducted to assess the effect of the exogenous variables *contractor reputation*, *asset specificity*, and *uncertainty* on the mediator *post-contractual opportunism* and the dependent variable *outsourcing success*. In this study, success was operationalized as six-item reflective construct. All items, *focus on core business*, *increase IS competence*, *access to skilled personnel*, *cost savings on human resources*, *cost savings on technological resources*, and *control of IS expenses* are closely related to SET satisfaction which will be discussed in Sect. 2.2.3.3 (Wang 2002).

To sum up, several studies related to this stream of research are either mathe-matical (e.g. Banker and Kemerer 1992; Zhang and Seidmann 2010) or conceptual (e.g. Hsieh and Huang 2012; Walther et al. 2012) in nature. For instance, taking a vendors perspective, on-premises and on-demand licensing is compared and impli-cations for software quality is derived (Choudhary 2007a, b). Due to the fact that an empirical study is conducted in this work, conceptual and mathematical papers are not further taken into consideration. In addition, organizational level studies (e.g. Malladi and Krishnan 2012a, b) were dropped. The above outlined business process performance conceptualization of Grant (2003) as well as Shang and Seddon (2002) encompasses the definition of Nidumolu (1995). Consequently, this study adds little value to the business process performance concept and is not further discussed. The remaining studies related to this stream of research stress the importance of considering sourcing performance of software related to a corpo-rate's IT function (e.g. Susarla et al. 2003, 2009; Wang 2002). In order to enrich the discussion of this concept, previous studies on outsourcing performance are discussed in the following subsection.

2.2.3.3   Studies on IT Outsourcing Performance

As outlined above, the notion of performance is typically vague in nature (Dibbern et al. 2004). Looking at more than 20 years of IT outsourcing research, a huge body of literature deals with the outcomes of sourcing arrangements for client firms. Over the years, scientists adopted a wide dispersion of dependent concepts (Dibbern et al. 2004; Mahnke et al. 2005). In this section, previous findings are classified based on their focus of investigation into studies on sourcing success, project performance, process performance, and organizational performance. It has to be noted that a complete discussion of dependent constructs applied in IT outsourcing research is beyond the scope of this work. Interested readers may refer to works of Dibbern et al. (2004) and Lacity et al. (2010).

Sourcing success is most frequently operationalized in terms of satisfaction (Dibbern et al. 2004) with perceived benefits derived from IT outsourcing arrange-ments (e.g. Grover et al. 1996; Koh et al. 2004; Lacity and Willcocks 1998; Lee et al. 2004; Wang 2002). Lacity et al. (2010) found that sourcing success is the predominant performance construct in IT outsourcing research. In sum, more than 170 out of 376 investigated studies relied on outsourcing success measures (Lacity et al. 2010). Satisfaction is defined as "*a positive affective state resulting from the appraisal of all aspects of a firm's working relationship with another firm*" (Ander-son and Narus 1984: 66). Previous studies relied on overall measures of (perceived) outsourcing success in terms of satisfaction with a sourcing arrangement in general and the intention to retain a particular service vendor (e.g. Koh et al. 2004; Saunders et al. 1997). Other studies added more granularity to the discussion. For instance, Lacity and Willcocks (2001) categorized such perceived benefits in terms of *financial restructuring*, *core competences*, *technological catalyst* (e.g. greater flex-ibility in technology), *business transition* (e.g. support of organizational change), *business innovation* (e.g. innovation of processes and skills), and *new markets* (e.g. joint ventures). This notion was eventually limited to fewer factors in quantitative performance measurement. Lee et al. (2004) identified SET satisfaction in terms of *cost efficiency* (former *financial restructuring*), *technological catalysis*, and *strategic competence* (former *core competence*) as most salient for IT outsourcing success research. *Strategic competence* refers to "*redirecting the business and IT into core competencies*" (Lacity and Willcocks 2001: 316). It is a measure of outsourcing's contribution to refocus on core competences, increasing IT competence, access to skilled IT personnel, as well as a changed focus on strategic activities (Grover et al. 1996; Lee et al. 2004; Saunders et al. 1997). *Technology catalysis* refers to "*strengthening resources and flexibility in technology service to underpin business' strategic direction*" (Lacity and Willcocks 2001: 317). It evaluates outsourcing's contribution to reducing risks of technological obsolescence, to transform traditional IT infrastructures, to access key technologies, to incorporate new technologies and skills, as well as to increase technological flexibility (Grover et al. 1996; Lacity and Willcocks 2001; Lee et al. 2004; Saunders et al. 1997). Finally, *cost efficiency* refers to "*improving the business' financial position*" (Lacity and Willcocks 2001: 315). It captures the avoidance of major capital expenditures, the increases in economies of scale in human and technological resources as well as the extent of greater control over IT-related expenditures (Grover et al. 1996; Lee et al. 2004; Saunders et al. 1997).

Project performance refers to outcomes directly attributed to a particular sourcing arrangement. In contrast to success measures, which typically rely on Likert-scale scores (Dibbern et al. 2004), project performance measures are frequently quantifiable in nature. For instance, Gopal et al. (2002) evaluated performance of outsourcing software development projects in terms of *time elapsed* (project duration), *quality* (software rework), and *costs* (effort). It was found that these three concepts are interdependent with each other. Domberger et al. (2000) evaluated the realization of expectations from outsourcing contracts. This contract performance was captured in terms of the eight items *service availability and timeliness, out-of-hours availability, response in emergencies, provision at expected cost, delivery to expected quality, accuracy of advice, correctness of error fixes*, and *minimization of system downtime*. Dibbern et al. (2008) measured performance of offshored software development and maintenance projects by the means of extra costs. These expenditures in terms of *control, coordination, design*, and *knowledge transfer* are costs that occur on top of a particular outsourcing arrangement. In addition, Nidumolu (1995) evaluated performance of software development projects by measuring *project performance* (labelled as *process performance*) in terms of learning, control, and quality.

Process performance is defined as "the level of performance of a process, such as process costs, operational efficiency, quality, or level of customer satisfaction" (Lacity et al. 2010: 426). In a study by Downing et al. (2003) the perceived business process improvements of IT outsourcing by business process managers was investigated.

Firm performance refers to "the degree to which a client organization reports business performance improvements as a result of an outsourcing decision, such as stock price performance, return on assets, expenses, and profits" (Lacity et al. 2010: 425). For instance, Agarwal et al. (2006) conducted an event study to analyse the impact of e-business outsourcing announcements on abnormal returns. In another event study, Gewald and Gellrich (2007) measured the impact of outsourcing statements on organizational performance. In their event study, performance was measured in terms of market reaction. The influence of outsourcing-specific risks such as transaction size, contract length, and outsourcing experience was investigated. Mojsilović et al. (2007) developed a model for analysing IT outsourcings' long-term impact on client's business. In addition, Wang et al. (2008a) emphasized the importance to include process level performance metrics such as sales per employee, total sales, and expenses in performance measurement. Performance on this level may be transformed into firm-level outcomes. In measuring performance on firm level, the authors relied on measures such as return on assets and return on investment (Wang et al. 2008a).

To sum up, a huge body of research on IT outsourcing outcomes exists. Concepts related to firm performance are concerned with capturing outcomes on an organizational level in terms of abnormal returns or other financial measures (e.g. Agarwal et al. 2006; Gewald and Gellrich 2007; Wang et al. 2008a). Variables related to this concept are particularly useful when investigating the position of certain companies within a competitive environment. As have been outlined, this study focused on process level performance outcomes. Consequently, firm performance is beyond the scope of this investigation. Concepts related to project performance determined the value of specific IT outsourcing tasks (e.g. Dibbern et al. 2008; Domberger et al. 2000; Gopal et al. 2002). Such tasks have an inherent duration with an explicit or an implicit completion date. Studies in this area rather focused on the realization of tasks related to the IT function and their impact on process or organizational value than on the performance of a particular enterprise system itself. Consequently, project performance concepts are less relevant for this research work.

The identified study on process performance by Downing et al. (2003) shows great overlap with the perceived performance concepts of Grant (2003) as well as Shang and Seddon (2002). However, the latter ones were found to be more explicit in defining a range of indicators identifying the contribution of process-centric software on business processes. Therefore, the concept by Downing et al. (2003) is not further investigated.

In contrast to this, the remaining sourcing success measures are more essential for the endeavour of this study. Most frequently IT outsourcing performance studies relied on the notion of *sourcing success* in terms of SET satisfaction (Goo et al. 2008; e.g. Grover et al. 1996; Lee et al. 2004). SET satisfaction provides a comprehensive measure to evaluate perceived performance from a strategic, economic, and technological point of view. It is frequently used to evaluate sourcing outcomes related to a corporate's IT function (e.g. Lacity and Willcocks 2001; Lee et al. 2004; Saunders et al. 1997). Against this background, SET satisfaction is identified as most valuable outcome concept for measuring sourcing performance of software.

2.2.3.4 Summary and Definition of Performance Outcome Concepts

This study focuses on a specific type of software artefacts. In particular, process-centric enterprise systems like ERP and CRM systems are investigated (Grant 2003; Shang and Seddon 2002; Strong and Volkoff 2010). Such software artefacts generate their primary impact on corporate business processes but also generate a strong secondary effect on a corporate's IT function (Swanson 1994) in terms of system development, system operation, and management (Heinzl 1993). Consequently, performance measurement has to capture both impacts of process-centric enterprise systems.

Drawing upon the literature review, two performance concepts were identified. First, business process performance assesses software's value within the business units (Grant 2003; Shang and Seddon 2002). The definition of this concept is given in Table 2.3. Second, sourcing performance in terms of SET satisfaction determines enterprise system's impact on the IT function (e.g. Goo et al. 2008; Grover et al. 1996; Lacity and Willcocks 2001; Lee and Kim 1999; Lee et al. 2004; Saunders et al. 1997). It measures the strategic, economic, and technological benefits of software. The definition of the three subconcepts related to software sourcing performance is given in Table 2.4. By including two concepts within this study, both, the primary value within the business units and the secondary impact on corporate's IT function can be investigated.

2.2.4 Previous Contribution on Software Alignment

In the presented study, software alignment is measured in terms of fit between software and business process (Strong and Volkoff 2010). Misfits occur as "*(. . .) the result of differences between the structures embedded in the package and those embedded in the organization*" (Soh and Sia 2004: 375). From a RIT perspective, such misfits are cases where elements of the real world are not adequately represented by an application (Sia and Soh 2007). In previous research, three perspectives of fit between software and business process structures emerged

Table 2.3 Definition of business process performance

Construct	Definition	Sources
Business process performance	Contribution of process-centric software to business process performance in terms of operational and managerial benefits identified by Grant (2003) as well as Shang and Seddon (2002)	Grant (2003), Shang and Seddon (2002)

Table 2.4 Definition of sourcing performance

Construct	Definition	Sources
Strategic benefits	A client organization's degree of satisfaction with software in terms of redirecting IT function into core competencies	E.g. Goo et al. (2008), Grover et al. (1996), Lacity and Willcocks (2001), Lee and Kim (1999), Lee et al. (2004), Saunders et al. (1997)
Economical benefits	A client organization's degree of satisfaction with software in terms of improving cost position of the IT function	
Technological benefits	A client organization's degree of satisfaction with software in terms of strengthening IT function's technological flexibility	

(Maurer et al. 2012; Nöhren et al. 2014). These three notions are discussed subsequently in order to derive an appropriate concept to evaluate software-business process fit.

2.2.4.1   The Sia-Soh-Notion of Software-Organization Fit

The first one is a taxonomy developed by Sia and Soh (2007). Based on institutional theory and RIT, four types of software misfits were derived (see Fig. 2.11). According to Sia and Soh (2007), misfits arise from differences in the actual organizational structures and the structures anticipated by a software developer. Drawing upon the institutional theory organizational structure can either be imposed or voluntarily acquired (Scott 1987). Imposed structures result from external sources such as the authoritative of a government (laws and regulations) and specific industry characteristics necessary to remain and perform in business (DiMaggio and Powell 1983; Soh and Sia 2004). Voluntary structures are deliberately adopted by an organization over time (Soh and Sia 2004). These structures arise from internal contingencies and encompass organizational norms and routines associated with efficient and effective resource acquisition and utilization (Scott 1987). Voluntarily acquired structures distinguish firms from each other (Soh and Sia 2004).

By including a RIT perspective, Sia and Soh (2007) enriched their discussion of imposed and voluntarily acquired structures by further differentiating between deep and surface structures of the software artefact. Thereby, four types of software-organization misfits were derived. First, *imposed deep structure misfits* refer to deficiencies of an enterprise system in capturing central elements of an organizational reality resulting in reduced levels of operational efficiency. Second, *imposed surface structure misfits* are less severe but require workarounds when operating the

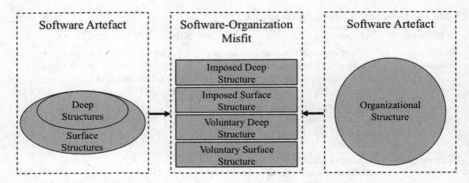

Fig. 2.11 Software-organization-misfit typology by Sia and Soh (2007)

user interface. Third, *voluntary deep structure misfits* result from the idiosyncratic processes of an organization conflicting with the core of an enterprise system. Finally, *voluntary surface structure* misfits are related to inappropriate or missing access, input, or output of software packages conflicting with organizational idiosyncrasies (Sia and Soh 2007).

2.2.4.2 The Strong-Volkoff-Notion of Software-Organization Fit

A second taxonomy was proposed by Strong and Volkoff (2010). Based on grounded theory, the authors identified six sources of software misfits—functionality, data, usability, role, control, and organizational culture—embedded within an enterprise system (see Fig. 2.12). In their study, surface structure was defined by software usability. *Usability misfits* occur, when the interaction with an enterprise system is confusing or inconvenient. Deep structures were defined by software functionality and data representation. *Functionality misfits* arise when particular functionalities are needed but missing. *Data misfits* occur, when data stored in an enterprise system leads to reduced quality in terms of timeliness, inaccessibility, or inappropriateness. Beside a deep and surface structure dimension, it was found that misfits also arise from latent structures. These latent structures, in terms of organizational culture, role, and control, are not directly designed within an application—like deep and surface structures—but arise from them as second order structures. Roles define the responsibilities of people within an organization. If the roles embedded in an enterprise system are inconsistent with the organizational responsibilities, *role misfits* occur. *Organizational culture misfits* result from an application that requires ways of working contrary to organizational norms. Finally, *control misfits* arise, when the control carried out by the system provides too much or too little opportunities (Strong and Volkoff 2010).

Strong and Volkoff (2010) further differentiated these sources of misfits into *deficiencies* and *impositions*. The former one refers to problems that arise when software features are needed but missing. The latter one specifies those

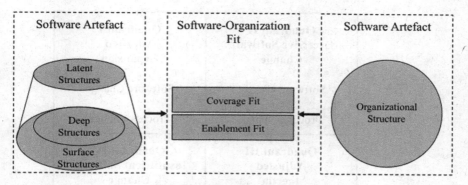

Fig. 2.12   Software-organization-fit typology by Strong and Volkoff (2010)

complications that result from the inherent structure of software that requires ways of working conflicting with the organizational reality. Drawing upon this classification, two fit constructs were developed. The first one, referred to as **coverage fit**, means that an application is free from functionality, data, usability, role, and control deficiencies. The second construct, termed **enablement fit** emerges from the absence of functionality, data, usability, role, control, and organizational culture impositions. Organizational culture misfits can only occur as impositions. Furthermore, enablement fit describes a situation where a company is better off with the existing system than with its legacy system (Strong and Volkoff 2010).

2.2.4.3   The Nöhren-Heinzl-Kude-Notion of Dynamic Software-Business Process Fit

Drawing upon a RIT perspective, IT is seen as representation of a corporate reality. Consequently, in the light of process and software structure change (e.g. Maltz and Kohli 1996; Nissen and Burton 2011; Nöhren et al. 2014; Zajac et al. 2000), software alignment must be seen as non-deterministic and dynamic process (Sabherwal et al. 2001; Vessey and Ward 2013). In particular, both, software as well as corporate's business processes must be adaptive in nature in order to coevolve with each other (Benbya and McKelvey 2006; Vessey and Ward 2013).

In general, change can be seen as a function of magnitude, direction, and timing of shifts in business process and software structures (Nissen and Burton 2011; Nöhren et al. 2014; Zajac et al. 2000). *Magnitude* expresses the extent of transformation. It describes whether business process or software reality experiences an incremental or a radical shift (Luo and Strong 2004; Orlikowski 1993). *Direction* expresses the course of an transformation. It describes to the path and the content of business process or software structure change. Finally, *timing* refers to date and frequency of transformation. It explains whether periods of stability with no change are rather long or short (Sabherwal et al. 2001).

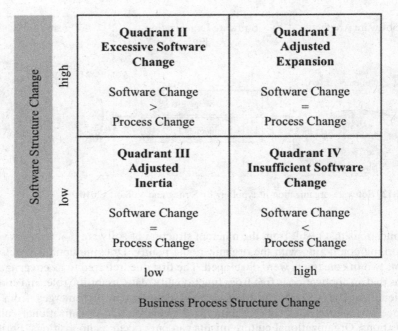

Fig. 2.13 Nöhren-Heinzl-Kude notion of dynamic software-process fit

If software structure change occurs in line with business process structure change, dynamic fit is established. In contrast to this, if software structure change is greater than business process structure change, or vice versa, companies suffer from dynamic misfit. These situations are illustrated in Fig. 2.13 (Nöhren et al. 2014; Zajac et al. 2000).

Figure 2.13 defines two ways to establish dynamic fit. Quadrant I describes the situation in which both, business process structures and software structures experience a high level of change resulting in a beneficial stage for a company. This situation is further referred to as *adjusted expansion*. Quadrant III represents the contrary situation wherein both, business process and software faces little or no change in their structures. A company benefits from persistence. This stage is branded *adjusted inertia*.

Additionally, there are two ways to suffer from dynamic misfit. Quadrant II represents the situation wherein software structure change is high but business processes fail to respond adequately. For organizations in this category, the nonoccurrence of such necessary business process change may be a result of either an organizational inability or unwillingness to change, or business process structures do not suggest the need to change (Zajac et al. 2000). This situation is further referred to as *excessive software change*. Quadrant IV describes the contrary situation in which business process structure change is high but software fails to respond adequately. It captures a condition wherein software has become obsolete, outdated, or otherwise inappropriate in light of business process transformation.

Dynamic misfit is the consequence of the nonoccurrence of required software structure change. This situation is labelled *insufficient software change*.

2.2.4.4   Summary and Development of Software-Business Process Fit Measure

Having outlined three recently published notions of software-business process fit, this section continues with a development of a fit measure for the endeavour of this study. In comparing the fit concepts of Strong and Volkoff (2010) with those of Sia and Soh (2007), the following conclusions can be made. First, the two studies differ with respect to their classification of misfit. Sia and Soh (2007) grouped software misfits with respect to their environmental source. It was found that while voluntarily acquired organizational structure misfits are less severe, companies suffer if imposed structures are not adequately mirrored by their software artefact. Sia and Soh (2007) did not further elaborate what deep and surface structures misfits are. In contrast to this, Strong and Volkoff (2010) added more granularity to the discussion of the software artefact. In particular, the "black box" of deep and surface structures is opened and the authors identified six types of misfits. Second, Strong and Volkoff (2010) provided a novel understanding of the enterprise software artefact. This definition accounts for an incorporation of latent structures that are not directly designed within an application but emerge as second-order structures from deep and surface elements. Third, the typology of Sia and Soh (2007) primarily focuses on why software-business process misfits emerge from environmental forces and how to overcome imposed and voluntarily acquired deep and surface structure misfits.

Against this background, the notion of Strong and Volkoff (2010) appears to be more appropriate to capture a holistic picture on software-business process fit. However, the derived fit constructs show two significant weaknesses. First, it has to be noted that coverage and enablement fit are not free of overlap. In particular, deficiencies—related to the coverage fit construct—"*are problems arising from [software] features that are missing but needed. Empirically, these problems take the form of actions users cannot take because the [enterprise system] is missing functionality, data fields, controls, etc., necessary for those actions.*" (Strong and Volkoff 2010: 737). Impositions—related to the enablement fit construct—"*are problems arising from the inherent characteristics of [software] such as integration and standardization. (. . .) Empirically, impositions take the form of the [software structure] requiring ways of working that are contrary to organizational norms and practices.*" (Strong and Volkoff 2010: 737). Consequently, deficiencies and impositions often emerge from the same sources in terms of functionality, data, usability, role, and control misfits. Second, enablement fit "*means the [software] permits and enables the organization to operate more effectively, and users to do their work more efficiently, than was the case without [the software]. (. . .) the organization is better off as a result of implementing the [software]*" (Strong and Volkoff 2010: 746). While coverage fit is independent from a performance anchor, enablement fit

Table 2.5 Definition of dynamic fit

Construct	Definition	Sources
Dynamic fit	Degree to which software is free from deficiencies in terms of functionality, data, usability, role, and control misfits	Based on Nöhren et al. (2014), Strong and Volkoff (2010)

takes a criterion-specific perspective (see Sect. 2.2.2 for a definition of performance anchoring). Based on this discussion, only coverage fit is taken into further consideration for measuring the fit between software and business process structure.

Neither the concepts of Strong and Volkoff (2010) nor those of Sia and Soh (2007) take changing business process or software structures into account. This shortcoming was addressed by the notion of dynamic fit of Nöhren et al. (2014) (see Fig. 2.13). If a company suffers from dynamic misfit in terms of excessive or insufficient software change, software and business process structures are drifting apart. In this situation, an organization experiences deficiencies by the means of functionality, data, usability, role or control misfits. In contrast to this, if company realizes dynamic fit in terms of adjusted expansion or inertia, business process and software structures coevolve with each other. In such conditions, organizations benefit from coverage fit. The definition of dynamic fit is given in Table 2.5. In order to understand how dynamic fit is generated Sect. 2.2.5 investigates concepts related to the dynamic fit process.

2.2.5   The Dynamic Alignment Process

Dynamic fit was defined taking a RIT perspective (Nöhren et al. 2014). Both, RIT and institutional theory sees an organization as a set of structures (Scott 1987; Wand and Weber 1990). These theoretical lenses are closely linked to each other but differ with respect to their focus. While RIT emphasizes on the structures of particular IT artefacts in relationship to other structures of a firm (Sia and Soh 2007; Strong and Volkoff 2010; Wand and Weber 1990), institutional theory takes a more holistic, aggregated, and dynamic view on organizational structures in general (including the IT artefact) and their relationship to changing environmental conditions (Berente and Yoo 2012; Jones and Karsten 2008; Scott 1987). Consequently, by linking RIT with institutional theory, shifts in software and business process structures that result in dynamic fit can be conceptualized.

This section investigates the process by which dynamic fit is established. As outlined above, software alignment must be seen as a non-deterministic and dynamic process (Sabherwal et al. 2001; Vessey and Ward 2013). "*Alignment is not desirable as an end in itself since the business must always change*" (Chan and Reich 2007: 298).

Dynamic fit refers to the coevolution between software and business process structures over time (Nöhren et al. 2014). A change in corporate's business process structures must go along with software structure change and vice versa in order to benefit from adjusted expansion or adjusted inertia (Nöhren et al. 2014; Sabherwal et al. 2001; Zajac et al. 2000). Consequently, dynamic fit possesses two necessary conditions: software structure change and business process structure change (Nöhren et al. 2014).

2.2.5.1   Software Structure Change

Starting with an investigation of **software structure change**, different parties are involved in sourcing applications: a client company that uses the software artefact to support its business processes and—if a packaged enterprise system is sourced— a software vendor that develops the application. Consequently, software structure change can either occur client-driven or vendor-driven (in on-premises and on-demand settings).

Innovation literature tags these types of software structure change as technology push and business pull innovation (Currie et al. 2004; Davern and Kauffman 2000; Horbach et al. 2012). Vendor-driven software structure change is related to *technological push* innovation (e.g. Carmel and Sawyer 1998; Davern and Kauffman 2000; Kim et al. 2009; Lin and Chen 2012). It describes a situation in which a software vendor performs deep or surface structure transformations of an enterprise system. Software change is governed outside a firm's hierarchy.

Client-driven software structure change is related to *business pull* innovation (e.g. Carmel and Sawyer 1998; Davern and Kauffman 2000; Kim et al. 2009; Lin and Chen 2012). It describes a situation in which deep or surface structure transformation of an enterprise system is either performed by a corporate's IT unit or by a subcontracted external third-party vendor under control of the client. Software innovation is governed within a firm's hierarchy.

Software structure change can either occur client-driven or vendor-driven. Table 2.6 gives the definition of the related technological push and business pull innovation concepts (Carmel and Sawyer 1998; based on Davern and Kauffman 2000; Kim et al. 2009; Lin and Chen 2012).

2.2.5.2   Business Process Structure Change

The second necessary condition of dynamic fit is **business process structure change**. A process is *"a series of actions or steps taken in order to achieve a particular end"* (Oxford Dictionaries 2014b). A specific kind of a process is a business process (Heinrich et al. 2011). Drawing upon institutional theory business processes can be seen as a set of organized and established structures (Berente and Yoo 2012; Sia and Soh 2007; Strong and Volkoff 2010). Business processes link functions for creating a business outcome in a chronological and factual manner (Heinrich et al. 2011). They are sets of logically related tasks, rules, and procedures

Table 2.6 Definition of software structure change

Construct		Definition	Sources
Software structure change	Technology push innovation	Technology push innovation occurs, when software innovation developed by a software vendor is implemented within a firm	Based on Carmel and Sawyer (1998), Davern and Kauffman (2000), Kim et al. (2009), Lin and Chen (2012)
	Business pull innovation	Business pull innovation occurs, when software innovation developed by a client is implemented within its firm	

Table 2.7 Definition of business process change

Construct	Definition	Sources
Business process structure change	Business process structure change occurs, when an organization transforms the structure of its tasks, rules and procedures	Based on Blum (2006), Maltz and Kohli (1996)

that are required for realizing a desired business goal (Blum 2006; Davenport and Short 1990; Maltz and Kohli 1996; Melville et al. 2004).

Like software structures, business process structures are not assumed to be static in nature. Institutional theory argues that most structures are exposed to change over time (Berente and Yoo 2012; Jones and Karsten 2008; Scott 1987). As shown in Table 2.7, business process structure change can be defined as transformation in the structure of tasks, rules, and procedures within an organization (Blum 2006; Maltz and Kohli 1996).

2.2.5.3   Environmental Change

The stimulus for software and business process structure change can be found within the environmental setting of an organization (Scott 1987). Changes in the structures of business processes and software are caused by fluctuations in organization's competitive context (e.g. length of product and service life cycles, customer turnover, and market share), by variations of industry-specific rules or procedures, or by shifts in regulatory frameworks and country-specific laws (e.g. Gemino et al. 2007; Maltz and Kohli 1996; Soh and Sia 2004; Son and Benbasat 2007; Tallon and Pinsonneault 2011; Tiwana and Keil 2009; Wang et al. 2006).

Institutional theory differentiates between imposed and voluntary structural change (Scott 1987; Sia and Soh 2007; Soh and Sia 2004). Imposed change is a result of external forces such as the government or established industry best practice (DiMaggio and Powell 1983; Sia and Soh 2007). It can be distinguished between changes in the firm-specific, the industry-specific, and the country-specific imposed context (Scott 1987; Sia and Soh 2007). The latter one refers to shifts in the socio-

Table 2.8 Definition of environmental change

Construct		Definition	Sources
Macro environmental change	Imposed country context	Changes in the socio-political system, economic configuration, or cultural practices within a country	Based on Maltz and Kohli (1996), Scott (1987), Sia and Soh (2007), Soh and Sia (2004)
	Imposed industry context	Changes in practices specific to firm's industrial sector	
Micro environmental change	Imposed firm context	Changes in structures related to a firm's trading partners	
	Voluntary context	Changes in the idiosyncratic organisational structures	

political system, economic configuration, or cultural practices within a country (Sia and Soh 2007). The introduction of a new national identification number or the inception of SEPA are examples for country-specific changes. Changes in the imposed industry-specific context are transformations in practices specific to firm's industrial sector (Sia and Soh 2007). An example would be a new and more stringent accountability requirement within the pharmaceutical industry (Sia and Soh 2007). Finally, changes in the imposed firm-specific context result from a firm's working relationship with its trading partners (Melville et al. 2004; Scott 1987; Sia and Soh 2007).

While shifts within the imposed setting comes from outside of an organization, changes in the voluntary context result from internal forces (Scott 1987). The voluntary context is idiosyncratic to a particular firm (Sia and Soh 2007). It includes such processes, rules, or procedures that organisations develop as a result of their experience, strategy, and management preferences (Scott 1987; Sia and Soh 2007).

In contrast to shifts in the voluntary context, which are always idiosyncratic to a particular firm (Sia and Soh 2007), imposed context change either occurs within the macro or the micro environment of an organization (Melville et al. 2004). Macro environmental changes are shifts in the imposed country-specific or the imposed industry-specific context (Sia and Soh 2007). These changes impact all companies within a nation or a particular sector. Micro environmental changes are unique to a particular company. They encompass shifts in the imposed firm-specific or the voluntary context of an organization (Scott 1987; Sia and Soh 2007). Table 2.8 gives the definition of macro and micro environmental change.

2.2.5.4 Contextual Factors Related to Software and Business Process Structure Flexibility

Dynamic fit is not merely a result of software and business process structure change (Nöhren et al. 2014). These changes must take place with an adequate timing, magnitude, and direction to be beneficial for a company (Zajac et al. 2000). If a company experiences an environmental change which results in a business process transformation, its enterprise systems needs to change equipollently and isochronally (Berente and Yoo 2012; Maltz and Kohli 1996; Scott 1987; Sia and Soh 2007). Consequently, software structures need to be flexible.

"Software is flexible if it can be efficiently and rapidly adapted because of a change in business needs." (Wang et al. 2008b: 438). This flexibility, which can be seen as an inherent and specific characteristic of a sourced software artefact, can be discussed by the help of TCE (Benlian et al. 2009; Winkler and Brown 2014).

TCE is a widely used theoretical lens in IT outsourcing research. It supports researchers by investigating decision, success, and failure of sourcing arrangements (e.g. Benlian et al. 2009; Dibbern et al. 2008; Schwarz et al. 2009). TCE provides a theoretical view on one major characteristic of software sourcing: application specificity (Winkler and Brown 2014). If an application is specific to a particular firm's requirements (high asset specificity), economic benefits from outsourcing decreases (Kern et al. 2002a, b; Winkler and Brown 2014). This application specificity *"is reflected in the degree that specific applications can be customized, integrated, and modularized prior to and in the outsourcing relationship"* (Benlian et al. 2009: 360). It serves as a measure for software's flexibility and its ease of customization (Winkler and Brown 2014). Application specificity was found to impact the adoption of on-demand software (Benlian et al. 2009) as well as the internal governance structure of applications (Winkler and Brown 2014). Its relationship with software alignment has not been studied so far.

In order to meet their idiosyncratic requirements and to realize fit, deep and surface attributes of software are frequently customized by client companies (e.g. Domberger et al. 2000; Maurer et al. 2012; Sarker et al. 2012; Xin and Levina 2008). Enterprise systems can be differentiated according to their customizability. This **software customizability** can be measured in terms of application specificity (Benlian et al. 2009; Winkler and Brown 2014). Customizations are frequently required to embed an enterprise system within an organization (Sia and Soh 2007; Soh and Sia 2004; Strong and Volkoff 2010). Software vendors differentiate themselves from their competitors by the degree to which their applications allow for individual adaptations of deep and surface structures (Slaughter and Levine 2006). Table 2.9 gives the definition of software customizability (Benlian et al. 2009; Wang et al. 2008b; Winkler and Brown 2014).

If an environmental change results in software transformation, organizational business processes must change equipollently and isochronally (Berente and Yoo 2012; Maltz and Kohli 1996; Scott 1987; Sia and Soh 2007). Consequently, not

Table 2.9 Definition of software customizability

Construct	Definition	Sources
Software customizability	Degree to which deep and surface structures of software can be rapidly and extensively customized by a client	Based on Benlian et al. (2009), Wang et al. (2008b), Winkler and Brown (2014)

Table 2.10 Definition of business process adaptability

Construct	Definition	Sources
Business process adaptability	Degree to which structures of business processes can be rapidly and extensively modified and adapted	Based on Lacity et al. (2011), Tatikonda and Montoya-Weiss (2001), Yang and Papazoglou (2000)

only software but also business process structures need to be flexible in nature in order to cope with changing software structures.

"*Process adaptability refers to flexibility (. . .) to meet emerging circumstances*" (Tatikonda and Montoya-Weiss 2001: 155). This flexibility, which can be seen as an inherent characteristic of organization's business processes, can be discussed by the help of RBV (Barney 1991; Tatikonda and Montoya-Weiss 2001).

RBV differentiates between human, physical, and organizational resources (Barney 1991; Grant 1991). Physical resources are assets like a company's technology, its equipment, and its geographical position (Barney 1991; Nöhren and Heinzl 2012). Human resources include skills and experience of managers and workers within the firm (Barney 1991). Organizational resources are assets such as an internal planning, controlling, and coordinating system as well as processes to fulfil customers' needs (Barney 1991; Nöhren and Heinzl 2012). Consequently, business processes (Heinrich et al. 2011) are organizational resources.

"To remain competitive organizations must be able to move fast and quickly adapt to change. Moreover, they must be able to reconfigure their key business processes as changing market conditions dictate." (Yang and Papazoglou 2000: 43). Organizational business processes differ with respect to their adaptability (Tatikonda and Montoya-Weiss 2001; Yang and Papazoglou 2000). **Business process adaptability** serves as a measure for business process structure flexibility and its ease of adaptation (Tatikonda and Montoya-Weiss 2001; Yang and Papazoglou 2000). Table 2.10 gives the definition of this construct (Lacity et al. 2011; Tatikonda and Montoya-Weiss 2001; Yang and Papazoglou 2000).

2.2.5.5   Summary

Software-business process fit is non-deterministic and dynamic in nature (Sabherwal et al. 2001; Vessey and Ward 2013). It expresses the coevolution between software and business process structure over time (Nöhren et al. 2014; Sabherwal et al. 2001; Zajac et al. 2000). This section discusses components of the process by which this coevolution in terms of dynamic fit is generated. Drawing upon institutional theory in combination with RIT, software structure change and business process structure change were identified as necessary conditions for dynamic fit. The latter one is defined as transformation in the structure of tasks, rules, and procedures within an organization (Blum 2006; Maltz and Kohli 1996). Software structure change can occur client-driven and vendor-driven. Vendor-driven software structure change refers to technology push innovation and expresses the implementation of a software innovation developed by a software vendor within a firm (Carmel and Sawyer 1998; based on Davern and Kauffman 2000; Kim et al. 2009; Lin and Chen 2012). Client-driven software structure change refers to business pull innovation and describes the implementation of a software innovation, which is developed by a client (Carmel and Sawyer 1998; based on Davern and Kauffman 2000; Kim et al. 2009; Lin and Chen 2012).

Both, business process structure and software structure change are results of shifts in environmental conditions (Scott 1987). These shifts are either firm-specific and result from internal or external environment (micro environmental change) or impact all companies within a country or industrial sector (macro environmental change) (Maltz and Kohli 1996; Scott 1987; Sia and Soh 2007; Soh and Sia 2004).

Due to the fact that dynamic fit is not merely a result of change in software and business process structure but also that these changes take place with an adequate timing, magnitude, and direction (Nöhren et al. 2014; Zajac et al. 2000), two contextual factors related to flexibility of software and business process structures were identified. Software customizability was defined as the degree to which deep and surface structures of software can be rapidly and extensively customized by a client (Benlian et al. 2009; Wang et al. 2008b; Winkler and Brown 2014). Business process adaptability describes the degree to which structures of business processes can be rapidly and extensively modified and adapted (Lacity et al. 2011; Tatikonda and Montoya-Weiss 2001; Yang and Papazoglou 2000).

2.3   Summary

The presented study aims to contribute to the discussion of how software sourcing modes impact software sourcing value in terms of alignment and performance and how these outcomes are interrelated with each other. No strong and precise definition of in-house, on-premises, and on-demand software was found in previous researches. Drawing upon the representational view of IT (Sia and Soh 2007; Strong and Volkoff 2010; Wand and Weber 1990), software sourcing modes were defined based on client company's ownership of physical, deep, and surface structures. In an in-house setting, physical, deep, and surface structures of the software artefact are held within a firm's hierarchy. In contrast to this, the ownership on deep and surface structures of packaged applications is held by a software vendor. On-premises and on-demand software differ with respect to their physical structures in terms of their deployment. Whereas on-premises applications are installed on a firm's own IT infrastructure (internal physical structure ownership), on-demand applications are hosted at a software vendor (external physical structure ownership) and are accessed via Internet. In a consequence, the extent of ownership on physical, deep, and surface structures decreases from in-house through on-premises to on-demand sourcing.

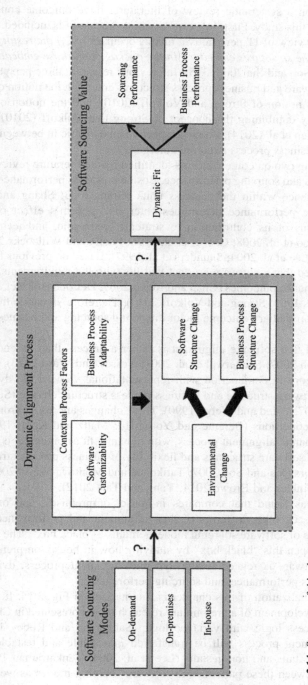

Fig. 2.14 Summary of this chapter

Drawing upon a systematic review of literature, three outcome concepts are encompassed in this study. First, software-business process fit is included. Taking a representational view of IT perspective, misfits occur as "(. . .) *the result of differences between the structures embedded in the package and those embedded in the organization*" (Soh and Sia 2004: 375). In previous research, three perspectives of fit between software and business process structures emerged: the notion of Sia and Soh (2007), the notion of Strong and Volkoff (2010), and the notion of Nöhren et al. (2014). By combining the concept of Strong and Volkoff (2010) with the concept of Nöhren et al. (2014), a new perspective on dynamic fit between software structure and business process structure emerged.

The remaining two outcome concepts identified by the literature review refer to business process and sourcing performance. Business process performance captures software's influence within the business units (Grant 2003; Shang and Seddon 2002). Sourcing performance determines enterprise system's effect on the IT function in terms of its contribution to strategic, economic, and technological benefits (e.g. Goo et al. 2008; Grover et al. 1996; Lacity and Willcocks 2001; Lee and Kim 1999; Lee et al. 2004; Saunders et al. 1997). Based on previous findings it can be concluded that a software artefact that fits with the requirements of a firm impacts performance outcomes (Chan and Reich 2007; DeLone and McLean 1992; Soh and Markus 1995; Strong and Volkoff 2010). Therefore, dynamic fit is attributed to be an intermediary outcome factor impacting sourcing and business process performance.

It was found that software alignment is rather a process than an end in itself (Chan and Reich 2007; Sabherwal et al. 2001; Vessey and Ward 2013). Based on institutional theory in conjunction with representational view of IT, dynamic fit results from software structure and business process structure change (Scott 1987; Sia and Soh 2007; Wand and Weber 1990). These changes are results from shifting environmental conditions (Berente and Yoo 2012; Maltz and Kohli 1996; Scott 1987). This dynamic alignment process, with dynamic fit as outcome, is impacted by flexibility of software structures and flexibility of business process structures as contextual factors (Sia and Soh 2007; Tatikonda and Montoya-Weiss 2001; Wang et al. 2008b; Winkler and Brown 2014; Yang and Tate 2012).

No study was found that compares in-house, on-premises, and on-demand software with each other in terms of their alignment and performance. Consequently, the role of software sourcing modes remains a "black box". The presented study aims to open this "black box" by studying how in-house, on-premises, and on-demand software is related to the dynamic alignment process, dynamic fit, business process performance, and sourcing performance.

The conceptualization of this chapter is summarized in Fig. 2.14. It forms the basis for the development of a preliminary research model presented in Chap. 3. By combining process logic with variance logic (Sabherwal and Robey 1995), the dynamic alignment process will be transferred into stable and testable clusters grouped into gestalts and non-gestalts (Lee et al. 2004; Venkatraman 1989). The relationship between these patterns and software sourcing modes as well as their influence on software sourcing value will be discussed.

Chapter 3
Preliminary Research Model

Having specified software sourcing modes, software sourcing value, and the components of the dynamic alignment process, this section continues with the development of a preliminary research model. Following the guidelines by Sabherwal and Robey (1995), a combined process and variance model approach is applied. This section starts with an introduction to model logic in Sect. 3.1. Section 3.2 continues with a transformation of the dynamic alignment process into alignment clusters (Sabherwal and Robey 1995). These alignment clusters encompass patterns of environmental change, software structure change, business process structure change, software customizability, and business process adaptability. Alignment clusters are grouped into *gestalts* and *non-gestalts*. Gestalt clusters are supposed to establish dynamic fit. Four such gestalts are proposed drawing upon the literature review conducted in the previous chapter. A preliminary research model is developed in Sect. 3.3. Chapter summary is given in Sect. 3.4.

3.1 Logical Structures of Research Models

When looking at research in social sciences, studies are either positioned as process or as variance approaches (Dibbern 2004; Mohr 1982). The difference between these two types of logical structures can be found in the relationship among antecedences and outcomes as shown in Table 3.1 (Markus and Robey 1988).

Variance logic assumes a world which *"is made up of fixed entities with varying attributes"* (Poole et al. 2000: 32). It explains dependent variables with at least two values attached (Dibbern 2004). Alterations in these values are caused by independent variables which also vary along some range of values (Sabherwal and Robey 1995; Webster and Watson 2002). These independent variables are causally linked to the dependent variables (Sabherwal and Robey 1995). Therefore, questions about the relationship between antecedences and consequences are naturally variance questions (Pentland 1999).

© Springer International Publishing Switzerland 2016
M. Nöhren, *Enterprise Software Sourcing Performance*, Progress in IS,
DOI 10.1007/978-3-319-23926-2_3

Table 3.1 Logical structures based on Markus and Robey (1988)

	Variance theory	Process theory
Definition	Cause is necessary and sufficient for outcome	Causation consists of necessary conditions in sequence that are impacted by change and random events
Assumption	Outcome will inevitably occur when necessary and sufficient conditions are present	Outcome may not occur even if all conditions are present
Elements	Dependent variables	Discrete outcomes
Role of time	Static	Longitudinal
Logical form	If X then Y; if more X then more Y	If not X then not Y; it cannot be extended to "more X" or "more Y"

The key focus of a variance logic is on a probabilistic prediction of alterations in the magnitude of a particular outcome under study (Adomavicius et al. 2008; Langley 1999; Soh and Markus 1995). The explanation of this outcome is based on necessary and sufficient causality (Poole et al. 2000). An outcome inevitably occurs if independent variables are different from zero. It is assumed that the underlying causal process that generates this outcome operates continuously over time (Poole et al. 2000). Consequently, time is negligible and variance models are static in nature (Markus and Robey 1988).

Following a variance logic, a dependent variable O can be seen as a function of $i = 1, \ldots, n$ independent variables V_i (Sabherwal and Robey 1995):

$$O = f(V_1, V_2, \ldots, V_n)$$

Opposed to this, **process logic** provides an explanation of temporal orders in which discrete outcomes occur instead of explaining variances in dependent concepts (Dibbern et al. 2004; Gregor 2006; Orlikowski 1993). Following a process logic, the world is assumed to be made up of entities which participate in events (Poole et al. 2000). Such events are the central units in process theories (Poole et al. 2000). In conjunction with contextual factors, events unfold other subsequential events towards a final outcome under study (Poole et al. 2000; Sabherwal and Robey 1995).

A process approach is of particular interest, when studying a dynamic phenomenon (Langley 1999). An observed sequence of events with underlying mechanisms that—under particular circumstances—result in a subsequential event are explained (Van de Ven and Huber 1990). Consequently, process theories identify necessary conditions for outcomes under study. These outcomes only occur if certain conditions were met, but even if all necessary conditions are present, the outcome does not inevitably occur (Markus and Robey 1988).

In algebraic terms, a process approach studies an outcome event O that is generated starting with the first event E_1 in the sequence, followed by a second event E_2 until the event E_n, which causes the final event O (Sabherwal and Robey 1995):

$$E_1 \rightarrow E_2 \rightarrow \ldots \rightarrow E_n \rightarrow O$$

Mohr (1982) argued that the logical structures of variance and process approaches can hardly be combined because variables and events are conceived in different ways. However, due to the fact that both model logics share the same epistemological assumptions about an objectively given and observable real world (see Chap. 4), different researchers have combined process and variance approaches in their studies (e.g. Robey and Farrow 1982; Sabherwal and Robey 1995). This allows to address more complex phenomena within a research model by understanding the sequence in which events occur and interpreting antecedences and outcomes of this process (Sabherwal and Robey 1995).

This study follows the guidelines by Sabherwal and Robey (1995) by combining process and variance logic within a research model. As outlined in Chap. 2, software-business process fit must be treated as a process (Chan and Reich 2007; Sabherwal et al. 2001; Vessey and Ward 2013) in which dynamic fit (Nöhren et al. 2014; Zajac et al. 2000) is generated in two consecutive steps starting with environmental change (Maltz and Kohli 1996; Scott 1987; Sia and Soh 2007; Soh and Sia 2004) as necessary condition for software structure and business process structure change (Blum 2006; Davern and Kauffman 2000; Maltz and Kohli 1996; Nöhren et al. 2014). This process is impacted by two contextual factors in terms of software customizability and business process adaptability (Tatikonda and Montoya-Weiss 2001; Wang et al. 2008b; Winkler and Brown 2014). Instead of focusing on how individual environmental changes, such as the introduction of SEPA or a new industry norm, leads to software structure and business process structure change, this study identifies and examines configurations that emerges to stable patterns (Sabherwal and Robey 1995). These patterns allow for transferring the dynamic alignment process into clusters and discuss the resulting model by the means of a variance logic (Markus and Robey 1988; Sabherwal and Robey 1995). Patterns of process event configurations are further classified into gestalts and non-gestalts (Lee et al. 2004; Venkatraman 1989).

3.2   Transforming the Dynamic Alignment Process into Alignment Clusters

As described in Chap. 2, software-business process fit must be understood as a process (Chan and Reich 2007; Sabherwal et al. 2001; Vessey and Ward 2013). Consequently, dynamic fit serves as an outcome of the dynamic alignment process (Poole et al. 2000; Sabherwal and Robey 1995). It captures the degree of coevolution between software and business process realities (Nöhren et al. 2014). Dynamic fit is generated by two previous events in the sequence: software structure and business process structure change (Blum 2006; Davern and Kauffman 2000; Maltz and Kohli 1996; Nöhren et al. 2014). The latter one describes transformations in process-related tasks, rules, and procedures within an organization (Blum 2006; Maltz and Kohli 1996). It expresses whether business process structure change occurs or not (Nöhren et al. 2014). Software structure change can either occur client-driven (business pull) or vendor-driven (technology push). Technology push innovation refers to the implementation of a software innovation within a firm that is developed by a software vendor (Carmel and Sawyer 1998; Davern and Kauffman 2000; Kim et al. 2009; Lin and Chen 2012). Business pull innovation describes the implementation of a software innovation, which is developed by a client (Carmel and Sawyer 1998; Davern and Kauffman 2000; Kim et al. 2009; Lin and Chen 2012). Both, business process structure and software structure change are results of environmental shifts (Scott 1987). These shifts are either firm-specific and result from a corporate's internal or external environment (micro environmental change) or impact all companies throughout a country or within an industrial sector (macro environmental change) (Maltz and Kohli 1996; Scott 1999; Sia and Soh 2007; Soh and Sia 2004).

As outlined above, the aim of this study is not an investigation of how particular environmental shifts result in software structure and business process structure change, which impacts dynamic fit or misfit (Burn 1993; Sabherwal et al. 2001). This study surface patterns of the dynamic alignment process and discusses their relationship with software sourcing modes as well as their impact on software sourcing value. Specifications of the five concepts related to the dynamic alignment process are specified in Sect. 3.2.1. Based on these specifications, different alignment clusters are defined in Sect. 3.2.2.

3.2.1 Specification of Concepts Related to the Dynamic Alignment Process

It is anticipated that companies differ with respect to the source of business process and software structure change (Scott 1987). Such shifts are either caused by macro or by micro environmental shifts (Maltz and Kohli 1996; Scott 1999; Sia and Soh 2007; Soh and Sia 2004). By differentiating between these two sources of change, empirical profiles can be positioned within the environmental change matrix presented in Fig. 3.1. The horizontal axis refers to shifts in the imposed firm context and the voluntary context of an organization (Scott 1987; Sia and Soh 2007). It expresses whether a company faces constant pressures through changes in its micro environment. Shifts in the imposed country context and the imposed industry context are given on the vertical axis (Scott 1987; Sia and Soh 2007). It states whether a company faces constant pressures through changes in its macro environment. Drawing upon the matrix in Fig. 3.1, companies can be classified based on

Fig. 3.1 Environmental change matrix

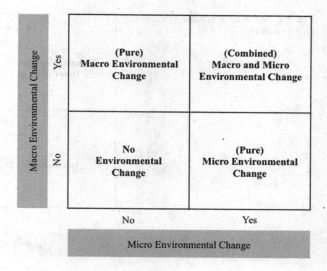

whether they constantly experience pure macro environmental change, pure micro environmental change, combined macro and micro environmental change, or no environmental change.

While some companies act very dynamically, other firms are rather stable with respect to their business processes. Previous studies found that companies within different industrial sectors differ with respect to their innovator rate. The innovator rate expresses the share of companies within an industry sector that introduces at least one new product or process within a period of 3 years (Rammer and Köhler 2012; Rammer and Ohnemus 2011). While the innovator rate of high-tech companies amounted to 74 % in 2010, organizations offering knowledge intensive services possessed a ratio of only 47 % (Rammer and Köhler 2012). Despite the fact that these rates are subject to change, they remain relatively stable for many years (Rammer and Köhler 2012). In this study, it is differentiated between organizations that constantly perform major or minor adaptations to their business processes and those where business process structures are stable over longer periods of time (Maltz and Kohli 1996; Sabherwal et al. 2001; Scott 1987).

Software structure change either occurs in terms of business pull or technology push innovation (Carmel and Sawyer 1998; Davern and Kauffman 2000; Kim et al. 2009; Lin and Chen 2012). Like for environmental change, empirical profiles can be positioned based on their sources of software structure change as presented in Fig. 3.1. The horizontal axis gives the occurrence of business pull innovation (Carmel and Sawyer 1998; Currie et al. 2004; Davern and Kauffman 2000). It expresses whether a company constantly performs client-driven software structure changes. The occurrence of technology push innovation is given on the vertical axis (Carmel and Sawyer 1998; Currie et al. 2004; Davern and Kauffman 2000). It states whether a company constantly implements vendor-driven software structure adaptations. Drawing upon the matrix in Fig. 3.2, companies can be classified based on

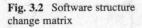

Fig. 3.2 Software structure change matrix

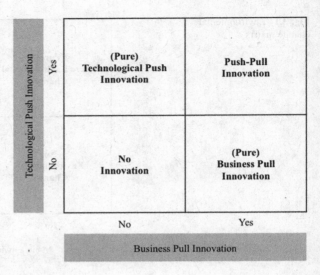

whether they experience pure business pull innovation, pure technology push innovation, push-pull innovation, or no innovation in their software structures.

Having defined business process adaptability and software customizability based on RBV and TCE, both concepts are assumed to be highly stable over time. Software customizability is an inherent and persisting specificity of particular software assets (Benlian et al. 2009; Wang et al. 2008b; Winkler and Brown 2014). Business process adaptability is seen as valuable and sustainable organizational resource (Barney 1991; Tatikonda and Montoya-Weiss 2001). The three concepts of dynamic fit, software customizability, and business process adaptability are rated into high, medium, and low levels. A detailed description of assessment of constructs is given in Chap. 4.

To sum up, with business process structure change possessing two specifications (yes and no), environmental change (macro, micro, macro and micro, and stable) and software structure change (technology push, push-pull, business pull, and no innovation) taking four specifications each, and business process adaptability as well as software customizability holding three values (high, medium, and low), the total number of possible combinations between these five concepts amounts to 288. According to Sabherwal and Robey (1995), it is postulated that the specifications of the five concepts related to the dynamic alignment process can be transferred into constant and stable clusters. Due to the fact that the presented study focuses on an investigation of the value of enterprise software, clusters are formed with respect to the four types of software structure change in Sect. 3.2.2. Figure 3.3 shows the specifications of the five concepts related to the dynamic alignment process.

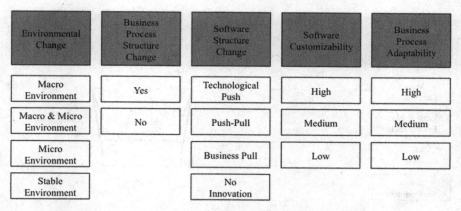

Fig. 3.3 Specifications of concepts related to the dynamic alignment process

3.2.2 Definition of Alignment Clusters and Gestalts

This section provides a definition of alignment clusters and gestalts. A cluster is a "*subgroup of a population, used for statistical sampling or analysis*" (Oxford Dictionaries 2014a). As outlined above, clusters are formed based on the type of software structure change. It is assumed that each of these types can be harmful and beneficial for companies, depending on others variables of the dynamic alignment process. The mere occurrence of environmental change, software structure change, or business process structure change as well as the level of software customizability and business process adaptability has no individual impact on alignment. This impact is generated by the organization of all elements of the dynamic alignment process. In such cases, where the whole shape of elements is not the same as the sum of its parts researchers speak of "gestalts" (Bernstein 2015; Weisberg and Reeves 2013). A "gestalt" is a collection of physical, biological, psychological, and symbolic elements that creates a whole, unified concept or pattern which is other than the sum of its parts, due to the relationship between its parts (Ellis 1938; Wertheimer 1923). Gestalts or "good" gestalts are feasible and desirable patterns of variables (Brown and Magill 1994; Lee et al. 2004; Venkatraman 1989). In contrast to this, "bad" gestalts or non-gestalts are patterns of variables that are undesirable for a company (Lee et al. 2004). A deeper discussion of the related "fit as gestalt"--concept is given in Chap. 4.

In this study, gestalts and non-gestalts are defined for each type of software structure change (Chakraborty et al. 2007; Chan and Reich 2007; Lee et al. 2004; Venkatraman 1989). Gestalts are those patterns of business process structure change (Blum 2006; Maltz and Kohli 1996), software structure change (Carmel and Sawyer 1998; Davern and Kauffman 2000; Kim et al. 2009; Lin and Chen 2012), environmental change (Maltz and Kohli 1996; Scott 1999; Sia and Soh 2007; Soh and Sia 2004), business process adaptability (Tatikonda and Montoya-Weiss 2001; Yang and Papazoglou 2000), and software customizability (Wang

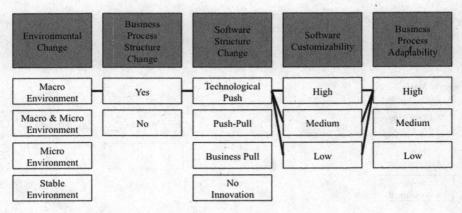

Fig. 3.4 Gestalt 1: pioneer innovator

et al. 2008b; Winkler and Brown 2014) that are expected to establish dynamic fit. Patterns that are anticipated to be undesirable are referred to as non-gestalts (Lee et al. 2004). Such non-gestalt clusters are supposed to result in dynamic misfit.

3.2.2.1 Pioneer Innovator Gestalt and Technology Push Non-gestalt

The first gestalt is referred to as a **pioneer innovator** (see Fig. 3.4). Empirical profiles within the pioneer innovator cluster rely on pure market governance of innovation in terms of technology push innovation.

The change impetus of empirical profiles within the pioneer innovator gestalt results from the macro environment. Companies within this cluster experience constant changes within their imposed country or their imposed industry context (Sia and Soh 2007; Soh and Sia 2004). No changes within the imposed firm context or the voluntary context occurred over longer periods of time (Scott 1999; Sia and Soh 2007). These environmental shifts are addressed by constant business process structure change and software structure change.

Empirical profiles within the pioneer innovator cluster constantly face such environmental changes that are not idiosyncratic to their company (Scott 1987). In a consequence, multiple companies within a country or a particular industry sector have to face similar change efforts (Scott 1987). Drawing upon TCE, this situation favours a market solution of software structure change (Williamson 1973, 1998) in terms of technology push innovation (Davern and Kauffman 2000; Kim et al. 2009).

In order to cope with such vendor-driven software structure changes, business process adaptability has to be on a high level (Tatikonda and Montoya-Weiss 2001; Yang and Papazoglou 2000). The role of software customizability is negligible and can be on a low, medium, or high level, due to the fact that no client-driven software change occurs (Wang et al. 2008b; Winkler and Brown 2014).

All other specifications of the concepts related to the dynamic alignment process in which company relies on a pure market governance of innovation are linked to the **technology push non-gestalt** cluster. In particular, these are cases in which constant technology push innovation occurs while company experience environmental changes that are not purely macro environmental, where business process structures are stable, or where business process adaptability is on a low or medium level. Empirical profiles related to the pioneer innovator gestalt are supposed to establish dynamic fit in terms of adjusted expansion. In contrast to this, dynamic alignment processes related to technology push non-gestalt are proposed to result in dynamic misfits.

3.2.2.2 Cautious Innovator Gestalt and Business Pull Non-gestalt

The second gestalt is referred to as a **cautious innovator** (see Fig. 3.5) and describes the contrary case to the pioneer innovator gestalt. Empirical profiles within the cautious innovator cluster rely on pure hierarchical governance of innovation in terms of business pull innovation.

The change stimulus of empirical profiles within the cautious innovator gestalt results from the micro environment. Companies within this cluster experience constant changes within their imposed firm or their voluntary context (Sia and Soh 2007; Soh and Sia 2004). No changes within the imposed country or the imposed industry context over longer periods of time (Scott 1999; Sia and Soh 2007). These environmental shifts are addressed by constant business process structure change and software structure change.

Empirical profiles within the cautious innovator cluster face environmental change that is idiosyncratic to their company (Scott 1987). In a consequence, no other or only a very limited number of firms within a country or a particular industry sector have to address similar change efforts (Scott 1987). Drawing upon TCE, this

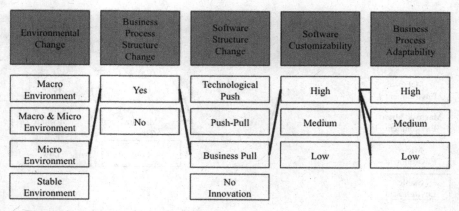

Fig. 3.5 Gestalt 2: cautious innovator

situation favours a hierarchical governance of software structure change (Williamson 1973, 1998) in terms of business pull innovation (Davern and Kauffman 2000; Kim et al. 2009).

In order to meet required client-driven software structure changes, software customizability has to be on a high level (Wang et al. 2008b; Winkler and Brown 2014). The role of business process adaptability is negligible and can be on a low, medium, or high level, due to the fact that no vendor-driven software change occurs (Tatikonda and Montoya-Weiss 2001; Yang and Papazoglou 2000).

All other specifications of the concepts related to the dynamic alignment process in which companies rely on a pure hierarchical governance of innovation are linked to the **business pull non-gestalt** cluster. In particular, these are cases in which constant business pull innovation occurs while company experience environmental changes that are not purely micro environmental, where business process structures are stable, or where software customizability is on a low or medium level. Empirical profiles related to the cautious innovator gestalt are supposed to establish dynamic fit in terms of adjusted expansion. In contrast to this, dynamic alignment processes related to business pull non-gestalt are proposed to result in dynamic misfits.

3.2.2.3 Ambidextrous Innovator Gestalt and Push-Pull Non-gestalt

The third gestalt is referred to as **ambidextrous innovator** (see Fig. 3.6) and describes a combination between pioneer and cautious innovator gestalts. Empirical profiles within the ambidextrous innovator rely on a hybrid governance of innovation in terms of push-pull innovation.

The change impetus of empirical profiles within the ambidextrous innovator gestalt results from the macro and micro environment. Companies within this cluster experience constant changes within their imposed firm or their voluntary

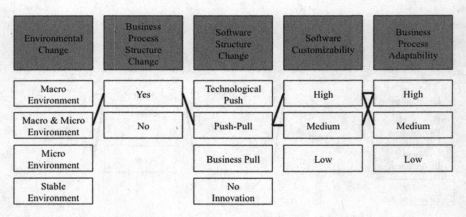

Fig. 3.6 Gestalt 3: ambidextrous innovator

context as well as within the imposed country or the imposed industry context (Scott 1999; Sia and Soh 2007). These environmental shifts are addressed by constant business process structure change and software structure change.

Empirical profiles within the ambidextrous innovator cluster constantly face idiosyncratic environmental changes as well as such changes that impact multiple companies within an industry sector or country (Scott 1987). These changes are addressed by combining technology push with business pull innovation (Davern and Kauffman 2000; Kim et al. 2009). Due to this amalgamation of client-driven and vendor-driven software change, either business process adaptability or software customizability is proposed to be high while the other one is anticipated to be at least on a medium level.

All other specifications of the concepts related to the dynamic alignment process in which a company relies on hybrid governance of innovation are linked to the **push-pull non-gestalt** cluster. In particular, these are cases in which technology push and business pull innovation occurs constantly while company either experience pure macro, pure micro, or no environmental change, where business process structures are stable, or where business process adaptability as well as software customizability are on a low or medium level. Empirical profiles related to the ambidextrous innovator gestalt are supposed to establish dynamic fit in terms of adjusted expansion. In contrast to this, dynamic alignment processes related to push-pull non-gestalt are proposed to result in dynamic misfits.

3.2.2.4 Conservative Gestalt and No Innovation Non-gestalt

The fourth gestalt is referred to as **conservative** (see Fig. 3.7) and describes the contrary case to the ambidextrous innovator cluster. It can be seen as a special case of hierarchy governance of innovation in which empirical profiles rely on structural persistence.

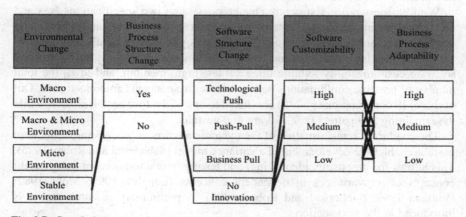

Fig. 3.7 Gestalt 4: conservative

Conservative gestalt companies do not experience any changes within their micro and macro environment over an extended period of time (Scott 1999; Sia and Soh 2007; Soh and Sia 2004). In a consequence, neither business process structure, nor software structure change occurs. The role of software customizability (Wang et al. 2008b; Winkler and Brown 2014) as well as business process adaptability (Tatikonda and Montoya-Weiss 2001; Yang and Papazoglou 2000) is negligible and can be on a low, medium, or high level, due to the absence of structural change.

All other specifications of the concepts related to the dynamic alignment process in which companies rely on a pure hierarchy governance of innovation in terms of persistence are linked to the **no innovation non-gestalt** cluster. In particular, these are cases in which companies experience environmental change and business process structure change. Empirical profiles related to the conservative gestalt are supposed to establish dynamic fit in terms of adjusted inertia. In contrast to this, dynamic alignment processes related to no innovation non-gestalt are proposed to result in dynamic misfits in terms of an insufficient software change.

3.2.3 Summary

Drawing upon Sabherwal and Robey (1995), it is postulated that the dynamic alignment process can be transferred into clusters (Fig. 3.8). Due to the fact that the presented study focuses on an investigation of the value of enterprise software, patterns are clustered with respect to the four type of software structure change. For each type of software structure change, ideal patterns of environmental change, business process structure change, software customizability, and business process adaptability are derived in Sect. 3.2.2. These ideal patterns are referred to as gestalts (Lee et al. 2004; Venkatraman 1989). The remaining patters are labelled non-gestalts (Lee et al. 2004; Venkatraman 1989).

With business process structure change possessing two specifications (yes and no), environmental change (macro, micro, macro and micro, and stable) and software structure change (technology push, push-pull, business pull, and no innovation) taking four specifications each, and business process adaptability and software customizability holding three values (high, medium, and low), the total number of possible combinations between these five concepts amounts to 288. Out of these, 19 combinations ($\approx$7 %) are linked to one of the four gestalt clusters while the remaining 269 patters ($\approx$93 %) are non-gestalts.

The conducted transformation of the dynamic alignment process into alignment gestalts enables the development of a variance model (Sabherwal and Robey 1995). This allows for proposing, identifying, and testing how alterations in independent concepts effect variances in dependent concepts (Langley 1999; Mohr 1982; Pentland 1999; Sabherwal and Robey 1995). A preliminary research model is introduced in the next section.

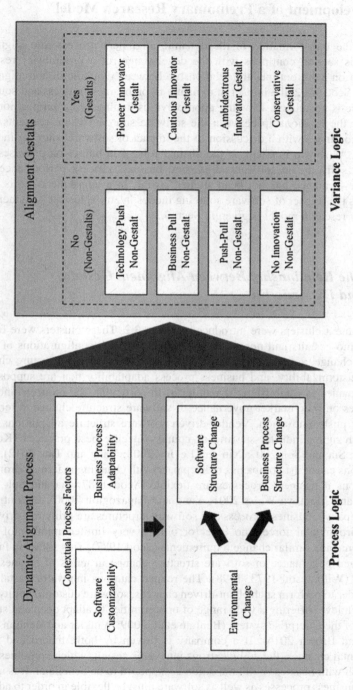

Fig. 3.8 Relationship between dynamic alignment process and alignment gestalts

3.3 Development of a Preliminary Research Model

Following the transformation of the dynamic alignment process into alignment gestalts, this section continues with the development of a preliminary research model. Section 3.3.1 outlines the relationship between dynamic fit and alignment gestalts. In Sect. 3.3.2, the impact of dynamic fit on business process and sourcing performance is postulated. Drawing upon previous findings, four propositions are derived for the relationship between the software sourcing value concepts. Section 3.3.3 continues with a discussion of the impact of software sourcing in value generation. As shown in Chap. 2, the distinct role of in-house, on-premises, and on-demand software on software alignment, business process performance, and sourcing performance has not been studied so far. In a consequence, this study investigates the impact of software sourcing modes in an exploratory manner. The preliminary research model is given in Sect. 3.3.4.

3.3.1 The Relationship Between Alignment Gestalts and Dynamic Fit

Eight alignment clusters were introduced in Sect. 3.2. These clusters were further classified into gestalts and non-gestalts. Gestalts are such configurations of environmental change, software structure change, business process structure change, software customizability, and business process adaptability that are supposed to assist companies in establishing dynamic fit. In particular, the pioneer innovator gestalt relies on pure market governance of software structure change in terms of technology push innovation. Vendor-driven software structure adaptations are a result of changing industry-specific or country-specific best practices (Koehler et al. 2010; Sia and Soh 2007; Xin and Levina 2008; Yang and Tate 2012). Such modifications can assist companies to keep pace with changing macro environmental conditions if business processes are flexible (Scott 1987; Sia and Soh 2007; Tatikonda and Montoya-Weiss 2001; Yang and Papazoglou 2000). In contrast to this, if company's business process and software structures are primarily driven by micro environmental forces, no other or only a very limited number of other organisations face similar change requirements (Scott 1987). This situation favours a hierarchical governance of software structure change in terms of business pull innovation (Williamson 1973, 1998). The related cautious innovator gestalt proposes in order to perform such client-driven changes, software customizability must be on a high level offering a wide range of opportunities to adapt deep and surface structures of the enterprise system (Benlian et al. 2009; Winkler and Benlian 2012; Winkler and Brown 2014). If a company is driven by both, macro and micro environmental changes, the ambidextrous innovator gestalt, which combines technology push with business pull innovation is supposed to be beneficial. It is argued that both, business processes as well as software must be flexible in order to adapt to due to this amalgamation of client-driven and vendor-driven software structure change, either business process adaptability or software customizability is proposed to be high while the other one is anticipated to be at least on a medium level. A special type of hierarchical governance is the conservative gestalt. In the absence of macro and micro environmental changes, persistence of business process and software structures is beneficial for companies. It can therefore be concluded that all for gestalt clusters are favourable for companies. In particular, it is proposed that pioneer innovator, cautious innovator, ambidextrous innovator, and conservative gestalts outperform technology push, business pull, push-pull, and no innovation non-gestalts with respect to dynamic fit.

| Proposition 1 | Alignment gestalts positively impact dynamic fit |

As outlined in the previous section, the total number of possible combinations between these five concepts amounts to 288 as a result of business process structure change possessing two specifications, environmental change and software structure change taking four specifications each, and business process adaptability as well as software customizability holding three values. Out of these, 19 combinations ($\approx$7 %) are linked to the four gestalt clusters while the remaining 269 patters ($\approx$93 %) are non-gestalts.

3.3.2 The Impact of Dynamic Fit

Dynamic fit expresses the coevolution between business process and software structure (Benbya and McKelvey 2006; Nöhren et al. 2014; Sia and Soh 2007; Strong and Volkoff 2010). A company suffers from dynamic misfit if it experiences an insufficient or excessive software structure change (Nöhren et al. 2014). Such misfits are instances, where the structures embedded within the system conflicts with an organizational reality (Sia and Soh 2007; Strong and Volkoff 2010). Drawing upon RIT, such a drifting apart between business process and software structures is destructive for a company (Wand and Weber 1990). In contrast to this, a fit between business process and software structures "*enables the organization to operate more effectively, and users to do their work more efficiently*" (Strong and Volkoff 2010: 746). It contributes to efficiency and effectiveness of corporate's processes (Sia and Soh 2007; Strong and Volkoff 2010). In a consequence, it can be proposed that dynamic fit is positively associated with business process performance.

| Proposition 2 | Dynamic fit positively impacts business process performance |

So far, nothing is known about the link between dynamic fit and sourcing performance (e.g. Grant 2003; Maurer et al. 2012; Ravishankar et al. 2011; Sia and Soh 2007; Soh and Sia 2004; Strong and Volkoff 2010). Sourcing performance is measured in terms of SET benefits in this study (e.g. Goo et al. 2008; Grover et al. 1996; Lee and Kim 1999; Lee et al. 2004; Saunders et al. 1997). Strategic benefits capture software's contribution to increase IT competence and IT function's ability to refocus on its core competencies (Lacity and Willcocks 2001; Lee et al. 2004). Economic benefits measure software's influence on economies of scale and costs related to a corporate's IT function (Lacity and Willcocks 2001; Lee et al. 2004). Technological benefits assess software's role in reducing the risk of technological obsolescence and in accessing key information technologies (Lacity and Willcocks 2001; Lee et al. 2004). Companies strive to resolve misfits in order to increase software's value contribution (Maurer et al. 2012; Sia and Soh 2007; Soh and Sia 2004). If a company suffers from software misalignment with constant levels of dynamic misfits that cannot be resolved by business process or software structure change, it has to search for and to invest in alternative software-centric solutions (Sia and Soh 2007). These investments are likely to reduce the level of economic, strategic, and technological outcomes from software. In contrast to this, if a company benefits from a coevolution of business process and software structures, SET benefits are expected to be high (Benbya and McKelvey 2006; Nöhren et al. 2014; Sabherwal et al. 2001). Therefore, the following propositions on the relationship between dynamic fit and sourcing performance are postulated:

Proposition 3a	Dynamic fit positively impacts strategic sourcing performance
Proposition 3b	Dynamic fit positively impacts economic sourcing performance
Proposition 3c	Dynamic fit positively impacts technological sourcing performance

In summary, this study is the first that investigates software-business process fit in a dynamic fashion (Nöhren et al. 2014). Previous research on alignment shows conflicting results on whether fit is always desirable and good for companies (Chan and Reich 2007). It was found that these conflicting findings are a result of treating the alignment phenomenon as static in nature (Sabherwal et al. 2001; Vessey and Ward 2013). However, "alignment is not desirable as an end in itself since the business must always change" (Chan and Reich 2007: 298). In a consequence, despite the fact that little is known on the relationship between dynamic fit and performance outcomes, a positive relationship is postulated and tested in the presented study. It is argued that a coevolution between business process and software structures are beneficial for companies (Benbya and McKelvey 2006; Nöhren et al. 2014; Sabherwal et al. 2001).

3.3.3 The Impact of Software Sourcing

Previous studies on software-business process fit have not incorporated different sourcing modes (e.g. Grant 2003; Maurer et al. 2012; Ravishankar et al. 2011; Sia and Soh 2007; Soh and Sia 2004; Strong and Volkoff 2010). In a consequence, nothing is known about the relationship between in-house, on-premises, and on-demand sourcing and software alignment.

It can be argued that software sourcing modes have different relationships with alignment gestalts. Due to the internal ownership of physical, deep, and surface structures, in-house sourcing is related to business pull innovation and a hierarchy governance of software structure change (Carmel and Sawyer 1998). Companies relying on this sourcing mode can establish software alignment by following a cautious innovator gestalt. In contrast to this, on-demand software is rather related to technology push innovation and a market governance of software structure change (Currie et al. 2004; Currie 2004). In an on-demand setting updates are constantly and automatically implemented by a software vendor (Koehler et al. 2010; Xin and Levina 2008; Yang and Tate 2012). Companies relying on this sourcing mode can realize dynamic fit by relying on a pioneer innovator gestalt. Benefiting from adjusted inertia in terms of a conservative gestalt is not possible in on-demand settings as a consequence of a constant occurrence of technology push innovation (Koehler et al. 2010; Xin and Levina 2008; Yang and Tate 2012). Finally, on-premises sourcing is related to push-pull innovation and a hybrid governance of software structure change (Carmel and Sawyer 1998). Therefore, companies sourcing enterprise systems on-premises can benefit from software alignment by following an ambidextrous innovator gestalt.

Previous studies on software alignment frequently focused on packaged applications (e.g. Grant 2003; Ravishankar et al. 2011; Sia and Soh 2007; Soh and Sia 2004; Strong and Volkoff 2010). It is argued that the inherent and indispensable standardization of such enterprise systems are a major source of structural misfits (Sia and Soh 2007; Strong and Volkoff 2010). In a consequence, it can be argued that lower ownership on physical, deep, and surface structures (see Fig. 2.4) results in an increasing standardization with less opportunities for integration, which negatively impact software alignment. However, outsourcing of software structures can also be beneficial for companies. Due to the external development of packaged applications, software providers adapt their enterprise systems on a regular basis and provide modifications to their customers based on industry best practices (Koehler et al. 2010; Sia and Soh 2007; Xin and Levina 2008; Yang and Tate 2012). Such modifications can assist companies to keep pace with changing macro environmental conditions (Scott 1987; Sia and Soh 2007). Therefore, it can also be proposed that ownership on physical, deep, and surface structures result in an increasing provision of industry best practices, which positively impact dynamic.

Looking at the relationship between software sourcing and performance outcomes, no study was found that directly compares in-house, on-premises, or on-demand sourcing with each other. Previous contribution investigates the impact of the three sourcing modes on performance related to business processes or the IT function individually from other sourcing arrangements (e.g. Nidumolu 1995; Susarla et al. 2003; Wang 2002). Consequently, little is known about the relationship between software sourcing and performance outcomes. Standardization and enforcement of industry best practices of packaged applications can support business processes "*to be more efficient and effective*" (Strong and Volkoff 2010: 746) but also "*requiring ways of working that are contrary to organizational norms and practices or that negatively affect organizational performance*" (Strong and Volkoff 2010: 737). In-house applications do not possess such standardizations and best practice structures. Therefore, it can be assumed that the ownership on physical, deep, and surface structures impact business process performance mediated by software alignment (Nöhren et al. 2014; Sia and Soh 2007; Strong and Volkoff 2010).

Higher degree software structure outsourcing reduces costs (economic benefits), helps to refocus the IT function on its core competences (strategic benefits), and reduces the risk of obsolescence due to constantly provided modifications based on industry best practices (technological benefits) (Koehler et al. 2010; Lee et al. 2004; Xin and Levina 2008). Therefore, sourcing performance could be higher in on-demand than in on-premises and in-house settings. However, an increase in outsourcing software structures might lower corporate's IT competence (reduced strategic benefits), lower its economies of scale in internal resources (reduced economic benefits), and lower software's interoperability (reduced technological benefits) (Lacity and Willcocks 2001; Lee et al. 2004). This could account for lower levels of sourcing performance from on-demand through on-premises to in-house settings. As discussed above, it was found, that this effect is mediated by the software fit (Nöhren et al. 2014).

To sum up, the impact of software sourcing modes on software sourcing value has not been studied so far. The relationship between dynamic fit, business process performance, and sourcing performance and the three sourcing settings in-house, on-premises, and on-demand remained undiscovered. In a consequence, propositions on the relationship between software sourcing and its value are not postulated *a priori* but will be derived based on triangulation of qualitative data in the presented study (Eisenhardt 1989; Yin 2009).

3.3.4   Summary

The preliminary research model is given in Fig. 3.9. It is postulated that alignment gestalts are positively associated with dynamic fit of software artefacts (proposition 1). In a consequence, alignment gestalts are expected to be a key success factor in the value generation of enterprise software. This value generation starts with the dynamic fit of a software artefact. Dynamic fit is seen as central mediator positively impacting business process performance (proposition 2) as well as sourcing performance in terms of strategic (proposition 3a), economic (proposition 3b), and technological benefits (proposition 3c).

This study is the first one investigating the impact of in-house, on-premises, and on-demand software on alignment and performance. In a consequence, the role of

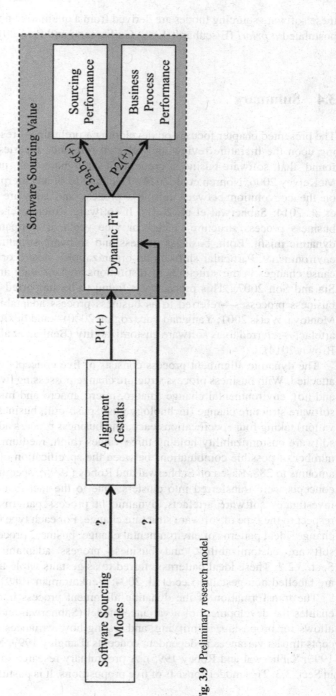

Fig. 3.9 Preliminary research model

these software sourcing modes are derived from a qualitative field study and are not postulated *a priori* (Eisenhardt 1989; Guillemette and Paré 2012).

3.4 Summary

The presented chapter focuses on developing a preliminary research model. Drawing upon the literature review and selected reference theories in Chap. 2, it was found that software-business process fit is dynamic in nature (Benbya and McKelvey 2006; Nöhren et al. 2014). Dynamic fit of an enterprise system depends on the coevolution between business process and software structures (Nöhren et al. 2014; Sabherwal et al. 2001). If software structure change is greater than business process structure change or vice versa, a company will suffer from dynamic misfit. Both, business process and software structures depend on their environments. Particular shifts in an organization's macro or micro environment cause changes in the structures of institutions and software artefacts (Scott 1987; Sia and Soh 2007). This process was found to be supported by the flexibility of business processes—referred to as business process adaptability (Tatikonda and Montoya-Weiss 2001; Yang and Papazoglou 2000)—and flexibility of the software artefact—referred to as software customizability (Benlian et al. 2009; Winkler and Brown 2014).

The dynamic alignment process consists of five concepts with different values attached. With business process structure change possessing two specifications (yes and no), environmental change (macro, micro, macro and micro, and stable) and software structure change (technology push, push-pull, business pull, and no innovation) taking four specifications each, and business process adaptability as well as software customizability holding three values (high, medium, and low), the total number of possible combinations between the specification of these five concepts amounts to 288. Based on Sabherwal and Robey (1995), specifications of these five concepts were transferred into clusters. Due to the fact that the presented study investigates software artefacts, dynamic fit process patterns are clustered with respect to the type of software structure change. For each type of software structure change, ideal patterns of environmental change, business process structure change, software customizability, and business process adaptability are derived in Sect. 3.2.2. These ideal patterns referred to as gestalts while the remaining patters are labelled non-gestalts (Lee et al. 2004; Venkatraman 1989).

The transformation of the dynamic alignment process into alignment gestalts enables the development of a variance model (Sabherwal and Robey 1995). This allows for proposing, identifying, and testing how variances in independent concepts impact variances in dependent concepts (Langley 1999; Mohr 1982; Pentland 1999; Sabherwal and Robey 1995). A preliminary research model was introduced in Sect. 3.3. This model consists of five propositions. It is postulated that gestalts are positively associated with dynamic fit of a software artefact. This dynamic fit is proposed to positively impact business process performance as well as sourcing performance. Due to the fact that the impact of software sourcing modes on software alignment and performance outcomes has merely been studied so far and due to the fact that this study is the first that provides a novel definition of the software sourcing taking a representational view of IT perspective, propositions on the relationship between in-house, on-premises, and on-demand software and their value are not postulated *a priori* but will be derived from based triangulation in Chap. 7 (Eisenhardt 1989; Yin 2009).

Chapter 4
Research Design

This study aims to contribute to research in the field of software alignment and software sourcing. A discussion of previous literature led to the development of a preliminary research model. An exploratory field study (Guillemette and Paré 2012) has been conducted in order to test *a priori* postulated propositions and to extend the research model. The related ontological and epistemological stance of this study is discussed in Sect. 4.1. Section 4.2 continues with a conceptualization of fit. Previous studies differentiated between six distinct perspectives of fit (Chan and Reich 2007; Venkatraman 1989). These perspectives are discussed and dynamic fit as well as alignment clusters are positioned. Section 4.3 outlines the data collection and the data analysis approach. The sampling procedure is discussed and the coding and interpretation of qualitative field study data is introduced. In addition, the applied statistical tests for evaluating associations among concepts is presented. A summary on research design is given in Sect. 4.4.

4.1 Philosophical Stance of Study

"Although philosophical ideas remain largely hidden in research (...), they still influence the practice of research and need to be identified" (Creswell 2009: 5). Before conducting an empirical study, each scientific work needs to outline its philosophical stance in terms of its inherent ontological and epistemological viewpoints.

Ontology refers to researcher's assumption about how the real world is made up and what the nature of things is (Guba and Lincoln 1994; Weber 2012). It clarifies what is there to know about and what kind of theories can be established (Gregor 2006; Guba and Lincoln 1994). Epistemology is derived from the ontological stance. It refers to how and what kind of knowledge can be obtained in theory construction and testing (Gregor 2006). In the information systems field, researchers most frequently classify their works as positivist or interpretative

© Springer International Publishing Switzerland 2016
M. Nöhren, *Enterprise Software Sourcing Performance*, Progress in IS,
DOI 10.1007/978-3-319-23926-2_4

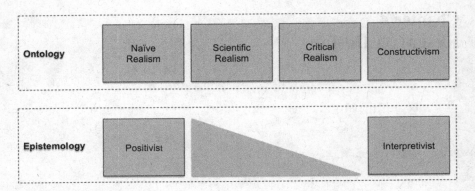

Fig. 4.1 Philosophical stances

(Dibbern et al. 2004; Orlikowski and Baroudi 1991). Figure 4.1 summarizes different ontological and epistemological stances related to these positions.

Positivists rely on the ontological stance of the (naïve) realism (Guba and Lincoln 1994). It is assumed that a reality is objectively given by quantifiable properties (Myers 2009). Therefore, knowledge referred to the "way things are" in terms of cause-effect models can be derived (Guba and Lincoln 1994). From an epistemological stance, the observer and the object under study are seen as independent entities (Guba and Lincoln 1994). Positivist studies build on *a priori* fixed relationships within a phenomenon in order to test theories and laws and thereby increase the predictive understanding of a phenomenon (Myers 2009; Orlikowski and Baroudi 1991).

Contrary to this, interpretivist studies rely on the ontological stance of (social) constructivism (Creswell 2009; Guba and Lincoln 1994). The existence of one single objective reality is rejected (Creswell 2009; Guba and Lincoln 1994). Instead, the real world is seen as socially constructed by the complexity of human sense-making (Myers 2009). From an epistemological point of view, researchers strive to understand the deeper structure of a phenomenon in its cultural and situational context (Dibbern et al. 2004; Orlikowski and Baroudi 1991). A generalization of findings in terms of universal laws and theories is not intended (Orlikowski and Baroudi 1991).

A central difference in interpretivist and positivist research can be found in the type of question a researcher examines and the types of conclusions he or she is striving for (Lin 1998). While positivist studies focus on testing *a priori* fixed relationships within a phenomenon (Chalmers 1999; Dubé and Paré 2003; Orlikowski 1993), interpretivist studies are concerned with understanding a phenomenon itself (Creswell 2009; Dibbern et al. 2004). *"While both in the end can comment about general principles or relationships, positivist work does so by identifying general patterns, while interpretivist work does so by showing how the general pattern looks in practice"* (Lin 1998: 163). Consequently, these two philosophical stances are often seen as two different extremes of worldviews.

Over the years, the strong boundaries between positivist and interpretivist stances were softened up and several positions evolved bridging between these two extremes. One of these positions is referred to as post positivism (Guba and Lincoln 1994). Post positivist relies on the ontology of critical realism that, on the one hand—like positivist—assumes the existence of one real world but on the other hand rejects the assumption that this reality is completely ascertainable due to the fact that a researcher's access to this world is imperfect and always mediated by his or her perception or a theoretical lens (Guba and Lincoln 1994; Mingers et al. 2013; Strong and Volkoff 2010; Volkoff and Strong 2013). While positivists trust that a researcher and the researched entities are independent from each other, post positivists assume that prior knowledge of an investigator can have an influence on what is observed (Bunge 1993). Unlike naïve realism, critical realists *"see scientific models and theories not as literal pictures of reality but as partial, tentative representations of what there is"* (Murphy 1990: 296).

Closely related to critical realism is scientific realism with its epistemological stance of soft positivism (Kirsch 2004; Madill et al. 2000; Ravishankar et al. 2011). *"Scientific realism is a refined version of critical realism"* (Bunge 1993: 231). The key difference between these two worldviews is that while scientific realism believes that a researcher can reveal true representations of the world, critical realism admits an inherent subjectivity in knowledge generation and is therefore closer related to constructivism (Bunge 1993; Madill et al. 2000). While relying on realist ontology and thereby assuming that a phenomenon objectively exists, this approach is not limited to *"preidentified constructs, but is designed to surface other constructs as well, in the manner of interpretivists or grounded theorists"* (Kirsch 2004: 378). It is particularly useful in combining an inductive with a deductive approach, when certain parts of a study are derived from theory but the researcher intends to enrich a model with laws that directly emerge from data (Ravishankar et al. 2011).

The aim of this study is to open the "black box" between software sourcing modes and their value. In doing so, this study bridges between realism and constructivism. It builds upon prior theories in terms of representational view of IT (Wand and Weber 1990), institutional theory (Scott 1987), resource-based view of IT (Barney 1991), and transaction cost economics (Williamson 1979), but *"(. . .) also allowing some unexpected findings and explanations to emerge from the data"* (Ravishankar et al. 2011: 41). Key informants were executives responsible for management of a particular software artefact under study (see Sect. 4.3). Their statements were interpreted in the light of identified theoretical lenses and constructs while being open to unexpected findings (Eisenhardt 1989; Kirsch 2004; Ravishankar et al. 2011; Yin 2009). While *"science is derived from facts"* (Chalmers 1999: 41), it is assumed that these facts are quantifiable in nature, are objectively given, and are measurable independently of the observer (Chalmers 1999; Myers 2009; Sabherwal and Robey 1995). The developed model should allow for statistical tests of relationships and will be generalizable to similar context settings.

4.2   Conceptualization of Fit

Each study on alignment needs to specify its perspective on fit. It was found that studies that neglect or lack a thorough specification frequently measured another type of fit as conceptually desired, which leads to inconsistent, mixed, or erroneous results (Bergeron et al. 2001; Chan and Reich 2007).

Venkatraman (1989) introduced six conceptualizations of fit that had most widely been used in previous research. In particular, fit can be studied as (1) moderation, (2) mediation, (3) matching, (4) covariation, (5) profile deviation, and (6) gestalts (Chakraborty et al. 2007; Chan and Reich 2007; Venkatraman 1989). These types of fit were differentiated according to their anchoring to performance (criterion-free versus criterion-specific) and their specificity of form (two versus many variables) (Strong and Volkoff 2010; Venkatraman 1989). The criterion anchoring separates "*fit that is intrinsically connected to specific criterion variables [from fit] which has universal applicability*" (Venkatraman 1989: 424).

Three types of fit are linked to the criterion-specific dimension (Venkatraman 1989). *Fit as moderation* defines fit as the interaction between two variables (Bergeron et al. 2001). In this view, the impact of a predictor on a criterion depends on a third variable referred to as moderator (Venkatraman 1989). *Fit as mediation* assumes the existence of an intervening variable between one or multiple antecedences and the criterion (Bergeron et al. 2001). This intervening effect accounts for a significant amount of the relationship between independent and dependent variable (Venkatraman 1989). Third, *fit as profile deviation* postulates the existence of an ideal profile, which is positively anchored to performance (Venkatraman 1989). In this perspective, any deviation from the ideal profile results in lower performance outcomes (Bergeron et al. 2001). These three conceptualizations related to the criterion-specific dimension understand fit as naturally connected to a particular performance anchor. For instance, in applying both, a moderation as well as a profile deviation perspective, Tallon (2007) defined fit between business strategy and IT concentration as performance.

The remaining three conceptualizations define fit as not directly anchored to a performance criterion (Venkatraman 1989). *Fit as matching* explains fit as balance between two variables (Bergeron et al. 2001). *Fit as covariance* understands the term as "*pattern of covariation or internal consistency among a set of underlying theoretically related variables*" (Venkatraman 1989: 435). In contrast to this, *fit as gestalts* are "*based on an internal congruence conceptualization, whereby fit is seen as a pattern*" (Bergeron et al. 2001: 127). Both, fit as covariation and fit as gestalts, are similar to each other. The basic difference is that covariance is rather a result of factor analysis whereas gestalts can be arrived at via cluster analysis (Venkatraman 1989). Consequently, fit as covariation assumes linear relationships between a set of variables, whereas fit as gestalts differ from this specificity of form (Lee et al. 2004; Venkatraman 1989).

While different conceptualizations of fit can be applied simultaneously within one study, one type of performance anchoring should be selected (Tallon 2007).

This study is related to the criterion-free dimension of performance anchoring and possesses two definitions of fit. First, dynamic fit is assessed in terms of fit as matching. In positioning their fit constructs as well as the constructs of Sia and Soh (2007) within the typology of Venkatraman (1989), Strong and Volkoff (2010) argued that software-business process fit does not completely match with one of the six perspectives because it is "*(. . .) tailored to IT artifacts, that is, they capture how the IT artefact [instead of a performance concept] affects the conceptualization of fit, rather than being fit forms of generic variables as in Venkatraman's forms*" (Strong and Volkoff 2010: 748). Coverage fit, which serves as a measure for the degree of dynamic fit in this study, can be seen as an extension of fit as matching to multiple sub-variables in terms of deep, surface, and latent structure elements (Strong and Volkoff 2010). In a consequence, dynamic fit is operationalized by the means of **fit as matching**.

Second, specifications of concepts related to the dynamic alignment process—environmental change, software structure change, business process structure change, business process adaptability, and software customizability—form alignment clusters (Sabherwal and Robey 1995). These clusters are linked to the **fit as gestalt** perspective (Venkatraman 1989). Gestalts seek for configurationally explanations of relationships among a set of two or more concepts (Bacharach 1989; Venkatraman 1989). The specification of these concepts form holistic pattern, archetypes, or strategic groups (Boyd et al. 2012). In other words, gestalts express feasible and strategically desirable patterns of variables (Brown and Magill 1994; Lee et al. 2004) "*defined in terms of the degree of internal coherence among a set of theoretical attributes*" (Venkatraman 1989: 432). Consequently, gestalts provide a multi-dimensional assessment of a context and are particularly useful when observing a large number of variables with multiple or at least more than one specifications (McLaren et al. 2011).

4.3   Data Collection and Data Analysis

The presented work aims to increase our understanding of how software sourcing modes contribute to software sourcing value in a post-implementation phase. It was found that previous studies on software-business process fit has not addressed the dynamic nature of the phenomenon (Grant 2003; Sia and Soh 2007; Soh and Sia 2004; Strong and Volkoff 2010). The dynamic process of software alignment has merely been studied so far (Nöhren et al. 2014). In addition, no study was found that provides a holistic definition of software sourcing and that investigates how different sourcing arrangements impact value in terms of alignment and performance. Consequently, both, the role of software sourcing and the dynamics of software alignment remained "black boxes" in previous research. In order to open these "black boxes", this study bridges among positivist and interpretivist research to ensure that—while having defined a preliminary research model—additional "*(. . .) findings and explanations (, . .) emerge from the data*" (Ravishankar et al. 2011: 41).

All *"science is derived from facts"* (Chalmers 1999: 41). Social science encompasses a multitude of research methods to gather these facts in order to answer particular research questions. Research methods can be classified into qualitative and quantitative paradigms (Creswell 2009). A selection of an appropriate method among all existing methods is a multi-criteria decision. According to Yin (2009), a central criteria in selecting a certain research paradigm is the type of research question a scientist strives to answer. It is differentiated between questions of "who", "what", "where", "how", and "why". Research questions related to "how" and "why" are typically exploratory in nature. These questions favour qualitative research approaches. In contrast to this, research questions of "who" and "where" are best answered by a quantitative method. Finally, exploratory "what" questions can be investigated by the means of qualitative and quantitative studies (Yin 2009).

This study posed the research questions of "how" software sourcing impacts value in terms of alignment and performance and "how" these outcomes are interrelated with each other. For this research endeavour, a qualitative exploratory field study according to Guillemette and Paré (2012) was conducted. It is a particular form of case-based qualitative research that bridges between traditional in-depth case study investigation and quantitative large-scale survey studies (Guillemette and Paré 2012; Yin 2009). This method was chosen in order to combine a testing of the theoretically deduced propositions and gestalts from the preliminary research model in Chap. 3 with the opportunity to include new findings that directly emerge from data triangulation (Yin 2009). Qualitative field study design allows for an incorporation of a larger number of empirical profiles than traditional case study research (Guillemette and Paré 2012; Yin 2009). This reduces the risk of overweighting idiosyncrasies of individual empirical profiles and increases the predictive nature and generalizability of findings (Eisenhardt 1989). In addition, a larger data set allows for a statistical test of relationships among concepts.

This section is organized as follows. Section 4.3.1 introduces the data sampling approach. Subsequently, the collection and interpretation of the qualitative field study data is outlined in Sect. 4.3.2. A detailed discussion of which data had been gathered and how the investigated facts were analysed is given. Finally, Sect. 4.3.3 gives an introduction to the applied statistical tests for the relationships among the concepts.

4.3.1   Sampling Procedure

In this study, the unit of analysis are process-centric enterprise systems as part of a corporate's IT function. Software sourcing was defined from an ownership on physical, deep, and surface structure perspective. Consequently, key informants were executives responsible for managing a particular software artefact under study (Guillemette and Paré 2012).

In outlining the explicit restrictions of this study, temporal and spatial boundaries are defined (Bacharach 1989). According to Swanson and Ramiller (2004), the process of organizational innovation—such as the implementation of an enterprise system—proceeds in four consecutive steps. It starts with a comprehension phase, in which a firm gets aware of the potential benefits of an enterprise system. In a second stage, a business case is created. This business case can result in an implementation of an enterprise system, which constitutes the third step in the innovation process. Following the implementation phase, the final assimilation phase starts, when the enterprise system *"begins to be absorbed into the worklife of the firm and to demonstrate its usefulness"* (Swanson and Ramiller 2004: 558). In order to understand the dynamic nature of software performance in post-implementation phase, only such empirical profiles were incorporated, that completed the implementation phase and entered the final stage of the innovation process. The presented study focuses on enterprise systems designed to support primary and secondary business processes within a firm (Grant 2003; Shang and Seddon 2002; Swanson 1994). Therefore ERP systems as well as individual modules for CRM, warehousing, or procurement were investigated. The decision was made in close cooperation with the key informants based on whether an organization has implemented a comprehensive ERP system or relied on heterogeneous process-centric software landscape.

A thorough selection of cases is a key challenge in qualitative research. In contrast to quantitative methods, case and field study design relies on a theoretical sampling of a population instead of a statistical one (Eisenhardt 1989). A random and large-scale sampling for the purpose of hypotheses testing only is neither required nor preferable (Eisenhardt and Graebner 2007; Eisenhardt 1989). Instead, researchers are able to focus on cases that extend existing theories (Eisenhardt 1989; Kirsch 2004; Yin 2009). Consequently, a central goal of this exploratory field study was to include data points as long as new insights emerged from the findings (Eisenhardt 1989). Three stopping criteria had been defined. First, a sufficiently large number of field study data has to be collected. Due to the fact that this study draws heavily on the qualitative field study design by Guillemette and Paré (2012), the minimum number of empirical profiles was set to be 33. The larger the empirical data set, the sounder the derived law (Chalmers 1999). Second, data should be observed under a wide variety of conditions (Chalmers 1999). Therefore, data was gathered for all three software sourcing modes, in different industrial sectors, within companies of different sizes, and for different process-centric applications. Third, empirical profiles that challenge the preliminary research model were included in order to extent existing literature. The properties of the exploratory field study according to Dubé and Paré (2003) are given in Appendix C.

4.3.2 Collection and Interpretation of Qualitative Data

Data was collected by semi-structured interviews and thereby a usage of pre-formulated questions as well as new questions that emerge during the conversations (Myers 2009). Each interview started with broad questions that asked the respondent to describe the IT function in general and his or her responsibility in software management. Then the interviewer asked more specific questions to ensure that the company has completed implementation phase and that all constructs of the preliminary research model were covered. In the second part of the interview, open questions were asked to capture data on all concepts under study. In order to differentiate between misfits that occurred during the implementation phase and those that arose over time (Strong and Volkoff 2010), a detailed description of the software implementation process and how the software evolved since entering the assimilation phase (Swanson and Ramiller 2004) was asked for. In the last part of the interview, open questions to evaluate software's value in terms of alignment and performance were asked. After each interview, transcripts were coded and interpreted. The high-level interview guideline is given in Appendix D.

The qualitative data from the field study was analysed using the software tools NVivo, Microsoft Excel, and Microsoft Access. This analysis implies *"identifying, coding, categorizing, classifying, and labeling the primary patterns in the data (by) analyzing the core content of interviews"* (Patton 2002: 463). Such codes are *"labels for assigning units of meaning to the descriptive or inferential information compiled during a study. Codes usually are attached to 'chunks' of varying size—words, phrases, sentences, or whole paragraphs"* (Miles and Huberman 1994: 56) reflecting the constructs within a study. The coding of constructs is introduced below.

4.3.2.1 Coding of Software Sourcing

In Chap. 2, software sourcing was defined taking a RIT perspective with respect to client's ownership of physical, deep, and surface structures (Sia and Soh 2007; Strong and Volkoff 2010; Wand and Weber 1990). This novel definition allows for treating the software sourcing concept as pure categorical variable (nominal scale of measurement) and as a discrete linear variable (ordinal scale of measurement) (Bortz and Schuster 2010; Racine and Li 2004). Categorical variables allow for *"splitting the sample into a number of subsets or cells"* (Racine and Li 2004: 100). Such categories have no numeric value attached and are not interpreted in a quantitative fashion (Bortz and Schuster 2010). Categorical variables are frequently extended to discrete linear variables (Racine and Li 2004). Such variables are ordinal in nature and allow to rank order entities based on their inherent value attached (Bortz and Schuster 2010).

Three distinct software sourcing modes in terms of in-house, on-premises, and on-demand categories were classified. These modes differ with respect to their allocation of physical, deep, and surface structure ownership. In an in-house setting all three types of software structures are held internally. Only the ownership on physical structures are held within a firm's hierarchy in an on-premises model. Finally, the on-demand setting expresses the contrary category to the in-house setting where all three types of software structures are owned by a software vendor. Beside such a pure categorical interpretation, software sourcing can also be understood as a discrete linear variable expressing the degree of software structure ownership. The extent of ownership on physical, deep, and surface structures decreases from in-house through on-premises to on-demand sourcing. Treating software sourcing as categorical or as discrete linear variable allows for different interpretations of the phenomenon. The latter one enables to study whether higher degrees of ownership on physical, deep, and surface structures positively or negatively impact software sourcing value. Treating software sourcing as categories with no numeric value attached gives the opportunity to investigate how in-house, on-premises, and on-demand settings are associated with alignment clusters and outcomes.

The coding of software sourcing presented in Table 4.1 allows for an categorical or as discrete linear interpretation of the concept. Software sourcing possesses three value-free categories in terms of in-house, on-premises, and on-demand modes. Based on the distinction between physical, deep, and surface structures, software sourcing can also been understood as outsourcing of software structures. Thereby, we see a decrease of ownership from in-house through on-premises to on-demand sourcing.

4.3.2.2   Coding of Concepts Related to the Dynamic Alignment Process

The dynamic alignment process encompasses five concepts: business process structure change (Blum 2006; Maltz and Kohli 1996), software structure change (Carmel and Sawyer 1998; Davern and Kauffman 2000; Kim et al. 2009; Lin and Chen 2012), environmental change (Maltz and Kohli 1996; Scott 1999; Sia and Soh 2007; Soh and Sia 2004), software customizability (Benlian et al. 2009; Winkler and Brown 2014), and business process adaptability (Tatikonda and Montoya-Weiss 2001; Yang and Papazoglou 2000). Table 4.2 gives the coding of environmental change. The codings of business process and software structure change are

Table 4.1 Coding of software sourcing

Construct	Specifications	Definition
Software sourcing	In-house (high ownership)	Ownership on physical, deep, and surface structures is held within a firm's hierarchy
	On-premises (medium ownership)	Ownership on physical structures is held within a firm's hierarchy while ownership on deep and surface structures is held outside a firm's hierarchy
	On-demand (low ownership)	Ownership on physical, deep, and surface structures is held outside a firm's hierarchy

Table 4.2 Coding of environmental change

Construct	Specifications	Definition
Environmental change	Macro environmental change	The company has to face constant changes in its imposed country context or in its imposed industry context
	Macro and micro environmental change	The company has to face constant changes in its imposed firm context or in its voluntary context and in its imposed firm context or in its voluntary context
	Micro environmental Change	The company has to face constant changes in its imposed firm context or in its voluntary context
	Stable environment	The company has to face no changes in its environmental context

Table 4.3 Coding of business process structure change

Construct	Specifications	Definition
Business process structure change	Yes	The company constantly transforms the structure of its tasks, rules and procedures
	No	The company performs no transformation of the structure of its tasks, rules and procedures

Table 4.4 Coding of software structure change

Construct	Specifications	Definition
Software structure change	Technology push innovation	The company constantly implements software innovations developed by a software vendor
	Push-pull innovation	The company constantly implements software innovations developed internally as well as software innovations developed by a software vendor
	Business pull innovation	The company constantly implements software innovations developed internally
	No innovation	The company implements no software innovations

presented in Tables 4.3 and 4.4. Tables 4.5 and 4.6 introduces the interpretation of the two contextual factors.

4.3.2.3   Coding of Concepts Related to Software Sourcing Value

Two concepts addressing the value in terms of performance outcomes are included in this study. First, business process performance measures software's value for business units (Grant 2003; Shang and Seddon 2002). The coding of this concept is given in Table 4.7. Second, sourcing performance captures software's contribution

Table 4.5 Coding of software customizability

Construct	Specifications	Definition
Software customizability	High	Software offers a wide range of opportunities to adapt its physical, deep, and surface structures to business process structures
	Medium	Software offers some opportunities to adapt its physical, deep, and surface structures to business process structures
	Low	Software offers very limited opportunities to adapt its physical, deep, and surface structures to business process structures

Table 4.6 Coding of business process adaptability

Construct	Specifications	Definition
Business process adaptability	High	Business process structures can be adapted to software structures
	Medium	Business process structures can partially be adapted to software structures
	Low	Business process structures can not be adapted to software structures

Table 4.7 Coding of business process performance

Construct	Specifications	Definition
Business process performance	Positive	Primarily positive impacts of software on business processes were reported
	Neutral	Positive and negative impacts of software on business processes were reported
	Negative	Primarily negative impacts of software on business processes were reported

to strategic (Table 4.8), economic (Table 4.9), and technological benefits (Table 4.10) of a corporate's IT function (Goo et al. 2008; Grover et al. 1996; Lacity and Willcocks 2001; Lee et al. 2004; Saunders et al. 1997). Examples of items from related quantitative constructs are given in Appendix B.

Finally, the coding of software-business process fit is given in Table 4.11. The related dynamic fit construct is a measure of coevolution between business process and software structures (Benbya and McKelvey 2006; Nöhren et al. 2014; Strong and Volkoff 2010; Zajac et al. 2000).

4.3.3   Introduction to Test Statistics of Categorical Data

This section gives a brief outline on the applied statistical tests on relationships among concepts. Data for this study was generated by the means of an exploratory

Table 4.8 Coding of sourcing performance—strategic benefits

Construct	Specifications	Definition
Strategic benefits	Positive	Primarily positive impacts of software on strategic returns were reported
	Neutral	Positive and negative impacts of software on strategic returns were reported
	Negative	Primarily negative impacts of software on strategic returns were reported

Table 4.9 Coding of sourcing performance—economic benefits

Construct	Specifications	Definition
Economic benefits	Positive	Primarily positive impacts of software on economic returns were reported
	Neutral	Positive and negative impacts of software on economic returns were reported
	Negative	Primarily negative impacts of software on economic returns were reported

Table 4.10 Coding of sourcing performance—technological benefits

Construct	Specifications	Definition
Technological benefits	Positive	Primarily positive impacts of software on technological returns were reported
	Neutral	Positive and negative impacts of software on technological returns were reported
	Negative	Primarily negative impacts of software on technological returns were reported

Table 4.11 Coding of dynamic fit

Construct	Specifications	Definition
Dynamic fit	Fit	Software is free from deficiencies in terms of functionality, data, usability, role and control misfits
	Misfit	Software constantly possesses deficiencies in terms of functionality, data, usability, role and control misfits

field study. As outlined above, data was analyzed by linking the qualitative content of interviews to the categories of constructs (Miles and Huberman 1994; Patton 2002). Therefore, values of these constructs must be interpreted as categorical in nature (Simonoff 2003).

Categorical data reflect variables that are measured on a scale that classifies data into a limited number of groups (Azen and Walker 2011). This distinguishes categorical variables from continuous variables with an infinite number of values attached (Powers and Xie 2008). If all data of interest is categorical in nature, it can be represented in terms of contingency tables (Kateri 2010). This section deals with statistical tests for such contingency tables. In Sect. 4.3.3.1, test statistics for two-way contingency tables are discussed, including the Chi-Square statistic, the Fisher's exact test, and the Phi test. Test statistics for moderating effects and related three-way contingency tables are introduced in Sect. 4.3.3.2. Finally, Sect. 4.3.3.3 summarizes on test statistics for categorical data and gives an outlook on which test is applied for interpretation in which data settings.

4.3.3.1 Test Statistics for Two Categorical Variables

To test significance of symmetric associations among categorical predictor and criterion variables, researchers most commonly rely on Chi-Square statistic and Fisher's exact test (Andersen 1997; Camilli 1995; Takane and Zhou 2013). Chi-Square statistic emerged as a preferred test of such relationships (Bortz and Schuster 2010). Fisher's exact test—that is only applicable for 2×2 matrixes in its original version—serves as a valuable alternative to Chi-Square statistic when dealing with small frequencies (Camilli 1995; Zar 1987). It was found that results from both tests are highly related to each other when testing 2×2 matrixes (Camilli 1995).

A Chi-Square test can be applied to test the significance of a relationship between two variables X and Y (Verma 2013). The following null hypothesis H_0 is tested against the alternative hypothesis H_1 (Bortz and Schuster 2010; Verma 2013):

H_0	X and Y are independent from each other
H_1	X and Y are associated with each other

If H_0 is rejected, the interpretation is that a significant relationship between X and Y exists (Bortz and Schuster 2010; Verma 2013). In order to apply a Chi-Square test, the following steps needs to be followed and are outlined below (Verma 2013):

1. Calculation of expected frequencies as shown in formula (4.1)
2. Calculation of Chi-Square statistic as shown in formula (4.2)
3. Calculation of degrees of freedom as shown in formula (4.3)
4. Identification of critical value as given in Appendix F
5. Interpretation and identification of level of significance

Assume that a population consists of $j = 1, \ldots, J$ mutually exclusive classes x_j of the variable X and $k = 1, \ldots, K$ mutually exclusive classes y_k of the variable Y, than the scores can be arranged in a contingency matrix as given in Table 4.12. Such a two-way contingency table expresses the observed absolute frequencies h_{kj} of two categorical variables related to the classes x_j and y_k for a sample size of $N = \sum_{1}^{K} \sum_{1}^{J} h_{kj}$ (Andersen 1997; Bortz and Schuster 2010). It indicates the cross-classification of all possible categories (Kateri 2010; Powers and Xie 2008).

Table 4.12 Contingency table on observed absolute frequencies

	x_1	x_2	...	x_J	Total
y_1	h_{11}	h_{12}	...	h_{1J}	$\sum\limits_1^J h_{1j}$
y_2	h_{21}	h_{22}	...	h_{2J}	$\sum\limits_1^J h_{2j}$
...	...	...	...	...	...
y_k	h_{K1}	h_{K2}	...	h_{KJ}	$\sum\limits_1^J h_{Kj}$
Total	$\sum\limits_1^K h_{k1}$	$\sum\limits_1^K h_{k2}$	...	$\sum\limits_1^K h_{kJ}$	$\sum\limits_{j=1}^J \sum\limits_{k=1}^K h_{kj}$

Based on the observed absolute frequencies, the expected absolute frequencies g_{jk} for the classes x_j and y_k are calculated and arranged in a second contingency matrix (Bortz and Schuster 2010):

$$g_{jk} = \frac{\sum\limits_{j=1}^J h_{kj} \cdot \sum\limits_{k=1}^K h_{kj}}{\sum\limits_{j=1}^J \sum\limits_{k=1}^K h_{kj}} \tag{4.1}$$

The Chi-Square (χ^2) statistic is computed based on the observed and the expected frequencies (Bortz and Schuster 2010; Heinzl 1993; Verma 2013):

$$\chi^2 = \sum\limits_{j=1}^J \sum\limits_{k=1}^K \frac{\left(h_{jk} - g_{jk}\right)}{g_{jk}} \tag{4.2}$$

The null hypothesis H_0 is rejected if the computed Chi-Square statistic χ^2 is bigger than the critical value $\chi^2_{critical}$ at a certain level of significance α and the related degrees of freedom df (Verma 2013). A table of critical values for Chi-Square statistic is given in Appendix F. Degrees of freedom are calculated based on the number of rows and column in the contingency table (Bortz and Schuster 2010):

$$df = (J - 1) \cdot (K - 1) \tag{4.3}$$

In this study, the following levels of significance were applied and were interpreted as given in Table 4.13 (Heinzl 1993).

It has to be noted that Chi-Square tests can only result in sufficient results if $g_{jk} > 5; \forall j = 1, \ldots, J; \forall k = 1, \ldots, K$ within the data set (Bortz and Schuster 2010). If

Table 4.13 Interpretation of significance

Symbol	Level of significance	Meaning
****	$\alpha \leq 0.001$	Extremely significant
***	$\alpha \leq 0.01$	Very significant
**	$\alpha \leq 0.05$	Significant
*	$\alpha \leq 0.1$	Weakly significant
ns	$\alpha > 0.1$	Not significant

this condition is not met, Fisher's exact test serves as an opportunity to Chi-Square statistic (Bortz and Schuster 2010).

Fisher's exact test is a procedure to obtain exact probabilities for statistical hypotheses in contingency tables with $k = j = 2$ (Johnson 1972; Zar 1987). The advantage of this test is that it does not rely on the assumptions of Chi-Square and is not based on Chi-Square distribution (Howell 2013). It is a valuable alternative to Chi-Square tests when dealing with small frequencies (Camilli 1995; Zar 1987). The probability value P is calculated as follows (Johnson 1972):

$$P = \frac{(h_{11} + h_{12})!(h_{11} + h_{21})!(h_{12} + h_{22})!(h_{21} + h_{22})!}{N!h_{11}!h_{12}!h_{21}!h_{22}!} \tag{4.4}$$

An approximation procedure is used to arrive at a two-tailed Fisher's exact test that addresses the same statistical hypotheses as 2×2 contingency matrixes tested by Chi-Square statistic (Berry et al. 2011; Zar 1987). A detailed description of this procedure can be found in Camilli (1995) and Zar (1987).

To test the strength of associations between variables, Phi Φ coefficients are calculated. The Phi coefficient measures the relationship between two binary variables. It is closely related to Chi-Square statistics as shown below (Bortz and Schuster 2010; Howell 2013).

$$\Phi^2 = \frac{X^2}{n} \tag{4.5}$$

Phi values range from -1 to $+1$ (Bortz and Schuster 2010). A Phi coefficient <0 identifies a negative relationship between two variables, while a Phi coefficient >0 indicates a positive association (Bortz and Schuster 2010). The closer the values are to zero, the weaker the relationship between the observed variables.

4.3.3.2 Test Statistics for Three Categorical Variables

"In general terms, a moderator is a qualitative (e.g. sex, race, class) or quantitative (e.g. level of reward) variable that affects the direction and/or strength of the relationship between an independent or predictor variable and a dependent

criterion variable." (Baron and Kenny 1986: 1174). When analyzing the effect of a moderator *W* in the relationship between two categorical variables *X* and *Y*, the two-way contingency table introduced above must be extended to a three-way contingency table (Powers and Xie 2008). It has to be differentiated between marginal and conditional contingency tables for the analysis of such three-way contingency tables (Azen and Walker 2011). Marginal contingency tables neglect the effect of the moderator variable *W* by adding all frequencies in a single two-way contingency table (Azen and Walker 2011; Tsuang et al. 2011). Conditional tables analyze the "*(. . .) relationship between three categorical variables by considering two-way contingency tables, known as partial tables, at fixed levels of a third variable*" (Azen and Walker 2011: 80). A partial table is a cross-classification of two variables, while a third variable is kept at a fixed level (Kateri 2010). In other words, conditional relationships identify associations separately for any given level of a third variable *W* (Azen and Walker 2011).

Due to the fact that such partial tables are two-way contingency tables, the statistical procedures described above can be applied to determine whether conditional relationships exist (Azen and Walker 2011). However, when applying traditional Chi-Square statistics to three-way contingency tables, conditional relationships are calculated for each of partial tables independently from the remaining ones (Janssen and Laatz 2003). An exception to this are Cochran- and Mantel-Haenszel statistics (Azen and Walker 2011; Howell 2013; Janssen and Laatz 2003).

The Mantel-Haenszel statistic is meaningful in analysing significance on two-way contingency tables while controlling for the effect of a third variable (Howell 2013). It is an extension of Chi-Square statistics for three-way contingency tables (Schumacher and Schulgen-Kristiansen 2002). The following null hypothesis H_0 is tested against the alternative hypothesis H_1 (Tsuang et al. 2011):

H_0	X and Y are independent from each other, given W
H_1	X and Y are associated with each other, given W

A detailed description of Mantel-Haenszel test statistic can be found in Howell (2013) and Azen and Walker (2011). It has to be noted that the Cochran test is similar to Mantel-Haenzel statistic, but is less frequently reported (Elliott and Woodward 2007). In this study, the Mantel-Haenszel statistic is applied, because it performs corrections for small sample sizes (Howell 2013; Janssen and Laatz 2003).

4.3.3.3 Summary on Test Statistics for Categorical Variables

Four test statistics are introduced in this section. As outlined above, Phi test is computed to test the strength of relationships between categorical variables (Bortz and Schuster 2010; Howell 2013). This test can be applied in two-way as well as in three-way contingency tables (Azen and Walker 2011). In two-way contingency

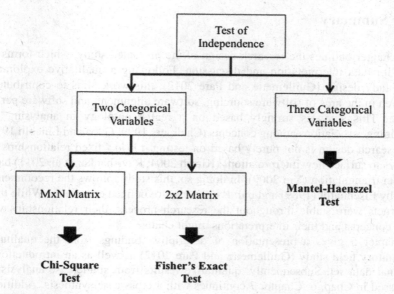

Fig. 4.2 Applied tests of independence

tables, researchers can rely on Chi-Square or Fisher's exact test to evaluate associations among categorical variables (Andersen 1997; Camilli 1995; Takane and
Zhou 2013). Chi-Square statistic emerged as a preferred test of such relationships
and is applicable to contingency tables with variables that have more than two
categories attached, referred to as $M \times N$ matrixes (Bortz and Schuster 2010;
Howell 2013). In contrast to this, Fisher's exact test is only applicable to 2×2
tables (Camilli 1995; Zar 1987). It was found that results from both tests are highly
related to each other when testing 2×2 contingency tables (Camilli 1995; Howell
2013). However, researchers report that Fisher's exact test should be preferred in
these settings (Howell 2013).

When analyzing the effect of a moderator in the relationship between two
categorical variables, the two-way contingency matrix is extended to incorporate
a third categorical variable (Azen and Walker 2011; Powers and Xie 2008). Despite
the fact that a Chi-Square test is applicable in such settings, the Mantel-Haenszel
statistic emerged as preferred test for three-way contingency tables (Azen and
Walker 2011; Howell 2013; Schumacher and Schulgen-Kristiansen 2002). Figure 4.2 summarizes on the tests of independence applied in Chap. 7.

4.4 Summary

This chapter outlines the research design of the presented study, which forms the basis for data interpretation and discussion. Following a qualitative exploratory field study design (Guillemette and Paré 2012), this work aims to contribute to research in the area of software sourcing, software alignment, and software performance. This study is strongly based on a realist ontology in analysing and explaining associations among concepts (Chalmers 1999; Guba and Lincoln 1994).

Research design is not purely based on testing *a priori* fixed relationships but ensures to surface new interpretations (Kirsch 2004; Ravishankar et al. 2011) based on data triangulation (Yin 2009). In doing so, this study follows the recommendations by Eisenhardt (1989) and builds upon a set of defined constructs. While these constructs were stable throughout the research process, their relationships with other concepts and their interpretations might change.

Chapter 5 gives a presentation of descriptive findings from the qualitative exploratory field study (Guillemette and Paré 2012) as well as an introduction to the final data set. Subsequently, qualitative results from single-case analysis are discussed in Chap. 6. Chapter 7 continues with a cross-case synthesis. Additional propositions on the impact of software sourcing modes and on emerging relationships among concepts are derived and tested statistically.

Chapter 5
Descriptive Findings

Following a discussion of the research design this chapter outlines descriptive results of the qualitative exploratory field study. Demographic data on case companies, interviewees, and empirical profiles in the overall sample is provided in Sect. 5.1. Section 5.2 gives the distribution of constructs in the final data set. Finally, Sect. 5.3 gives an overview of the empirical profiles included. All empirical profiles and related participating companies were anonymised.

5.1 Field Study Companies and Empirical Profiles

Data has been gathered within 43 field study companies. Among them, nine companies belong to the manufacturing sector. Out of these, four organizations were positioned within the automotive industry. One of them is a large international vehicle manufacturer (DELTA-MANUFACTURING) and three companies are suppliers of international car producers (BETA-, GAMMA-, and ETA-MANUFACTURING). The remaining five manufacturing companies offer products for industrial clients. Eight field study organizations are within the service industry. Among them, six companies were within the information and telecommunication sector offering IT-related services such as implementation, consulting, and outsourcing. Five companies are in the financial industry offering services like insurance, leasing, and funding of social projects. Four organizations belong to the transportation industry offering logistics, shipping, and carriage of people and goods. Additionally, four firms are positioned within the retail sector. These companies offer goods for end users and business clients. Three public institutions and three organizations within the energy sector were included. Furthermore, two firms offering construction services to large business clients and two associations such as sport confederations participated in the study. Moreover two companies focusing on research and development in the life science and pharmaceutical industry contributed to this investigation. Finally, a large group within the private

© Springer International Publishing Switzerland 2016
M. Nöhren, *Enterprise Software Sourcing Performance*, Progress in IS,
DOI 10.1007/978-3-319-23926-2_5

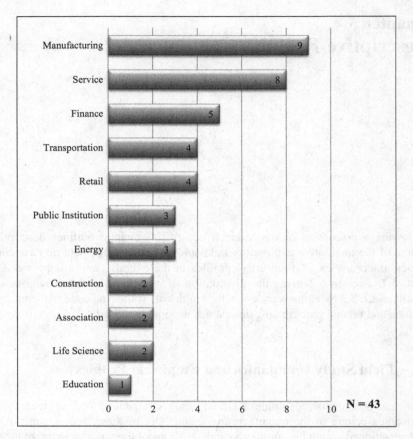

Fig. 5.1 Field study companies

education business was included. Figure 5.1 gives an overview of the high-level industry sector of the field study companies.

Beside an incorporation of different industrial sectors, companies of different sizes participated in the exploratory field study (see Fig. 5.2a). Out of the 43 companies, eight companies were small firms (less than 101 employees), 15 are medium-sized (101–1000 employees), 12 are large cooperations (1001–10,000 employees), and eight are huge companies with more than 10,000 employees. In the data set, the median value amounts for 608 employees. On an average, the case companies employed 7595 people at the time of data collection.

In sum, 51 interviews were conducted within the 43 case companies. It has to be noted that due to missing values, two interviewees at BETA-SERVICE and ETA-SERVICE were interviewed twice. Consequently, 49 people participated in the field study as shown in Fig. 5.2b. Among them, 19 were chief information officers (CIOs), 14 were high-level IT executives on the second-tier of IT management, seven were C-level executives and chief executive officers (CEOs), seven

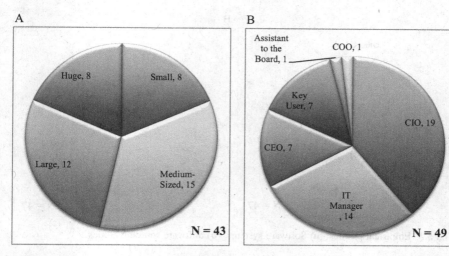

Fig. 5.2 Company size and roles of the interviewees. (**a**) Company size (headcount). (**b**) Interviewees roles

were high-level key users and business process owner, one was an assistant to the board of directors, and one was a chief operations officer (COO).

Empirical profiles within this study are process-centric enterprise systems. In sum, 47 applications were investigated. It must be noted that interviewees in four organizations provided an in-depth description of not only one but two enterprise systems. As shown in Fig. 5.3a, 30 ERP systems, 14 CRM applications and three others including one warehousing application, one procurement software, and one campus management system are observed. With respect to the software sourcing mode, six applications were sourced in an in-house setting ($\approx$13 %), whereas 41 enterprise system were packaged applications (see Fig. 5.3b). Of them, 26 applications were provided on-premises ($\approx$55 %) and 15 on-demand ($\approx$32 %). This share of "as-a-service"-applications within the data set was bigger than expected. Recent market data show that only 12 % of companies in the German market are using process-centric enterprise systems of the cloud (Niemann 2013).

ERP systems were most frequently sourced in an on-premises mode. In particular, out of 30 ERP systems, 20 were provided on-premises, nine were provided on-demand, and only one ERP system was sourced in-house. In contrast to this, a bigger share of on-demand software was found with respect to CRM applications. In particular six out of 14 CRM applications were provided on-demand, four in-house, and four were deployed in an on-premises mode.

A   B

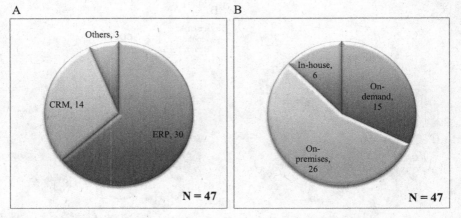

Fig. 5.3 Empirical profiles. (a) Software systems. (b) Software sourcing modes

5.2 Descriptive Analysis of Constructs

In the process of data analysis, three empirical profiles were dropped due to missing values. First, BETA-INNOVATION, a huge international research and development company within the life science industry was deleted due to the fact that this company was in the implementation phase of its on-premises CRM system at the time of the data collection. Second, GAMMA-ENERGY was dropped because the interviewee was not able to give a detailed report on the dynamic alignment process for the company's on-premises ERP system. Finally, DELTA-TRANSPORTATION was not incorporated in the final data set due to the fact that the interviewee lacked deep insights on business process performance outcomes of their on-premises ERP system. Consequently, the final data set consisted of 44 empirical profiles in 40 companies based on 48 interviews.

Looking at sourcing performance, Fig. 5.4 gives the distribution of the three subcomponents of SET satisfaction. It was found that for 24 ($\approx$55 %) out of the 44 empirical profiles, interviewees reported on positive strategic benefits. Negative strategic impacts were found for 18 enterprise systems ($\approx$41 %). A similar picture was captured with respect to technological benefits. Here, 30 ($\approx$68 %) applications realized positive impacts, whereas 12 systems ($\approx$27 %) where found to be negative. The situation looks different with respect to economic benefits. Most frequently, interviewees reported on negative impacts.

Looking at the distribution of business process performance, 32 ($\approx$73 %) out of 44 process-centric software systems contributed to efficiency and effectiveness of corporate's business processes. Interviewees reported on positive as well as negative outcomes for ten applications ($\approx$23 %). Business process performance contribution of these systems was rated neutral. Only two software systems ($\approx$4 %) were found to be harmful for business processes.

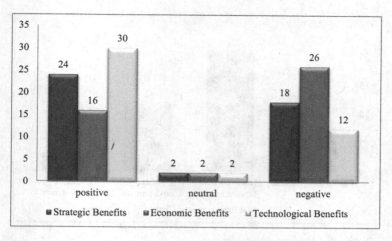

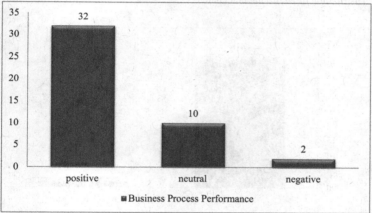

Fig. 5.4 Distribution of performance outcome constructs

Looking at concepts related to the dynamic fit process, in 21 cases (≈48 %), the impetus for change resulted from shifts in a company's macro and micro environment (see Fig. 5.5). Eight companies experienced pure macro environmental dynamics (≈18 %) and 12 firms were purely driven by idiosyncratic micro environmental volatility (≈27 %). Only three empirical profiles were found to be in a stable situation in which no structural change was required (≈7 %).

Most of the empirical profiles within the data set constantly experience large or small changes of their business process structures. As shown in Fig. 5.6, such business process structure change was found in 41 cases (≈93 %). Only three companies (≈3 %) reported on stable business process structures over longer periods of time. Constant software structure change was found in the cases of 39 applications. Technology push innovation with pure vendor-driven software changes was found in 11 cases (25 %). Nine empirical profiles (≈21 %) relied on

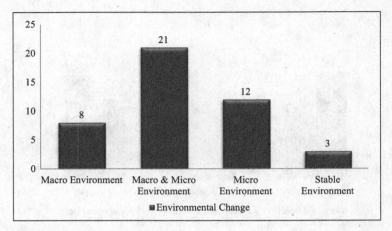

Fig. 5.5 Distribution of environmental change

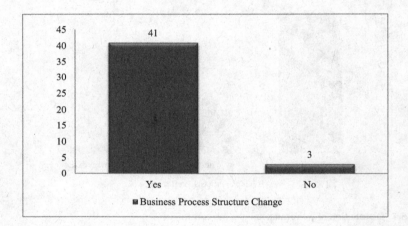

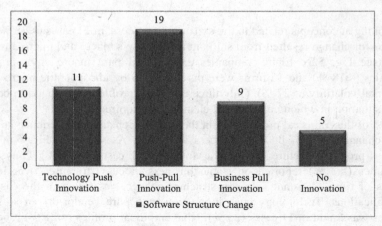

Fig. 5.6 Distribution of structural change constructs

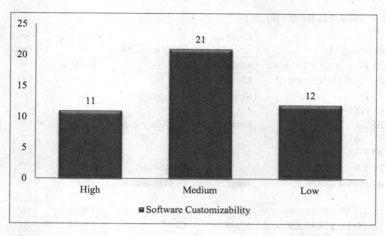

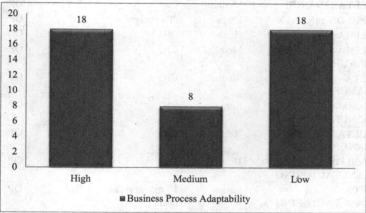

Fig. 5.7 Distribution of contextual factors

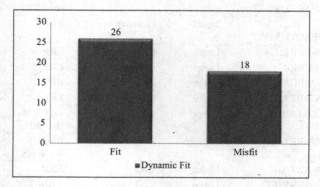

Fig. 5.8 Distribution of dynamic fit

Table 5.1 Final data set of field study

#	Company alias	Company size	Interviewee(s)	Software type	Sourcing mode
A1	ALPHA-ASSOCIATION	Medium	CIO	CRM	OP
A2	BETA-ASSOCIATION	Medium	CIO	ERP	OP
C1	ALPHA-CONSTRUCTION	Small	Assistant to the board	ERP	OD
C2	BETA-CONSTRUCTION	Large	CEO, key user	ERP	OP
E1	ALPHA-ENERGY	Medium	CIO	ERP	OP
E2	BETA-ENERGY	Medium	IT manager	ERP	OP
F1	ALPHA-FINANCE	Huge	IT manager, key user	ERP	OP
F2	BETA-FINANCE	Medium	CIO	CRM	OP
F3	GAMMA-FINANCE	Medium	CIO	CRM	IH
F4	DELTA-FINANCE	Medium	CIO	ERP	OP
F5	EPSILON-FINANCE	Large	IT manager	ERP	OP
I1	ALPHA-INNOVATION	Huge	CIO	CRM	OD
M1	ALPHA-MANUFACTURING	Medium	CIO	ERP	OP
M2	BETA-MANUFACTURING	Medium	CIO	ERP	OP
M3	GAMMA-MANUFACTURING	Large	CIO	ERP	OP
M4	DELTA-MANUFACTURING	Huge	CIO	ERP	OP
M5	EPSILON-MANUFACTURING	Huge	CIO	ERP	OP
M6	ZETA-MANUFACTURING	Large	IT manager, key user	ERP	OP
M7	ETA-MANUFACTURING	Medium	CIO	ERP	OP
M8	THETA-MANUFACTURING	Medium	IT manager	(a) CRM (b) ERP	(a) IH (b) OP
M9	IOTA-MANUFACTURING	Small	IT manager	ERP	OD
P1	ALPHA-PUBLIC	Large	IT manager	ERP	OP
P2	BETA-PUBLIC	Large	IT manager	ERP	OP
P3	GAMMA-PUBLIC	Large	IT manager	ERP	OP
R1	ALPHA-RETAIL	Small	CEO	ERP	OD
R2	BETA-RETAIL	Large	CIO	(a) CRM (b) ERP	(a) IH (b) OP
R3	GAMMA-RETAIL	Medium	CIO	(a) PCS (b) WHS	(a) IH (b) OP
R4	DELTA-RETAIL	Huge	CIO	ERP	IH
S1	ALPHA-SERVICE	Large	CIO	CRM	OD
S2	BETA-SERVICE	Small	CEO, key user	ERP	OD

(continued)

Table 5.1 (continued)

#	Company alias	Company size	Interviewee(s)	Software type	Sourcing mode
S3	GAMMA-SERVICE	Medium	CEO	ERP	OD
S4	DELTA-SERVICE	Small	CEO	CRM	OD
S5	EPSILON-SERVICE	Small	CEO	CRM	IH
S6	ZETA-SERVICE	Medium	Key user	CRM	OP
S7	ETA-SERVICE	Small	CEO	(a) CRM (b) ERP	(a) OD (b) OD
S8	THETA-SERVICE	Small	COO	CRM	OD
T1	ALPHA-TRANSPORTATION	Medium	IT manager	ERP	OP
T2	BETA-TRANSPORTATION	Huge	CIO	ERP	OP
T3	GAMMA-TRANSPORTATION	Large	IT manager	CRM	OD
U1	ALPHA-UNIVERSITY	Large	CIO	CMS	OP

CIO chief information officer, *CEO* chief executive officer, *COO* chief operations officer, *CMS* campus management system, *CRM* customer relationship management, *ERP* enterprise resource planning, *PCS* procurement system, *SCM* supply chain management, *WHS* warehousing system, *IH* in-house, *OD* on-demand, *OP* on-premises

the contrary business pull innovation with only client-driven software change. Most frequently, in 19 cases ($\approx$43 %), companies relied on push-pull innovation by combining technology push and business pull. Only five applications ($\approx$11 %) experienced no software structure innovation.

Figure 5.7 gives the distribution of the contextual factors in terms of software and business process flexibility. Software customizability was rated high in 11 cases (25 %) and low in 12 cases ($\approx$27 %). Most frequently, in 21 empirical profiles ($\approx$48 %), interviewees reported on medium opportunities to adapt deep and surface structures of the observed software artefact. Looking at business process flexibility, a high and a low level of business process adaptability was reported in 18 cases ($\approx$41 %) each. A medium rating was linked to eight profiles ($\approx$18 %).

The distribution of dynamic fit is given in Fig. 5.8. A constant coevolution between business process and software structures was found in 26 cases ($\approx$59 %). In the remaining 18 cases ($\approx$41 %) suffered from dynamic misfit.

5.3 Summary

In sum, 44 empirical profiles within 40 companies were included. All empirical profiles and participating companies were anonymised as outlined above. Three on-premises profiles were deleted due to missing values. The final data set consists on six in-house applications, 23 on-premises systems, and 15 on-demand software solutions. Table 5.1 gives an overview of the final data set including company alias, company size, role of interviewees, type of process-centric software artefact, and software sourcing mode.

The final data set serves as basis for data interpretation. Chapter 6 continues with a single-case analysis by an discussing exemplary empirical profiles. The cross-case synthesis is given in Chap. 7. Findings will be aggregated and a statistical test of the initially proposed and emerging associations will be provided.

Chapter 6
Single-Case Analysis

In order to explore and validate the value of software sourcing modes and to investigate the relationship between software alignment and performance, an exploratory field study (Guillemette and Paré 2012) in 40 organizations was conducted. It must be noted that participants in four organizations provided not one but two detailed descriptions of process-centric enterprise software. Consequently, the final sample was composed of 44 empirical profiles of software artefacts.

Despite the fact that qualitative field studies typically rely on cross-case triangulation only (Guillemette and Paré 2012), this chapter provides additional findings from single-case analysis (Eisenhardt 1989; Yin 2009). It must be noted that an in-depth description of all 44 empirical profiles is beyond the limits and scope of the presented work. Eight empirical profiles are discussed in greater detail in this chapter. The selection of these exemplary profiles was made subjectively with respect to their alignment cluster and their ability to illustrate the reference framework. Section 6.1 starts with an investigation of market governance of software structure change. Two empirical profiles on technology push innovation are given. The related pioneer innovator gestalt as well as the technology push non-gestalt is outlined. Section 6.2 continues with hybrid governance of software structure change. Exemplary profiles on push-pull innovation and the related ambidextrous innovator gestalt as well as the push-pull non-gestalt are discussed. The following two sections give empirical profiles for the clusters linked to market governance. Business pull innovation and examples on the related cautious innovator gestalt as well as the business pull non-gestalt are presented in Sect. 6.3. Section 6.4 discusses the absence of software structure change by empirical profiles on the conservative gestalt as well as the no innovation non-gestalt. Finally, Sect. 6.5 summarizes the single-case investigation and shows data on all 44 empirical profiles within the data set.

6.1   Technological Push Innovation

In this section, the role of software structure change in terms of technology push innovation is outlined. In sum, 11 empirical profiles rely on this type of software structure change. Among them, nine enterprise systems are sourced in an on-demand setting, while the remaining two applications are provided on-premises. Eight of the technology push innovation systems realize dynamic fit and three suffer from dynamic misfit.

Section 6.1.1 gives the example of a pioneer innovator gestalt. An exemplary empirical profile on a technology push non-gestalt is given in Sect. 6.1.2. Section 6.1.3 gives a brief summary on software structure change in terms of technology push innovation.

6.1.1   Pioneer Innovator Gestalt

An exemplary case of a pioneer innovator is given by ALPHA-FINANCE. ALPHA-FINANCE is a German statutory health insurance company. The German health care market is separated in private health insurance—for self-employed people and those with higher incomes—and in statutory health insurance by which all other people are insured (Roeder and Labrie 2012). Approximately 90 % of the German population is protected by statutory health insurances (Roeder and Labrie 2012). Among them, more than five million people are insured by ALPHA-FINANCE. As the interviewees reported, ALPHA-FINANCE is primarily driven by macro environmental changes in terms of shifts in their imposed country context.

> Health insurance companies depend on the legislator and there are several changes per year. Of course, the extend of these changes varies from year to year. Typically we see two regulatory changes within a one years time frame. Take SEPA as an example. (...) Health insurance is a financial service, so SEPA impacts our cash flows. We need SEPA functionalities within the system and we need to provide information on our customers bank accounts. IT Manager, ALPHA-FINANCE

These change requirements are addressed by relying on pure technological push innovation. ALPHA-FINANCE's ERP system is deployed in a private cloud setting. An external service provider is responsible for operating and updating the ERP system. ALPHA-FINANCE do not perform any client-driven software structure changes internally.

> [The provider] is responsible for all updates. It is standard software. (...) We get new releases two times a year with new features and functionalities. (...) Those updates are very extensive ones. (...) IT Manager, ALPHA-FINANCE

> It is standard software. We do not adapt it. IT Manager, ALPHA-FINANCE

In order to act in conformance with shifts in the imposed country context, ALPHA-FINANCE adapt its business processes frequently.

> There is a certain standard, that all health insurance companies rely on. So there is little room for individuality. So if a new law comes into force, we have to adapt to it. Key-User, ALPHA-FINANCE

Business process adaptability turned out to be high at ALPHA-FINANCE. The interviewees reported that frequently, software structure changes in terms of technology push innovation provides the company with opportunities for process modifications. These opportunities are used to reassess existing business processes in the light of changing software structures.

> With (the packaged software), we are highly restricted to what the software offers (...) When software change takes place, we get the opportunity to reassess our processes. (...) Frequently, this leads to process adaptations. Key-User, ALPHA-FINANCE

> Software drives our processes more than our processes drive software. (...) Our standard software offers certain processes and it is in our interest to adapt to these processes. IT Manager, ALPHA-FINANCE

No deficiencies were reported by the interviewees. Moreover, the IT manager at ALPHA-FINANCE informed that technological push innovation is accountable for preventing the company from the occurrence of software structure misfits. The health insurance company benefits from dynamic fit in terms of adjusted expansion.

> The releases [provided by the vendor] are necessary to ensure our ability to act in conformance with the law. (...) We get those releases on the first of January and the first of July each year because—in general—these are the dates when new laws for health insurance companies come into force. IT Manager, ALPHA-FINANCE

By relying on a pioneer innovator gestalt and realizing dynamic fit in terms of adjusted expansion, ALPHA-FINANCE's ERP system was found to be in line with business process structures. This situation results in a positively impact on business process performance.

> [The ERP system] supports the efficiency and effectiveness of our processes. Efficiency is always influenced by software. In our case, the influence is very strong. There are two key aspects when talking about efficiency: First, the agent who works with this software. How efficiently can he or she navigate through the software and how fast does he or she gets the information he or she needs. How intuitive is the software? How many steps does he or she needs to do a certain task. A second point of efficiency is: How much—we call it bad processing—can the software prevent? How good are the plausibility checks, etc. (...) That is what we get from the software. So that is why this software is essential for us. Key-User, ALPHA-FINANCE

Looking at sourcing performance, ALPHA-FINANCE's ERP system positively impacts strategic, economic, and technological benefits.

> We only need few people for software maintenance. IT Manager, ALPHA-FINANCE

> IT efficiency is influenced significantly. (...) In the end, it must be said that the economic benefits are just great. IT Manager, ALPHA-FINANCE

> The advantage is: The software is always developed proactively by the vendor. So we do not have to worry about it. Key-User, ALPHA-FINANCE

6.1.2   Technology Push Non-gestalt

While pioneering with technological push innovation was beneficial for ALPHA-FINANCE's ERP system, a different situation was found at ETA-SERVICE. ETA-SERVICE is a small vendor within the information technology industry. The company offered customized software development services to their clients. It turned out that while ETA-SERVICE is also impacted by shifts within their macro environment, the company is primarily driven by micro environmental dynamics.

> We grow at an annual rate of approximately 50% to 80% each year. (. . .) I would say that our goals change frequently and that is why we have to react to changing situations quite often. (. . .) Every time we see a change on the market we have to react to it by changing our goals. We launch a new product and we acquire new customers in new industries. (. . .) We compete with large international companies, so we constantly have to keep pace with market changes and technological revolutions. CEO, ETA-SERVICE

In 2011, ETA-SERVICE implemented an on-demand ERP system and relies on pure technological push innovation. No client-driven software structure changes occur.

> We get updates on a quarterly basis. (. . .) Typically one of these updates is a very extensive one. CEO, ETA-SERVICE

> We do not adapt the software. (. . .) Sometimes, we change a mask or adjust a parameter, but this is not a really customization. It is rather on a 'secretary level' of software adaptation. CEO, ETA-SERVICE

It was found that ETA-SERVICE adapts its business processes frequently. These adaptations are primarily a result of micro environmental shifts. ETA-SERVICE constantly launches new products and has to adjust its internal processes to these new service offerings.

> We are highly dynamic. (. . .) We do not have annual goals or something like that. Our goals change quarterly. We constantly bring new innovations on the way and we have to adapt our processes to it. When we launch a new product, we do know nothing about its value. We can hardly forecast such things. We have to verify its value on the market. (. . .) So if we experience that something changes on the market, we have to change as well. So we are highly dynamic. CEO, ETA-SERVICE

Business process adaptability turned out to be high at ETA-SERVICE. The company aims at learning from the industry best practices offered by its ERP system.

> The goal was not just to implement a specific ERP system but rather to improve our business-management knowledge. By implementing [the ERP system], we bought new

> processes (...) We are very flexible in our processes. (...) We adapted the processes to
> what the software offers, not vice versa. CEO, ETA-SERVICE

Dynamic Misfit is identified at ETA-SERVICE. The company's idiosyncratic
processes were not sufficiently mirrored by its ERP system. For instance, the ERP
systems lacks an integration of ETA-SERVICE's external accountant department.
In addition, software structure changes in terms of technology push innovation
frequently harms the organization's business processes.

> We have very specific processes that are not mirrored by the ERP system. (...) Most of
> these updates are not really beneficial for us. Sometimes we experience downtimes of up to
> one week (...) Of course you wish for more functionality, but you are restricted to what the
> system offers you. (...) The system could run faster. (...) See, we do not have an internal
> tax department (...) We have serious problems with the integration of our external tax
> accountant. (...). For instance, the control of task packages is inadequate within the system.
> CEO, ETA-SERVICE

Looking at business process performance contribution, ETA-SERVICE's ERP
system was not valuable, when it comes to the company's primary processes and
tasks such as project management or software development.

> [The ERP system], it is necessary to manage our business (...) Our key processes are not
> well represented by the system. We tried to incorporate processes such as project manage-
> ment and software development within the system but it was challenging so we stopped
> it. (...) So the administrative costs increased. Every employee now has to invest more time
> in administrative things CEO, ETA-SERVICE

Looking at sourcing performance, ETA-SERVICE's ERP system was found to
be negative from a strategic and technological point of view. The reduced strategic
benefits turned out to be a result of deficiencies from software updates.
ETA-SERVICE has to invest in rework constantly. In addition, the software vendor
recently announced that its on-demand ERP system is not further developed. This
increases the risk of structural obsolescence and reduces technological benefits.

> Typically, we have to invest up to three or four man-days after each update to get the system
> ready. (...) We had to rework after each update. In recent times, things are getting better.
> (...) It is better now, but it is still far away from being good. (...) CEO, ETA-SERVICE

> Recently, [the software vendor] announced that he stopped development of their
> [on-demand ERP system]. (...) It would have been great if we would get a HTML 5.0
> surface or something else that would make the software run faster and thereby increase its
> performance. This will not be the case within the next years. (...) It is sad. We really
> backed the wrong horse. CEO, ETA-SERVICE

In contrast to strategic and technological sourcing performance, economic
impacts of ETA-SERVICE's ERP system turned out to be positive. This was
reported to be a result of sourcing the software on-demand and thereby outsourcing
physical, deep, and surface structures to a software vendor.

> The ERP system is good from an economic point of view. Especially due to the fact that we
> have little operating costs. (...) It is good for this price. CEO, ETA-SERVICE

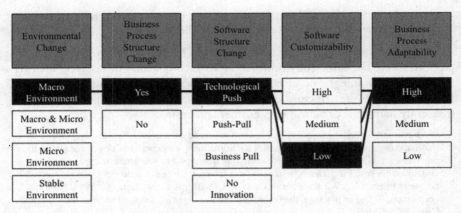

Fig. 6.1 Dynamic alignment process at ALPHA-FINANCE

6.1.3 Summary

This section discusses the role of software structure change in terms of technology push innovation by giving two exemplary empirical profiles sourcing their ERP systems on-demand. ALPHA-FINANCE established dynamic fit in terms of adjusted expansion. The company was found to be primarily driven by macro environmental shifts. These shifts are addressed by constant business process structure change and software structure change in terms of technology push innovation. Technology push innovation is supported by a high level of business process adaptability. Software customizability was found to be low. Figure 6.1 gives the specification of constructs related to the dynamic alignment process. The lines between specifications express the pioneer innovator gestalt as defined in Chap. 3. The specifications of ALPHA-FINANCE are shaded black.

By relying on a pioneer innovator gestalt, software structure of ALPHA-FINANCE is in line with business process structure. It was found that the ERP system contributed to business process performance. In addition, sourcing performance in terms of strategic, economic, and technological outcomes were found to be positive.

An example of a technology push non-gestalt is given by ETA-SERVICE. Driven by macro and micro environmental changes while being primarily impacted by the latter one, ETA-SERVICE suffers from dynamic misfit. Constant business process structure changes put pressures on related software structures. It was found that ETA-SERVICE do not perform any client-driven software modifications. In addition, technology push innovation is insufficient to address to constant changes within the company's micro environment. As a result, software structure is not in line with business process structure. Like above, Fig. 6.2 gives the specification of constructs related to the dynamic alignment process. The lines between specifications express the pioneer innovator gestalt as defined in Chap. 3. The specifications of ETA-SERVICE are shaded black.

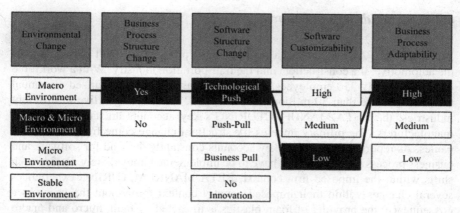

Fig. 6.2 Dynamic alignment process at ETA-SERVICE

By being a technology push non-gestalt, software structure of ETA-SERVICE is not in line with business process structure. ERP system's contribution to business process performance is rated neutral. On the one hand, the secondary business processes are supported well by the software. On the other hand, the application lacks certain features resulting in deficiencies for ETA-SERVICE's primary processes. In addition, sourcing performance in terms of strategic and technological outcomes were found to be negative. However, economic benefits are identified as a result of sourcing software on-demand.

6.2   Push-Pull Innovation

Following a discussion of technology push innovation in Sect. 6.1, this section continues with an investigation of push-pull innovation. In sum, 19 empirical profiles rely on this hybrid governance of software structure change. Among them, five enterprise systems are sourced in an on-demand setting, while the remaining 14 applications are provided on-premises. Nine of the push-pull innovation systems realize dynamic fit while ten suffer from dynamic misfit.

Section 6.2.1 gives the example of an ambidextrous innovator gestalt. An exemplary empirical profile on a push-pull non-gestalt is presented in Sect. 6.2.2. Section 6.2.3 provides a brief summary of software structure change in terms of push-pull innovation.

6.2.1 Ambidextrous Innovator Gestalt

BETA-MANUFACTURING is a medium-sized provider of foam plastics within the automotive, the construction, and the transportation industry. With a workforce of approximately 350 employees, the German-based company realized an annual turnover of more than 30 million Euros in 2013. While being active in different industries, the BETA-MANUFACTURING's key accounts are large global car manufacturers. The primary impetus for structural change come from these companies. As reported by the CIO, key accounts constantly demand for software and business process adaptations that have to be implemented immediately. Beside such shifts within the imposed firm context, BETA-MANUFACTURING experiences several changes within their imposed country context throughout the year. As a consequence, the provider of foam plastics is impacted by both, micro and macro environmental changes.

> Our market segment is quite challenging. We are a supplier within the automotive industry. Automotive companies are very huge organizations. (. . .) Automotive companies have very high and complex requirements with respect to quality, documentation, and several other things. (. . .) Nowadays, we do not only deliver products, we also deliver information to Daimler, BMW, and all the other companies. (. . .) We have to keep pace with changing electronic data transfer requirements of the automotive companies. In recent years, this is getting more and more challenging. For instance, in 1988, Daimler asked whether we could deliver some information electronically. Back in the days, electronic data transfer was a foreign word for us, so we told them: 'Yes, we take care of it and we will get back to you in one and a half years.' Today, they say we need this or that change and you have fourteen days to get your system ready. CIO, BETA-MANUFACTURING

> There are a lot of legal changes throughout the year. Especially in the area of human resources. CIO, BETA-MANUFACTURING

These macro and micro environmental shifts force BETA-MANUFACTURING to adapt its business processes frequently. The interviewee reported that changes in the structure of their business processes occurred more often in recent years.

> We have to adapt ourselves to changing requirements quite often. Such changes occur more frequently nowadays and it is even getting worse. (. . .) It is getting more complex. Often, when an automotive company demands for a particular adaptation to our [ERP system], our business units have to work differently because they have to provide other data or something like that. CIO, BETA-MANUFACTURING

An on-premises ERP system was implemented by BETA-MANUFACTURING in 2000. Since that time, software structure change has been realized by combining technology push innovation with business pull innovation. All ERP updates available are implemented by BETA-MANUFACTURING. However, due to changes within the imposed firm context, the provider of foam plastics has to perform client-driven software adaptations as well.

> (. . .) there are 'Enhancement Packages' adding new features to the current version. (. . .) We implement all these 'Enhancement Packages' available. CIO, BETA-MANUFACTURING

> From time to time, we have to adapt the system. (...) If necessary, we do some reprogramming. (...) That is always a huge effort for us. CIO, BETA-MANUFACTURING

A medium level of software customizability supports business pull innovation. BETA-MANUFACTURING ramped-up their internal IT capabilities in order to perform those required software structure changes.

> Last year, we learned that we had too little knowledge to make all those modifications to [the ERP system] that we would require. So we hired an additional [ERP system] programmer, who had several years of experience with the software. Since then, we have been able to make lots of adaptations on our own. CIO, BETA-MANUFACTURING

At the same time, business process adaptability was found to be high at BETA-MANUFACTURING. The interviewee reported that business processes are rather adjusted to the inherent software standard than vice versa.

> Our philosophy is to stick as close as possible to the standard. We rather adapt ourselves than [the ERP system]. (...) We use a lot of the standard functionalities. (...) CIO, BETA-MANUFACTURING

No software structure misfits were reported by the interviewee. BETA-MANUFACTURING is highly satisfied with the dynamic nature of their on-premises ERP system. Vendor-driven software structure change in combination with client-driven software structure change prevents the company from suffering from deficiencies.

> In the face of an potential production line standstill of our clients, we have to adapt our ERP system immediately. Our all-time record was that we did 800 kilometres in three hours. We got a call from the Hungarian site of one of our clients that all of our goods were consumed. We had three hours to deliver the raw materials to this site. We did it, but it was very expensive. There are a lot of these situations where something goes wrong, which could get expensive for us. So it is a good thing that we can adapt the system quite fast in order to prevent such things in the future. (...) [The software vendor] provides lots of updates when there are bugs within the system or if a new legislation comes into force. CIO, BETA-MANUFACTURING

Consequently, BETA-MANUFACTURING realized this dynamic fit by the means of an ambidextrous innovator gestalt. Software structure is in line business process structure, which contributes to business process performance.

> Processes became more agile and easier to handle (...) The biggest advantage of [the ERP system] is the automation within the production and the delivery department. It is way easier to link our internal units with those units of our clients. CIO, BETA-MANUFACTURING

The interviewee was satisfied with the technological benefits of their on-premises ERP system. A sophisticated technology push innovation reduces the risk of software obsolescence at BETA-MANUFACTURING.

> It is no longer how it was once. [The software vendor] improved its update strategy. In the past, we got a new release every second or third year. Now there are 'Enhancement Packages' adding new features the current version. This is way easier for us, because we get these updates more often. CIO, BETA-MANUFACTURING

A different picture was found with respect to the strategic and economic sourcing performance. The interviewee reported no increase in IT competence through sourcing the on-premises ERP system. In addition, client-driven software structure change turned out to be complex for BETA-MANUFACTURING. This situation limits the opportunity to focus on core competencies of the IT function.

> Our IT competence did not increase. Of course, it is quite difficult to assess what would have been if there was a crisis, but I think we could have managed it with the old software as well? (. . .) If we have to move one comma within the system, we need three man-days. Like I said, the system offers a lot of opportunities for us to adapt it to our needs, but we have to make changes at multiple locations within the system simultaneously and this is a huge effort for us. CIO, BETA-MANUFACTURING

Looking at the economic benefits, the CIO at BETA-MANUFACTURING reported that the company is not able to perform all required software structure changes internally. Often, external consultants have to support the IT unit, which is very expensive for the firm.

> Often, the software lacks important features and we have to build them on our own. To give you an example—despite the fact that we sourced the automotive version of [the ERP system]—form printouts are really bad within the system. In fact, dozens of forms are missing, (. . .) In such situations, we hire external consultants and this is really expensive. CIO, BETA-MANUFACTURING

6.2.2   Push-Pull Non-gestalt

An example of a push-pull non-gestalt is given by another manufacturing company. ZETA-MANUFACTURING is among the largest packaging steel producers in Europe. As part of a larger cooperation, ZETA-MANUFACTURING employs more than 2000 people that serve clients in 80 countries around the globe. Two people were interviewed at the packaging steel producer: a second tier IT executive, responsible for managing the firm-wide ERP system and a key-user, who is a process owner for handling user software change requests throughout the cooperation. Like in the case of BETA-MANUFACTURING discussed above, the impetus for change results from shifts within the macro as well as the micro environment of the company.

> In principle, we are on a niche market. Competition and market dynamic result from two key forces. First, the market volume remains stable since several years. So we compete with companies that offer similar products or substitute packaging materials. (. . .) From time to time, new competitors offering such substitutes—like Tetra-Pak—enter the market. (. . .) Second, we do not offer a standard product. Even though that cans of our clients seem to be similar for the eyes of the end users, they differ with respect to their ingredients, their surface properties, and their finishing. (. . .) So we offer customized products for all of our clients. That means, we have to link these clients with our sales and our productions department electronically. And that—in turns—means that we have to link our systems with those of our clients. IT Manager, ZETA-MANUFACTURING

Legislation and regulation continue to change. Especially in the area of human resources, constant changing legal requirements—take SEPA as an example; take ELENA as an example—impose a permanent need to transform our processes. Key-User, ZETA-MANUFACTURING

ZETA-MANUFACTURING adapts its business process structures when external forces demand for it. For instance, the key-user within the human resource department reported that each year in January, a multitude of new legislations come into force.

We adapt our processes whenever it is necessary, for instance, when a new legislation comes into force. In January, our employees have to get familiar with new laws and they have to implement the required procedures." Key-User, ZETA-MANUFACTURING

Software structure changes of ZETA-MANUFACTURING's on-premises ERP system were addressed by combining technology push innovation with business pull innovation. The interviewees reported that all software updates provided by the system vendor are implemented throughout the year. In addition, lots of client-driven customizations are installed.

"We are running the latest version of [the ERP system]. We implement all those updates available on a regular basis." IT Manager, ZETA-MANUFACTURING; "We implement smaller support packages every month. In addition, we have these huge 'Christmas Packages' with lots of adaptations adding legal changes. These adaptations have to be implemented right away and must be launched until the end of January." Key-User, ZETA-MANUFACTURING

"Our philosophy is to retain [IT] knowledge in-house. We have a lot of programmers that do all kind of customizations for us." Key-User, ZETA-MANUFACTURING; "Software customization is primarily driven by internal forces. We build add-ons. We do the programming." IT Manager, ZETA-MANUFACTURING

A medium level of software customizability supports business pull innovation. The IT manager at ZETA-MANUFACTURING reported on some opportunities to perform client-driven changes of software structures.

The enhancement concept of [the ERP system] is quite good. We have several opportunities to adapt and modify the system. (...) We use these opportunities quite a lot. We have several add-ons and we do a lot of additional programming to the system. IT Manager, ZETA-MANUFACTURING

However, business process adaptability was found to be low at ZETA-MANUFACTURING. The key-user reported that software structures and business process structures exist independently from each other. If the structures of their ERP system conflicts with those of corporate's processes, work around is needed to cope with this situation. ZETA-MANUFACTURING do not adapt its business processes to what the software offers.

There is the software and there is the process. Software offers a basic structure. In general, this structure is valuable to ensure integrity and regulatory compliance. (...) On the other hand, if the software processes conflict with how we do processes, it hampers our flexibility and we have to work around the system. Key-User, ZETA-MANUFACTURING

Dynamic misfit is identified at ZETA-MANUFACTURING. The interviewees reported on a multitude of deficiencies. A central factor impacting dynamic misfit was ZETA-MANUFACTURING's inability to adapt business processes towards changing software structures by the means of technology push innovation. The company experiences a constant shift towards a tighter standard with less functionalities available. This situation results in a constant occurrence of new deficiencies.

"This [document management system] is an add-on. It is like that: there are lots of potential functionalities that [the software vendor] will not deal with. They say: 'These functionalities are way too specific. We do not implement them [within the standard].' They [software vendor] stay out of many areas. [The software vendor] just offers one standard and within this standard they only offer very specific things. They stay out of certain topics. Auditing and compliance are examples, for this.", "[The software vendor] clearly stated: 'We do not change anything with respect to all this document stuff. Whatever document is created within the system, is created by Adobe. This is our partner. Get used to it' (...) We see an increasing shift towards the standard. [The software vendor] wants to get rid of all these special functionalities", "[The enterprise system] provides the legislative standard and that is even all. They do not address individual things. They say, 'we are not interested in tariff agreements'. They also say, 'certain things, which are not mandatory, are not important for the development of our standard'. To give you an example: Two years ago, there was the big topic of ELENA. ELENA was an automated reporting procedure where we would have had to transfer all data on employees that leave our company to the job centre—no matter whether she or he is some unskilled worker or an executive employee—because— theoretically spoken—she or he could apply for social welfare programs. That means that a tremendous amount of data would have had to be transmitted to the job centres so that they are able to better prove applications and to calculate such things like accommodation allowances and so on. It was not implemented back then, (...) but now the job centres woke up and say: 'We would like to have it.' Now there is some sort of an 'ELENA Light', which is called BEA. That means that we communicate these data to the labour administration directly by an automated procedure. And even today, [the software vendor] says: 'This is off interest for us. It is not mandatory. We know that you have to submit this data but you can still do it paper-based.' So, as long as a procedure is not mandatory, they are not interested in it.", "I just looked at an old presentation where they announced that usability would be improved significantly soon. However, the status today is that nothing has changed. (...) The user interface—to be honest—is not quite contemporary. Someone who grew up with Apple products would say: 'What is that?' (...) It is not structured in a way, a 'modern' human is used to work with an application. When I show this [user interface] to my kids—and I do that sometimes at home—and tell them that this is Germany's leading enterprise software, they laugh their heads off." Key-User, ZETA-MANUFACTURING

By relying on push-pull innovation while having a low level of business process flexibility, ZETA-MANUFACTURING suffered from misfits between business process and software structures. These misfits reduce ERP system's contribution to business process performance.

On the one hand, [the ERP system] supports our core processes quite good. It helps us in terms of effectiveness and 'doing the things right'. We have to follow a certain procedure in a particular order. And thereby, the system makes sure that we are not forgetting anything. However, whether this is always efficient or not remains questionable. Like I said, the system is not really flexible and it lacks a lot of features that would be helpful in executing our processes. As a consequence, we often need workarounds and this is neither efficient nor effective. Key-User, ZETA-MANUFACTURING

Looking at sourcing performance, ZETA-MANUFACTURING's ERP system do not contribute to strategic, economic, or technological benefits. In order to reduce software-business process misfit, the company has to invest time and efforts in customizing the software artefact towards their very specific requirements. Thereby, ZETA-MANUFACTURING is unable to refocus on its core competencies. Due to the fact that several software structure misfits cannot be resolved by package adaptation, the steel producer has to invest in alternative solutions, which reduces economic benefits derived from their on-premises ERP system. An increasing standardization of the software artefact driven by technology push innovation of the vendor increases misfits and reduced technological benefits.

> We invest a lot of time and effort in software customization. External consultants frequently support us. (...) An example: One of the most complex things within a firm is time management. An employee may work a maximum of ten hours a day. How do we capture this time within the system? How do we control that nobody exceeds his or her ten hours maximum? What happens to the overtime? How is overtime cut back? Key-User, ZETA-MANUFACTURING

> "There are several add-ons that provides us with most of the features we need. However, it often takes too much time to integrate these things. (...) It starts with the vendor selection. For example: Talent management is really a weak spot within [the ERP system]. So we implemented an add-on that was recommended by [the software vendor]. We learned that this was not sufficient for our needs and that we had no opportunity to adapt the source code. The system was a 'black box' for us. So we talked to the vendor, but they said: 'We will not tell you what is happening within the system.' (...) In the end, we experienced a lot of technical issues. We wasted a lot of money on this. It was one of the biggest flops we ever experienced. In the end, we lost a five-digit amount of money." Key-User, ZETA-MANUFACTURING

> "[The software vendor] focuses on hot topics and trend themes. In a consequence, the ERP system started a journey towards an increasing standardization with decreasing opportunities for us." IT Manager, ZETA-MANUFACTURING

6.2.3   Summary

This section discusses the role of push-pull innovation by offering two exemplary empirical profiles sourcing their ERP systems on-premises. BETA-MANUFACTURING creates dynamic fit in terms of adjusted expansion. The company is driven by macro and micro environmental shifts. These shifts are addressed by constant business process structure change and software structure change in terms of push-pull innovation. Technology push innovation is supported by a high level of business process adaptability. A medium level of software customizability supports BETA-MANUFACTURING in performing additional business pull innovations. Figure 6.3 gives the specification of constructs related to the dynamic alignment process. The lines between specifications express the

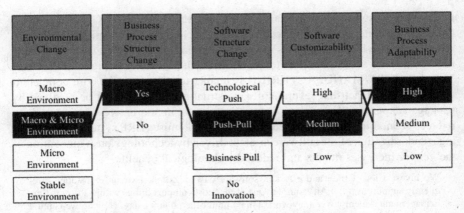

Fig. 6.3 Dynamic alignment process at BETA-MANUFACTURING

ambidextrous innovator gestalt as defined in Chap. 3. The specifications of BETA-MANUFACTURING are shaded black.

By relying on an ambidextrous innovator gestalt, software structure of BETA-MANUFACTURING is in line with business process structure. It was found that the ERP system contributed to business process performance. In addition, while technological outcomes are positive, BETA-MANUFACTURING's strategic and economic sourcing performance was rated negative.

An example of a push-pull non-gestalt is given by ZETA-MANUFACTURING. Driven by macro and micro environmental changes, ZETA-MANUFACTURING suffers from dynamic misfit. It was found that the company is unable to adapt its business processes to changing software standards provided by the ERP system's vendor. As a result, software structure is not in line with business process structure. Like above, Fig. 6.4 gives the specification of constructs related to the dynamic alignment process. The lines between specifications express the ambidextrous innovator gestalt as defined in Chap. 3. The specifications of ZETA-MANUFACTURING are shaded black.

By being a push-pull non-gestalt, software structure of ZETA-MANUFACTURING is not in line with business process structure. ERP system's contribution to business process performance was rated neutral. On the one hand, the software artefact supports business processes of ZETA-MANUFACTURING. On the other hand, the application lacks certain features resulting in deficiencies, which in turns reduces software's value contribution in corporate's business processes. Constant software misfits negatively impacts strategic, economic, and technological outcomes of the on-premises ERP system.

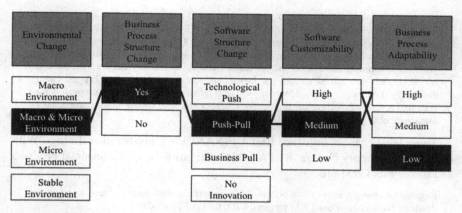

Fig. 6.4 Dynamic alignment process at ZETA-MANUFACTURING

6.3 Business Pull Innovation

This section continues with discussing the role of business pull innovation. In sum, nine empirical profiles rely on this type of software structure change. Among them, five enterprise systems are sourced in an in-house setting, while the remaining four applications are provided on-premises. Six of the business pull innovation systems realize dynamic fit and three suffer from dynamic misfit.

Section 6.3.1 gives the example of a cautious innovator gestalt. An exemplary empirical profile on a business pull non-gestalt is presented in Sect. 6.3.2. Section 6.3.3 provides a brief summary on hierarchy governance of software structure change in terms of business pull innovation.

6.3.1 Cautious Innovator Gestalt

An example of a cautious innovator gestalt is given by BETA-FINANCE. BETA-FINANCE is a leading international provider of tangible assets in the areas of real estate and aviation with a total investment volume of more than 15 billion Euros. Looking at the CRM process, the company is primarily impacted by shifts in the imposed firm context. Constant changes within the legal framework influence BETA-FINANCE indirectly. In particular, these changes do not impact the financial service provider itself but their clients and thereby the company's financial products.

> As mentioned before, we are in a niche segment. That means, we form the end of the entire investment portfolio. We always had a market environment with only few competitors. Since the financial crisis in 2009 and 2010, the number of competitors decreased. But nevertheless there are a couple of key players on the market that compete with us. (. . .) Most of the changes that we have to face are regulatory ones. The legislation—especially in

our market segment—is in a permanent flow. (...) These legal changes impact us indirectly. That means, we have to adapt our service offerings. (...) To give you another example: From the 90s of last century until the early 2000s, our products were rather a tax saving opportunity for wealthy customers. They could spread their tax charges over many years. In the mid of 2000 the legislator reacted and systematically cut back on those tax saving models and forced us into the investment section. That was the biggest change during the last years. Now, this year—as next great disruption—the European Union launched a new capital market regulation. (...) So you see, we are mainly impacted by regulatory changes. CIO, BETA-FINANCE

These legal changes influence BETA-FINANCE's idiosyncratic offerings. With each such regulatory change, BETA-FINANCE has to adapt its financial products and thereby its CRM process.

Regulatory changes impact our clients. This, in turns, means that we have to adapt our financial products and our CRM process. CIO, BETA-FINANCE

The required software structure change of the on-premises CRM system is performed by relying on pure business pull innovation. No vendor-driven software structure changes occurred in more than one decade.

Of course there is this entirely new version of the system available on the market, but we are not going to implement it; at least not before 2015. That would then be the first major disruption of the package. In fact, it would be like implementing a whole new system. You can certainly take over some of the things we have, but it would be the first upgrade in eleven or twelve years. CIO, BETA-FINANCE

We conduct all adjustment of the CRM-system ourselves. That is the most important thing for us (...) You simply have to know the system well. CIO, BETA-FINANCE

This internally executed software structure change is supported by a high customizability of the on-premises enterprise system. The interviewee at BETA-FINANCE reported on multiple opportunities to adapt the system according to the company's very specific needs.

This is why we have decided in favour of this system. It is completely parameterizable without traditional programming or development activities. That means that I can control workflows, extensions, and the entire business logic of it with a simple parameterizing tool. This is manageable with simple technical IT know-how. (...) That—ultimately—is the crucial strength of our CRM-system. CIO, BETA-FINANCE

BETA-FINANCE realizes dynamic fit in terms of adjusted expansion. A high level of software customizability supports the financial service provider in rapidly addressing required software structure changes as a result of shifts within the imposed firm context. Thereby, the company avoids the occurrence of deficiencies within their on-premises CRM system.

So, every regulatory change, finds a complete echo within the system. From a system's side, changing competition and the regulatory environment influence us intensively. (...) Timeliness is the most important thing for us. So, these changes often occur very short-dated. Due to the fact that all of these changes impact our funding concepts, it has to be implemented within a few days. As you have already heard, it is simply not acceptable that we cannot get a fund on the market on time due to technical reasons. That is an absolute 'no go' CIO, BETA-FINANCE

By relying on a cautious innovator gestalt, BETA-FINANCE's ERP system is in line with its business process structure. The software helps to address constant environmental changes in a timely manner. This dynamic fit positively impacts efficiency and effectiveness of BETA-FINANCE's CRM process.

The CRM system supports efficiency and effectiveness of our processes. Take the following example: A large international banking house decides to distribute an Airbus A380. That means, we talk about 300 to 350 million Euros. Imagine the amount of data that has to be handled if they decide to issue a public fund with a minimum amount of 10,000 Euros. (. . .) Once the partner [banking institution] agreed to sign a contract with us, we typically have less than two weeks to get the fund on the market. That means we change the system to support our sales processes. (. . .) So yes, the software contributes to efficiency and effectiveness of our sales process. CIO, BETA-FINANCE

Looking at sourcing performance, software-business process fit impacts outcomes related to BETA-FINANCE's IT function. The ERP system positively influences strategic benefits with respect to increasing IT competences, economic benefits in terms of gaining economies of scale, and technological benefits by reducing the risk of structural obsolescence.

And within our system, we can perfectly perform all these [required changes] ourselves. Actually, we can meet every interface requirement—no matter how obscure it is— relatively fast and with very small IT capabilities. So I would conclude: 'No matter what you need, you get it in less than two weeks.' CIO, BETA-FINANCE

From an economic point of view, we are highly satisfied with the system. We have been using this system for more than ten years now. We made several large adaptations to it without having any costs for external programmers and without having high development costs. This is just great. CIO, BETA-FINANCE

The software meets all our expectations. I am also responsible for business organization in my company. So I am aware of what is going on in the market. So far, we were able to satisfy all those requirements from changing business processes in a very, very effective manner. CIO, BETA-FINANCE

6.3.2   Business Pull Non-gestalt

DELTA-MANUFACTURING is headquartered in the United States of America. The company is a huge international vehicle producer with a global workforce of more than 60,000 employees. The change impetus at DELTA-MANUFACTURING results from both, macro and micro environmental shifts while the latter one turned out to be the key driver. The company constantly invests in new technologies in order to improve their products. In addition, DELTA-MANUFACTURING expands in new global regions where it faces different market situations.

> We are the global market leader with a share of 20% in Europe and more than 50% in the
> United States. (...) Our product life cycles are very, very long and our machines are
> extremely long-lasting. (...) Changes in market share are very unlikely and if they occur
> it is typically less than 1%. (...) The market around the machines is getting more and more
> important. Future competition will revolve around software and advanced technologies. We
> have an increasing number of machines that are controlled by satellites and we will extend
> our service offerings in that area significantly within the years to come. (...) We heavily
> invest in new markets such as Africa. There, we face a different market situation. They
> simply need machines that move. High-tech is not a big topic in this region. (...) From time
> to time there are new environmental standards or new restrictions on emissions. CIO,
> DELTA-MANUFACTURNG

Such changes within the company's macro and micro environment drives business process structure change. The interviewee reported that its business processes are constantly adapted as a result of product innovations as well as shifts in DELTA-MANUFACTURING's market environment.

> We are a high tech company. We have a large technology innovation centre here in
> Germany. There, we develop and implement value-adding components that go straight
> into our products. (...) Our market environment impacts our business processes. For
> instance, if we see an economic downturn in one country, we have to adapt to it. Take
> Russia as an example. If Russia's economic situation changes, its big enterprises will not
> get money from financial institutions. That means that these companies cannot effort our
> products any longer so that we have to offer own financial services to ensure the supply in
> this market. CIO, DELTA-MANUFACTURNG

More than 30 years ago, an on-premises ERP system was implemented within the EMEA region. Due to the idiosyncratic requirements of the firm, DELTA-MANUFACTURING set up an internal IT department with approximately 200 employees. Most of these employees were constantly working on business pull innovation.

> We reserve the right to know everything better than [the software vendor]. That is the
> reason why we do not rely on their updates but develop and implement our own features
> and improvements. CIO, DELTA-MANUFACTURNG

> I have more than 180 employees in my department who's key responsibility is to constantly
> adapt the system to our business needs. CIO, DELTA-MANUFACTURNG

The CIO at DELTA-MANUFACTURING reported that the system offers a wide range of opportunities to adapt it towards the company's business requirements. This is supported by a large headcount of ERP specialists. However, due to large changes in the past, the complexity of the software structure increased tremendously over the years. This situation lowers system's customizability significantly and forced DELTA-MANUFACTURING's IT department to switch from a project-driven software structure change policy to a release strategy with not more than two software updates per year.

> You can imagine that this coordination [between the IT department and our business line] is
> very costly and requires a lot of time. And then—of course—there is always a certain delay
> [in implementing new features]. When an idea is born, it takes a lot of time to implement it
> within the system. You cannot execute it on one weekend. (...) Larger changes take up to

two, three, five months or even several years, depending on how complex they are. (...)
Because it [project-driven software change] was no longer manageable—due to the high
complexity of our own customizations—we switched to a release strategy by having not
more than two updates per year. CIO, DELTA-MANUFACTURING

The decreasing customizability of DELTA-MANUFACTURING's ERP system
leads to a delay in implementing features required by the business units. This delay
constantly results in missing functionalities, which reduces dynamic fit of software.

Business often complains about missing features. They would like to get new features
projects-driven. That is how it was used to be in the past: There was a project and we
[IT department] directly implemented the required features within the system. CIO,
DELTA-MANUFACTURNG

ERP system's contribution to business process performance was rated neutral.
On the other hand, the software artefact positively impacts efficiency and effectiveness of DELTA-MANUFACTURING's internal processes. On the other hand,
the delay in implementing new features, which in returns results in dynamic misfits,
leads to severe extra costs within the business units.

The business needs a stable and functional system. We often hear that important functionalities are missing. (...) 'If we would have had these or that functionality earlier, we would
not have lost again hundreds of thousands of euros.' (...) We hear that quite often from the
business units. CIO, DELTA-MANUFACTURING

In some areas, lead time went down from two minutes to four seconds. So that is probably a
great thing for the stakeholders in the process. CIO, DELTA-MANUFACTURING

Mixed results were found with respect to sourcing performance. The interviewee
reported that strategic benefits are low. Client-driven software changes need a
coordination on a global scale. Larger software adaptations that are required at
one of DELTA-MANUFACTURING's global locations need to be evaluated for its
value at other locations. This coordination effort reduces the ability to refocus the
IT function on its core competencies in terms of software adaptation.

The coordination effort for software updates is quite huge. It is a complex and global
process. For instance, if someone here in Germany has a good idea for a project, we have to
check whether it is also good for our processes in the USA or at another global site. You can
imagine that this is very time-consuming. CIO, DELTA-MANUFACTURNG

In addition, a large IT workforce is needed to realize business pull innovation.
Thereby, the economic benefits of the software artefact are reduced.

We have approximately 180 IT employees in the EMEA region responsible for customizing
and upgrading our ERP system. We need such a high workforce to implement all
customizations required (...) This is quite expensive. CIO, DELTA-MANUFACTURNG

However, technological benefits of the on-premises software were found to be
positive at DELTA-MANUFACTURING. The company is satisfied with the interoperability of their ERP system. For instance, the interviewee reported on the
opportunity to link their ERP system with other IT innovations provided by the
software vendor.

Each of our [software update] activities is on improving things. It is always about being faster (. . .) or including new technologies. (. . .) Recently, we implemented [a new database system] provided by [the software vendor]. That is—of course—just a middleware but it was a quantum leap for us. It improved our IT flexibility significantly. CIO, DELTA-MANUFACTURNG

6.3.3   Summary

In this section, the role of business pull innovation is outlined by offering two exemplary empirical profiles. Both systems are sourced in an on-premises mode. BETA-FINANCE creates dynamic fit of their CRM system by the means of adjusted expansion. The company is primarily driven by micro environmental shifts. These shifts are addressed by constant business process structure change and software structure change in terms of business pull innovation. This client-driven software change is supported by a high level of software customizability. Business process adaptability turned out to be low. Figure 6.5 gives the specification of constructs related to the dynamic alignment process. The lines between specifications express the cautious innovator gestalt as defined in Chap. 3. The specifications of BETA-FINANCE are shaded black.

By following a cautious innovator gestalt, software structure of BETA-FINANCE is in line with business process structure of the company. The on-premises CRM system adds to business process performance as well as to sourcing performance in terms of strategic, economic, and technological benefits.

DELTA-MANUFACTURING is an example of a business pull non-gestalt. Driven by macro and micro environmental changes while being primarily impacted by the latter one, DELTA-MANUFACTURING suffers from dynamic misfit. Constant business process structure changes put pressures on related software structures. An increasing complexity of the company's ERP system reduces its

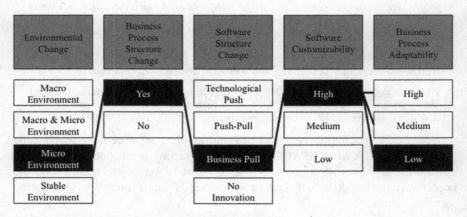

Fig. 6.5 Dynamic alignment process at BETA-FINANCE

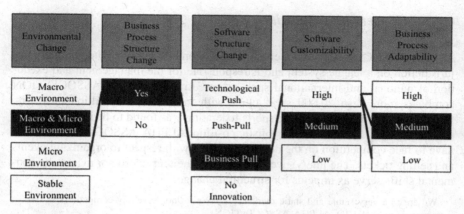

Fig. 6.6 Dynamic alignment process at DELTA-MANUFACTURING

customizability. In a consequence, business pull innovation is insufficient to address constant change requests from DELTA-MANUFACTURING's business units. As a result, software structure is not in line with business process structure. Like above, Fig. 6.6 provides the specification of constructs related to the dynamic alignment process. The lines between specifications express the cautious innovator gestalt as defined in Chap. 3. The specifications of DELTA-MANUFACTURING are shaded black.

Positive and negative impacts of DELTA-MANUFACTURING's ERP system on business process performance were reported. Negative impacts were found to be a result of dynamic misfit. While strategic and economic sourcing performance was rated negative, positive technological benefits were identified.

6.4 No Innovation

The previous sections investigates empirical profiles where either pure technology push innovation, pure business pull innovation, or both types of software structure change in terms of push-pull innovation occurs. This section discusses two empirical profiles in which no software innovation takes place. Such stable software structures are found in five cases. Among them, three enterprise systems are sourced in an on-premises setting, one is provided in-house, and one application is deployed in a private cloud mode. Three systems realize dynamic fit in terms of adjusted inertia, while two suffer from dynamic misfit.

Section 6.4.1 provides the example of a conservative gestalt. An exemplary empirical profile on a no innovation non-gestalt is presented in Sect. 6.4.2. Section 6.4.3 gives a brief summary on hierarchy governance in terms of stable software structures.

6.4.1 Conservative Gestalt

ALPHA-ASSOCIATION is a German-based sports federation. The company has jurisdiction on a league system and is responsible for the management and execution of national and international sport events. In sum, ALPHA-ASSOCIATION combines more than 20,000 sport clubs with more than six million members. Looking at the CRM process, the sports federation was found to be in a very stable market position. Due to its monopolistic position, ALPHA-ASSOCIATION do not have to face competition on the domestic market with respect to organizing events and selling tickets. The interviewee reported that neither micro nor macro environmental shifts serve as impetus for structural change.

> We are in a very stable and static market. (...) We do not have any competitors in our domestic market. CIO, ALPHA-ASSOCIATION

As a consequence of ALPHA-ASSOCIATION's stable market position, no changes to the structures of the company's CRM process occurs. The interviewee reported on structural persistence since the completion of the software implementation phase.

> We do not have to adapt to any market changes. CIO, ALPHA-ASSOCIATION

An on-premises CRM system was implemented. This system is responsible for supporting the business in managing marketing campaigns, in selling tickets, and in realizing cross-selling potentials. ALPHA-ASSOCIATION neither performs technology push innovation, nor business pull innovation of software structures. Their on-premises CRM system was adapted to the company's very specific needs during the implementation phase. An external consulting firm executed these adaptations. This consulting firm was eventually phased-out by entering the assimilation phase (Swanson and Ramiller 2004). No further software structure changes are intended.

> We were supported by a consulting company [during system implementation phase]. This company was responsible for project management and especially for change management. (...) We phased-out the consulting firm. (...) We did not change the system since that time. CIO, ALPHA-ASSOCIATION

The interviewee reported no deficiencies. Due to the absence of business process structure change, the initial software structure adaptation in the software implementation phase is still sufficient enough. As a consequence, ALPHA-ASSOCIATION creates dynamic fit in terms of adjusted inertia.

> The initial analysis [of our processes] was very intensive. This supported us in communicating change requests to the software vendor and the consulting firm. (...) In the end, we got what we needed. CIO, ALPHA-ASSOCIATION

ALPHA-ASSOCIATION provides an example of a conservative gestalt. Non-existence of environmental, business process, and software structure changes establish dynamic fit by structural persistence. Thereby, ALPHA-ASSOCIATION's CRM system adds to performance of the supported business process.

For instance, several employees contacted the same customers about the same marketing campaign. That is something that we can better manage and control now (...) So, these [ticketing] processes had been executed manually before implementing the CRM software. CIO, ALPHA-ASSOCIATION

In addition, the CRM system positively impacts sourcing performance. Strategic, economic, and technological benefits were found at ALPHA-ASSOCIATION. The system increases IT competence of the sports federation. Moreover, ALPHA-ASSOCIATION established a new technological agenda and increased software landscape's interoperability by linking its CRM system to a novel database system provided by the software vendor. Thereby, the company is able to handle a large number of customer data records.

In the past, our ticketing was operated by an external partner. We had no possibility to integrate it into our ERP system. CIO, ALPHA-ASSOCIATION

And I am convinced that we achieved an economic benefit simply through the structure of our entire data. CIO, ALPHA-ASSOCIATION

We are a flagship project of [the software vendor] because we are the first company that runs [the CRM system] on [software vendor's novel database system]. The system helps us to handle our customer data. CIO, ALPHA-ASSOCIATION

6.4.2   No Innovation Non-gestalt

BETA-ASSOCIATION is a federation of companies within the German books industry. The organization offers a wide range of services for stationary book stores. BETA-ASSOCIATION has to face severe changes within its micro environment. In recent years, new competitors offering substitute products such as eBooks or online books entered the market. This situation puts pressure on the existing business models within the books industry.

Our competitors are all those companies that do not directly belong to the books industry— especially online stores such as Amazon or others. These online stores do not simply compete with traditional book stores. They offer a new product—the eBook—that destabilize existing business models. (...) In recent years, online sales are on the rise while the traditional book market decreases. This led to an increasing consolidation on the market. (...) New competitors enter the market. EBooks are now offered by companies like Apple in their Appstores. These are competitors that have a way larger capital background than we have. And these companies start acting more and more aggressively on the market. (...) It is not just eBooks that put pressure on existing business models. Take Google books as an example: users have the opportunity to search and read specialist literature online. CIO, BETA-ASSOCIATION

These changes force BETA-ASSOCIATION to adapt its service offerings and related business processes. In order to cope with substitute products and to increase the competitive position of their clients, BETA-ASSOCIATION has to develop solutions to face market volatility.

These changes impact our business models. We have to act very dynamically. Currently, we are developing an own eBook reader for the stationary book stores. In contrast to Apple or Amazon, this reader has to be independent from a particular platform. (...) We have to develop unique selling propositions for the offline book stores. CIO, BETA-ASSOCIATION

Software structure change did not occur at BETA-ASSOCIATION. The interviewee reported that the last software update was in 2009. Since that time, neither technology push, nor business pull innovation occurred.

We often decide not to implement release changes provided by [the software vendor] (...) There is an entirely new version of the ERP system available, but we are not going to implement it. (...) Our last software update was in 2009. CIO, BETA-ASSOCIATION

We do not adapt the software ourselves. All customizations and adaptations are done by the software vendor. We can send them our change requests and they implement it. CIO, BETA-ASSOCIATION

The absence of software structure change turned out to be harmful for BETA-ASSOCIATION. The company is unable to overcome deficiencies and suffers from dynamic misfit in terms of insufficient software structure change.

It is getting problematic, each time, we require a certain software change. This is nothing we can do right away because we have to send change requests to the software vendor. Then, it takes some time and we get a service offering. Typically, these adaptations are very costly. A simple interface costs between 20,000 and 30,000 Euros, which is a lot of money for a company of our size. (...) In most cases we decide not to make these adaptations. CIO, BETA-ASSOCIATION

Business process performance contribution of BETA-ASSOCIATION's ERP system was rated neutral. On the one hand, the software artefact contributes to the efficiency of the company's standard processes. On the other hand, dynamic misfits leads to a drifting apart between business process and software structures. This results in a situation in which some processes are executed manually and outside BETA-ASSOCIATION's ERP system.

The software supports our standard processes very good. It contributes to the efficiency of our business. (...) [In most cases we decide not to make these adaptations.] That means, we rather go back to execute some of our processes manually instead of investing in software changes. CIO, BETA-ASSOCIATION

Sourcing performance of BETA-ASSOCIATION's ERP system turned out to be negative. Due to the inability to overcome software-business process misfit, BETA-ASSOCIATION increasingly shifts from a consolidated and integrated solution to a heterogeneous software landscape. This limits the ability to focus on core competencies. In addition, BETA-ASSOCIATION has to pay for each software update. This fact lowers economic and technological benefits of the ERP system.

We are about to move from a consolidated solution to more heterogeneous software landscape. (...) For instance, [the ERP system] offers a CRM component, but we decided in favour of another system. The price-performance ratio of this CRM system was way better. However, now we would have to build an interface that would link the ERP and the

CRM system with each other. (. . .) We bought a separate warehousing system and linked it to [the ERP system]. CIO, BETA-ASSOCIATION

The software vendor is good but expensive. We have to pay for everything. To give you an example: Next year, SEPA comes into force. This requires a wide range of adaptation to our ERP system (. . .) It will cost us at least 60,000 Euros. CIO, BETA-ASSOCIATION

The software only changes if we pay for it. So we only get an innovation or an update if we demand for it. CIO, BETA-ASSOCIATION

6.4.3   Summary

The role of stable software structures is investigated in this section. Two illustrative on-premises empirical profiles are introduced. ALPHA-ASSOCIATION establishes dynamic fit in terms of adjusted inertia. The monopolistic company acts on a stable market with no environmental shifts putting pressures on the corporate's CRM process. Neither business process structures, nor software structures are innovated. Figure 6.7 gives the specification of constructs related to the dynamic alignment process. The lines between specifications express the conservative gestalt as defined in Chap. 3. The specifications of ALPHA-ASSOCIATION are shaded black.

By relying on a conservative gestalt, software structure of ALPHA-ASSOCIATION is in line with business process structure. It was found that the CRM system contributes to business process performance as well as sourcing performance in terms of strategic, economic, and technological benefits.

An example of a no innovation non-gestalt is given by BETA-ASSOCIATION. Driven by micro environmental changes, BETA-ASSOCIATION suffers from dynamic misfit in terms of insufficient software change. While business process structures are changed, neither technology push, nor business pull innovation

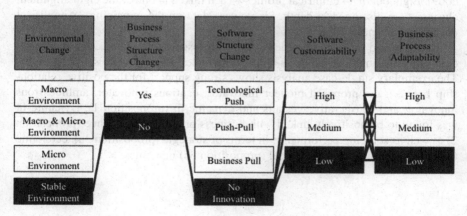

Fig. 6.7 Dynamic alignment process at ALPHA-ASSOCIATION

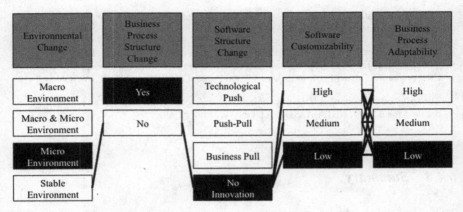

Fig. 6.8 Dynamic alignment process at BETA-ASSOCIATION

occurs. Like above, Fig. 6.8 gives the specification of constructs related to the dynamic alignment process. The lines between specifications express the conservative gestalt as defined in Chap. 3. The specifications of BETA-ASSOCIATION are shaded black.

BETA-ASSOCIATION realises dynamic misfit and a drifting apart between business process structures and software structures. This misalignment negatively impacts business process performance as well as strategic, economic, and technological sourcing outcomes.

6.5 Summary

This chapter provides evidence from single-case analysis (Eisenhardt 1989; Yin 2009). Eight out of 44 empirical profiles—each linked to one of the eight alignment clusters—are discussed in depth. Single-case data on the remaining 38 empirical profiles are given in Table 6.1.

The observed empirical profiles differ with respect to dynamic alignment process, software sourcing value, as well as the underlying software sourcing mode. The exemplary single-case analysis shows strong support for the positive relationship between the proposed pioneer innovator, cautious innovator, ambidextrous innovator, and conservative gestalts and dynamic fit (proposition 1). Dynamic fit was found to be positively linked with business process performance (proposition 2) as well as sourcing performance in terms of strategic (proposition 3a), economic (proposition 3b), and technological (proposition 3c) outcomes.

Table 6.1 Overview on single-case analysis

	Software sourcing mode	Environmental change	Bus. process structure change	Software structure change	Software customizability	Business process adapt.	Dynamic fit	Business process performance	Strategic sourcing performance	Economic sourcing performance	Technological sourcing performance
A1	On-premises	Stable	No	No innovation	Low	Low	Yes	Positive	Positive	Positive	Positive
A2	On-premises	Micro	Yes	No innovation	Low	Low	No	Neutral	Negative	Negative	Negative
C1	On-demand	Micro & macro	Yes	Push-pull	Low	Low	No	Positive	Positive	Negative	Positive
C2	On-demand	Macro	Yes	Technology push	Low	High	Yes	Positive	Positive	Positive	Positive
E1	On premises	Micro & macro	Yes	Push-pull	Medium	Medium	No	Positive	Negative	Negative	Negative
E2	On-premises	Micro & macro	Yes	Push-pull	Medium	High	Yes	Positive	Negative	Negative	Positive
F1	On-demand	Macro	Yes	Technology push	Low	High	Yes	Positive	Positive	Positive	Positive
F2	On-premises	Micro	Yes	Business pull	High	Low	Yes	Positive	Positive	Positive	Positive
F3	In-house	Micro & macro	Yes	Business pull	High	Low	Yes	Positive	Negative	Negative	Negative
F4	On-premises	Micro & macro	Yes	Push-pull	Medium	Low	No	Neutral	Negative	Negative	Positive
F5	On-premises	Macro	Yes	Push-pull	High	Low	No	Neutral	Negative	Negative	Negative
I1	On-demand	Micro & macro	Yes	Technology push	Medium	High	Yes	Positive	Positive	Positive	Positive
M1	On-premises	Micro & macro	Yes	Business pull	Medium	Low	No	Positive	Positive	Negative	Positive
M2	On-premises	Micro & macro	Yes	Push-pull	Medium	High	Yes	Positive	Negative	Negative	Positive

(continued)

Table 6.1 (continued)

	Software sourcing mode	Environmental change	Bus. process structure change	Software structure change	Software customizability	Business process adapt.	Dynamic fit	Business process performance	Strategic sourcing performance	Economic sourcing performance	Technological sourcing performance
M3	On-premises	Micro & macro	Yes	Push-pull	Medium	High	Yes	Positive	Positive	Negative	Positive
M4	On-premises	Micro & macro	Yes	Business pull	Medium	Medium	No	Neutral	Negative	Negative	Positive
M5	On-premises	Macro	Yes	Technology push	Medium	High	Yes	Positive	Positive	Positive	Positive
M6	On-premises	Micro & macro	Yes	Push-pull	Medium	Low	No	Neutral	Negative	Negative	Negative
M7	On-premises	Micro & macro	Yes	Push-pull	Low	Medium	Yes	Positive	Positive	Negative	Positive
M8a	In-house	Micro	Yes	Business pull	High	Low	Yes	Positive	Positive	Negative	Positive
M8b	On-premises	Macro	Yes	Push-pull	Medium	Low	No	Positive	Negative	Negative	Negative
M9	On-demand	Stable	No	No innovation	Medium	High	Yes	Positive	Negative	Positive	Positive
P1	On-demand	Macro	Yes	Push-pull	Low	Medium	No	Neutral	Negative	Negative	Positive
P2	On-premises	Micro & macro	Yes	Push-pull	Medium	Medium	No	Neutral	Neutral	Negative	Negative
P3	On-premises	Micro & macro	Yes	Push-pull	Low	Medium	Yes	Positive	Positive	Negative	Positive
R1	On-demand	Micro	Yes	Push-pull	High	High	No	Neutral	Positive	Negative	Positive
R2a	In-house	Stable	No	No innovation	High	Low	Yes	Positive	Positive	Positive	Negative
R2b	On-premises	Micro & macro	Yes	Push-pull	Medium	High	Yes	Positive	Positive	Positive	Positive

R3a	In-house	Micro	Yes	Business pull	High	Low	Yes	Neutral	Negative	Negative	Negative
R3b	On-premises	Micro	Yes	Business pull	High	Low	Yes	Positive	Negative	Negative	Negative
R4	In-house	Micro & macro	Yes	Business pull	High	Low	Yes	Positive	Negative	Negative	Positive
S1	On-demand	Micro	Yes	Push-pull	High	Medium	No	Positive	Positive	Neutral	Positive
S2	On-demand	Micro & macro	Yes	Technology push	Medium	High	Yes	Positive	Positive	Positive	Positive
S3	On-demand	Micro & macro	Yes	Technology push	Medium	Low	No	Negative	Negative	Negative	Positive
S4	On-demand	Micro	Yes	Technology push	Medium	High	No	Neutral	Positive	Positive	Positive
S5	In-house	Micro	Yes	Business pull	High	Low	Yes	Positive	Neutral	Negative	Positive
S6	On-premises	Micro	Yes	No innovation	Medium	High	No	Positive	Negative	Negative	Negative
S7a	On-demand	Micro	Yes	Technology push	Low	High	Yes	Positive	Positive	Positive	Positive
S7b	On-demand	Micro & macro	Yes	Technology push	Low	High	No	Negative	Negative	Positive	Negative
S8	On-demand	Micro & macro	Yes	Push-pull	Medium	Low	No	Positive	Positive	Positive	Neutral
T1	On-premises	Macro	Yes	Technology push	Low	High	Yes	Positive	Positive	Positive	Neutral
T2	On-premises	Micro	Yes	Push-pull	Low	Medium	Yes	Positive	Positive	Negative	Positive
T3	On-demand	Macro	Yes	Technology push	Medium	High	Yes	Positive	Positive	Positive	Positive
U1	On-premises	Micro & macro	Yes	Push-pull	Medium	High	Yes	Positive	Positive	Neutral	Positive

Based on the findings from the single-case investigation, Chap. 7 offers a cross-case synthesis and discusses the role of software sourcing modes in greater detail. In doing so, preliminary and emerging propositions are either corroborated or dropped by qualitative reasoning in combination with a statistical test of associations. The final explanatory research model is presented in Chap. 8.

Chapter 7
Cross-Case Synthesis

Following an individual discussion of the empirical profiles, this chapter offers an aggregated analysis of findings. The goal of this cross-case synthesis is to explore, validate, and test associations among concepts (Yin 2009). As a result of the aggregated analysis, the initial research model is refined and extended. In particular, the role of software sourcing modes in software alignment and their impact on performance outcomes are derived.

Section 7.1 starts with a validation of the five propositions in the initial research model. Subsequently, Sect. 7.2 outlines emerging associations among concepts. In sum, nine additional propositions are identified by cross-case synthesis. Statistical tests of associations among concepts are provided in each section. As outlined in Chap. 4, Chi-Square tests are applied to $M \times N$ two-way contingency tables (e.g. Bortz and Schuster 2010; Howell 2013). Contingency tables were aggregated to 2×2 matrixes, if the criterion of expected absolute frequencies of $g_{jk} > 5$ was not met (Bortz and Schuster 2010). This allows to calculate Fisher's exact score, which is a preferred test for 2×2 contingency tables (Howell 2013). Mantel-Haenszel test is computed for three-way contingency tables that observe the moderating effect of a third categorical variable (Azen and Walker 2011). Drawing upon these test statistics, propositions are either validated or dropped. Values were computed by using IBM SPSS Statistics version 23. Section 7.3 summarizes on the findings.

7.1 Investigation and Validation of Initial Propositions

This section starts with an investigation and validation of the initial research model. As outlined in Chap. 2, five propositions were derived from previous research. First, it is postulated that the proposed gestalts are positively associated with dynamic fit. The related proposition 1 is discussed in Sect. 7.1.1. Second, Sect. 7.1.2 continues with an investigation on the impact of dynamic fit on business process performance. Proposition 2 suggests a positive relationship. Third, the three propositions on dynamic fit's impact on strategic, economic, and technological sourcing performance are evaluated in Sect. 7.1.3. Finally, Sect. 7.1.4 summarizes the findings on the initial propositions.

7.1.1 Relationship Between Alignment Gestalts and Dynamic Fit

Software-business process alignment is dynamic in nature (Benbya and McKelvey 2006; Nöhren et al. 2014). Dynamic fit of an enterprise system results from a coevolution between the structures of corporate's business processes and those of a software artefact (Nöhren et al. 2014; Sabherwal et al. 2001). If software structure change is greater than business process structure change or vice versa, a company experiences dynamic misfit. Both, business process and software structures depend on their contexts. Particular shifts in an organization's macro or micro environment causes changes in the structures of institutions and software (Scott 1987; Sia and Soh 2007). The dynamic fit process is supported by the flexibility of business processes—referred to as business process adaptability (Tatikonda and Montoya-Weiss 2001; Yang and Papazoglou 2000)—and flexibility of the software artefact—referred to as software customizability (Benlian et al. 2009; Winkler and Brown 2014).

The dynamic alignment process is transferred into clusters based on Sabherwal and Robey (1995). With business process structure change possessing two specifications (yes and no), environmental change (macro, micro, macro and micro, and stable) and software structure change (technology push, push-pull, business pull, and no innovation) taking four specifications each, and business process adaptability as well as software customizability holding three values (high, medium, and low), the total number of process patterns amounts to 288. In Chap. 3, these patterns were grouped into eight clusters. Four of these clusters are referred to as gestalts, while the other four are labelled non-gestalts. First, pioneer innovator gestalt is proposed to establish dynamic fit by pure market governance of software structure change in terms of technology push innovation. Second, cautious innovator gestalt encompass patterns that are anticipated to realize dynamic fit by pure hierarchical governance in terms of business pull innovation. Third, the ambidextrous innovator gestalt bridges between pioneer and cautious innovator and combines both types of software structure change. While these three gestalts are proposed to establish dynamic in terms of adjusted expansion, a fourth conservative gestalt is supposed to benefit from dynamic fit in terms of adjusted inertia. Empirical profiles linked to this gestalt cluster profit from stable business process and software structures in the absence of environmental changes. These four gestalts encompass 19 process patterns. The remaining 269 patterns are linked to the technology-push, push-

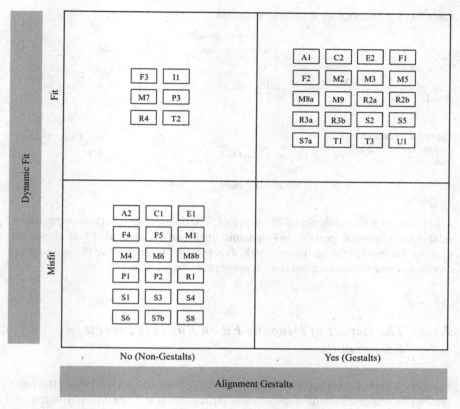

Fig. 7.1 Relationship between alignment gestalts and dynamic fit

pull, business pull, and no innovation non-gestalt clusters. It is anticipated that gestalts outperform non-gestalts with respect to dynamic fit.

It is proposed that alignment gestalts are positively associated with dynamic fit. Figure 7.1 illustrates this relationship. The horizontal axis shows gestalts and non-gestalts. Dynamic fit of enterprise systems is given on the vertical axis. The squares refer to the empirical profiles as defined in Table 5.1 (see Chap. 5).

Figure 7.1 shows a positive relationship between alignment gestalts and dynamic fit. Twenty empirical profiles were linked to one of the four gestalt clusters. For all of these software artefacts, business process structure was found to be in line with software structure. Only six out of 24 cases related to non-gestalts established dynamic fit. The dynamic alignment process of these empirical profiles differ from the related gestalts by the specification of one construct each. The residual 20 cases suffered from dynamic misfit.

Table 7.1 gives the contingency matrix on the relationship between gestalts and dynamic fit. As shown in Table 7.2, a Fisher's Exact Score of .000 was computed identifying proposition 1 as extremely significant at a probability level of

Table 7.1 2 × 2 contingency table on proposition 1

		Alignment gestalts		Total
		No (non-gestalt)	Yes (gestalt)	
Dynamic fit	Fit	6	20	26
	Misfit	18	0	18
Total		24	20	44

Table 7.2 Test statistics
proposition 1 for 2 × 2
contingency table

	Value	Exact sig. (2-sided)
Fisher's exact test		.000
Phi	.760	
No. of valid cases	44	

$1 - \propto \ \leq 99.9\%$. A calculated Phi value of .760 determines a very strong positive relationship between gestalts and dynamic fit. It can be concluded that alignment gestalts are positively associated with dynamic fit. In summary, the aggregated cross-case and single-case analysis support proposition 1.

7.1.2   The Impact of Dynamic Fit on Business Process Performance

A constant coevolution between business process structures and software structures prevents companies from experiencing deficiencies and establish dynamic fit (Nöhren et al. 2014; Sabherwal et al. 2001; Strong and Volkoff 2010). Drawing upon previous research, it was postulated that such dynamic fit positively impacts business process performance (DeLone and McLean 1992; Grant 2003; Nöhren et al. 2014; Sia and Soh 2007; Soh and Markus 1995; Strong and Volkoff 2010).

Figure 7.2 illustrates this relationship. The horizontal axis shows dynamic fit. Rating of business process performance contribution of enterprise systems is given on the vertical axis. The squares refer to the empirical profiles as defined in Table 5.1 (see Chap. 5).

Figure 7.2 shows a positive relationship between dynamic fit and business process performance. Twenty-five out of 26 empirical profiles in which business process structures and software structures were in line with each other, experienced a positive impact of their enterprise system on business process performance. In contrast to this, business process performance improvement was present in only seven out of 18 cases where software was not aligned. The remaining 11 empirical profiles experienced no improvements of their business processes. In two cases, GAMMA-MANUFACTURING (S3) and ETA-SERVICE's ERP system (S7b), the software artefact was harmful for corporate's business processes.

The contingency matrix for proposition 2 is given in Table 7.3. The expected absolute frequency of $g_{jk} > 5$ was not met for three of the cells within the matrix.

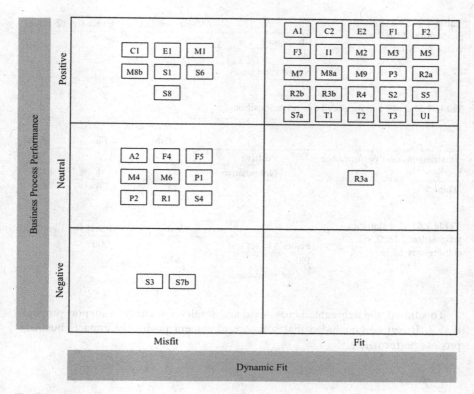

Fig. 7.2 Impact of dynamic fit on business process performance

Table 7.3 3 × 2 contingency table on proposition 2

		Dynamic fit		
		Misfit	Fit	Total
Business process performance	Positive	7	25	32
	Neutral	9	1	10
	Negative	2	0	2
Total		18	26	44

The minimum expected count is .82. Consequently, the calculated Chi-Square value shown in Table 7.4 is not used for data interpretation (e.g. Bortz and Schuster 2010; Howell 2013).

The concentrated 2 × 2 contingency matrix is given in Table 7.5. A Fisher's exact score of .000 was calculated determining proposition 2 as extremely statistically significant at a probability level of $1 - \propto \ \leq 99.9\%$. A Phi value of .632 identifies the association between business process performance and dynamic fit as strongly positive (Table 7.6).

Table 7.4 Test statistics proposition 2 for 3×2 contingency table

	Value	df	Exact sig. (2-sided)
Chi-Square	17.654	1	
Phi	.633		
No. of valid cases	44		

Table 7.5 2×2 contingency table on proposition 2

		Dynamic fit		
		Misfit	Fit	Total
Business process performance	Positive	7	25	32
	Not positive	11	1	12
Total		18	26	44

Table 7.6 Test statistics proposition 2 for 2×2 contingency table

	Value	Exact sig. (2-sided)
Fisher's exact test		.000
Phi	.632	
No. of valid cases	44	

To sum up, the aggregated cross-case and single-case analysis support proposition 2. It can be concluded that software alignment positively impacts business process performance.

7.1.3   Impact of Dynamic Fit on Sourcing Performance

Sourcing performance was measured in terms of SET satisfaction, which captures software's contribution to strategic, economic, and technological benefits (e.g. Goo et al. 2008; Grover et al. 1996; Lacity and Willcocks 2001; Lee et al. 2004). It was postulated that dynamic fit is positively associated with the three dimensions of sourcing performance.

Starting with an investigation of the relationship between dynamic fit and strategic benefits, Fig. 7.3 illustrates the association between these two concepts. The horizontal axis shows dynamic fit. Rating of strategic sourcing performance is given on the vertical axis. The squares refer to the empirical profiles as defined in Table 5.1 (see Chap. 5).

Interviewees reported on positive strategic sourcing performance in 18 out of 26 empirical profiles in which business process structure was in line with software structure. Strategic sourcing performance was rated negative in seven cases, where software was aligned. Negative strategic impacts were identified for most of the empirical profiles in which interviewees informed on a dynamic misfit between business process structure and software structure. Only six out of 18 misaligned cases realized a positive strategic outcome.

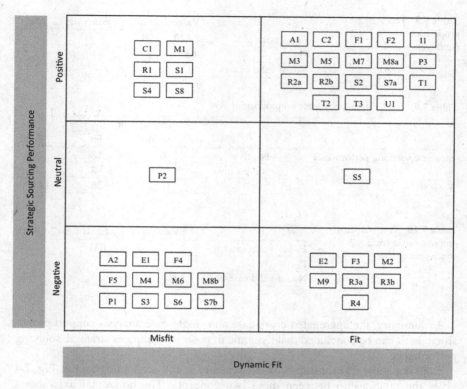

Fig. 7.3 Impact of dynamic fit on strategic sourcing performance

Table 7.7 3 × 2 contingency table on proposition 3a

		Dynamic fit		Total
		Misfit	Fit	
Strategic sourcing performance	Positive	6	18	24
	Neutral	1	1	2
	Negative	11	7	18
Total		18	26	44

The contingency matrix for proposition 3a is given in Table 7.7. Data analysis reveals that for three cells, the expected absolute count is less than 5. The minimum expected count is .82. Consequently, the calculated Chi-Square value shown in Table 7.8 is not used for data interpretation (e.g. Bortz and Schuster 2010; Howell 2013).

Table 7.9 gives the 2 × 2 contingency matrix related to proposition 3a. The calculated Fisher's exact score of .031 identifies proposition 3a as significant at a probability level of $1 - \propto \ \leq 95\%$. A Phi value of .354 determines a moderate positive association (Table 7.10).

Table 7.8 Test statistics proposition 3a for 3×2 contingency table

	Value	df	Exact sig. (2-sided)
Chi-Square	5.620	1	
Phi	.633		
No. of valid cases	44		

Table 7.9 2×2 contingency table on proposition 3a

		Dynamic fit		Total
		Misfit	Fit	
Strategic sourcing performance	Positive	6	18	24
	Not positive	12	8	20
Total		18	26	44

Table 7.10 Test statistics proposition 3a for 2×2 contingency table

	Value	Exact sig. (2-sided)
Fisher's exact test		.031
Phi	.354	
No. of valid cases	44	

In summary, the aggregated cross-case and single-case analysis support proposition 3a. It can be concluded that dynamic fit positively impacts strategic sourcing performance.

Looking at the relationship between dynamic fit and economic benefits, Fig. 7.4 gives the relationship between these two concepts. The horizontal axis shows dynamic fit. Rating of economic sourcing performance is given on the vertical axis. The squares refer to the empirical profiles as defined in Table 5.1 (see Chap. 5).

Half of the empirical profiles that benefited from dynamic fit realized positive economic outcomes, while economic sourcing performance of the remaining cases was rated neutral or negative. Interviewees reported on negative economic outcomes in 14 out of 18 software misalignment cases. Economic sourcing performance was rated high for only three empirical profiles, where software structure was not in line with business process structure.

The contingency matrix for proposition 3b is given in Table 7.11. Data analysis reveals that for two cells the expected absolute count is less than 5. Like above, the minimum expected count is .82. Consequently, the calculated Chi-Square value shown in Table 7.12 is not used for data interpretation (e.g. Bortz and Schuster 2010; Howell 2013).

Table 7.13 gives the 2×2 contingency matrix on the relationship between dynamic fit and economic sourcing performance. The calculated Fisher's exact score identifies proposition 3b as significant at a probability level of $1 - \propto \ \leq 95\%$. The related Phi value of .341 determines a moderate positive association (Table 7.14).

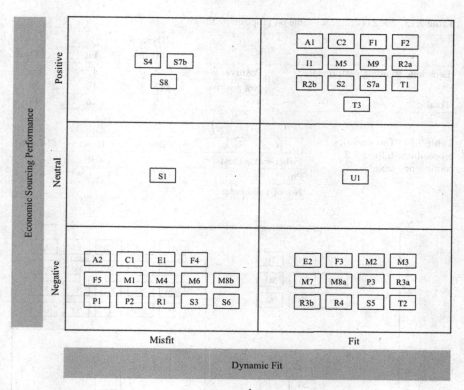

Fig. 7.4 Impact of dynamic fit on economic sourcing performance

Table 7.11 3 × 2 contingency table on proposition 3b

		Dynamic fit		Total
		Misfit	Fit	
Economic sourcing performance	Positive	3	13	16
	Neutral	1	1	2
	Negative	14	12	26
Total		18	26	44

Table 7.12 Test statistics proposition 3b for 3 × 2 contingency table

	Value	df	Exact sig. (2-sided)
Chi-Square	5.119	1	
Phi	.341		
No. of valid cases	44		

In summary, the aggregated cross-case and single-case analysis show support of proposition 3b. It can be concluded that dynamic fit positively impacts economic sourcing performance.

Table 7.13   2 × 2 contingency table on proposition 3b

		Dynamic fit		Total
		Misfit	Fit	
Economic sourcing performance	Positive	3	13	16
	Not positive	15	13	28
Total		18	26	44

Table 7.14   Test statistics proposition 3b for 2 × 2 contingency table

	Value	Exact sig. (2-sided)
Fisher's exact test		.030
Phi	.341	
No. of valid cases	44	

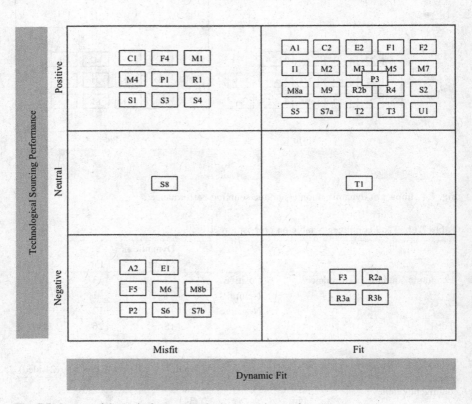

Fig. 7.5   Impact of dynamic fit on technological sourcing performance

Finally, Fig. 7.5 gives the relationship between dynamic fit and technological benefits. The horizontal axis shows dynamic fit. Rating of technological sourcing performance is given on the vertical axis. The squares refer to the empirical profiles as defined in Table 6.1 (see Chap. 5).

Table 7.15 3 × 2 contingency table on proposition 3c

		Dynamic fit		
		Misfit	Fit	Total
Economic sourcing performance	Positive	9	21	30
	Neutral	1	1	2
	Negative	8	4	12
Total		18	26	44

Table 7.16 Test statistics proposition 3c for 3 × 2 contingency table

	Value	df	Exact sig. (2-sided)
Chi-Square	4.839	1	
Phi	.322		
No. of valid cases	44		

Table 7.17 2 × 2 contingency table on proposition 3c

		Dynamic fit		
		Misfit	Fit	Total
Technological sourcing performance	Positive	9	21	30
	Not positive	9	5	14
Total		18	26	44

Table 7.18 Test statistics proposition 3c for 2 × 2 contingency table

	Value	Exact sig. (2-sided)
Fisher's exact test		.049
Phi	.325	
No. of valid cases	44	

The structure of 26 enterprise systems was found to be in line with business process structure. The interviewees reported on positive technological outcomes for 21 of these applications. Negative outcomes were found to be present in of these four cases. The pictures change when looking at the 18 dynamic misfit enterprise systems. Here, positive technological outcomes were found in only half of the cases.

The contingency matrix for proposition 3c is given in Table 7.15. Data analysis reveals that for three cells the expected absolute count is less than 5. Within the data set, the minimum expected count is .82. Consequently, the calculated Chi-Square value shown in Table 7.16 is not used for data interpretation (e.g. Bortz and Schuster 2010; Howell 2013).

Table 7.17 gives the contingency matrix. A calculated Fisher's exact score identifies proposition 3c as significant at a probability level of $1- \propto \ \leq 95\%$. The relationship between technological sourcing performance and dynamic fit is positive, classified by a Phi value of .325 (Table 7.18).

In summary, the aggregated cross-case and single-case analysis support proposition 3c. It can be concluded that dynamic fit positively impacts technological sourcing performance.

7.1.4   Summary

The initial research model encompassed five propositions. Proposition 1 postulates a positive relationship between dynamic fit and pioneer innovator, cautious innovator, ambidextrous innovator, and conservative gestalts. In addition, four propositions on the impact of dynamic fit on performance outcomes were derived. It is argued that dynamic fit positively impacts business process performance (proposition 2) as well as sourcing performance in terms of strategic (proposition 3a), economic (proposition 3b), and technological (proposition 3c) benefits. To sum up, the aggregated cross-case and single-case analysis supports all of the five propositions from the initial research model. Proposition 1 and proposition 2 were found to be extremely significant at a probability level of $1- \propto \ \leq 99.9\%$. Propositions 3a, 3b, and 3c are supported at a probability level of $1- \propto \ \leq 95\%$.

7.2   Extension and Refinement of Research Model

A qualitative reasoning in order to test and validate propositions of the preliminary research model was conducted in Sect. 7.1. Thereby, the initial propositions helped "*to focus attention on certain data and to ignore other data*" (Yin 2009: 130). Strong support was found with respect to proposition 1 and proposition 2. In addition, the aggregated cross-case and single-case analysis also supports the positive impact of dynamic fit on sourcing performance and the related propositions 3a, 3b, and 3c.

This section continues with an inductive data interpretation (Eisenhardt and Graebner 2007). All empirical profiles were reinvestigated and explanations that emerged out of the data were included (Eisenhardt 1989; Ravishankar et al. 2011). Section 7.2.1 starts with a discussion of the relationship between sourcing performance and business process performance. Subsequently, Sect. 7.2.2 continues with an outline of the role of software sourcing modes. The moderating effects of market and hybrid governance of software structure change is investigated in Sect. 7.2.3. Finally, Sect. 7.2.4 summarizes findings from the inductive data analysis.

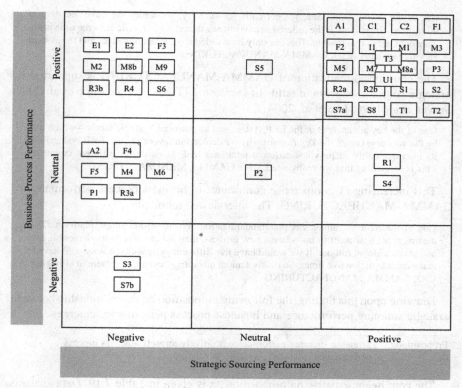

Fig. 7.6 Impact of strategic sourcing performance on business process performance

7.2.1 Emerging Relationship Between Sourcing and Business Process Performance

Findings from the cross-case analysis indicate an association between sourcing performance and business process performance. First, it can be postulated that strategic benefits positively impact business process performance. Figure 7.6 illustrates this relationship. The horizontal axis shows strategic sourcing performance. Rating of business process performance is given on the vertical axis. The squares refer to the empirical profiles as defined in Table 5.1 (see Chap. 5).

The relationship between strategic sourcing performance and business process performance can be illustrated by the help of GAMMA-MANUFACTURING (M3). GAMMA-MANUFACTURING is a supplier of synthetics within the automotive industry. The interviewee reported that the company constantly ramps up its delivery capabilities at the global locations of their clients.

> We have to change constantly. We are very much involved in the logistics of the manufacturers. If an automotive manufacturer sets up a new site somewhere in the world, we have to open a subsidiary at this location as well. Otherwise, we would lose the contract to

one of our competitors. See, we get calls for delivery, for which we have less than a 90-minutes timeframe. If the ordered item is not at a manufacturer's site after the time is up, we would get in real trouble. This can only be avoided if we adapt ourselves and the system very dynamically. CIO, GAMMA-MANUFACTURING

The constant globalization of GAMMA-MANUFACTURING is supported by strategic sourcing benefits in terms of increasing IT competence (Goo et al. 2008; Grover et al. 1996; Lee et al. 2004).

One of the key advantages of the ERP system and an essential strategic factor—which was by the way also one of the key reasons why we decided in favour of [this ERP system]—is its internationality. It provides different templates and standards for different countries. This is something that we really need. CIO, GAMMA-MANUFACTURING

This increasing IT competence contributes to business process performance of GAMMA-MANUFACTURING. The interviewee reported:

One of the main advantages is the standardization. We have one single platform. That means, if we now want to introduce a new process, then we are able to implement it here and make a global roll out. If we would have five different systems, then we would have to make the adaptation five times. So that is a major advantage and improvement in efficiency. CIO, GAMMA-MANUFACTURING

Drawing upon this finding, the following proposition on the relationship between strategic sourcing performance and business process performance emerges:

Proposition 4a	Strategic sourcing performance positively impacts business process performance

The contingency matrix on proposition 4a is given in Table 7.19. Data analysis reveals that for six cells the expected absolute count is less than 5. The minimum expected count is .09. Consequently, the calculated Chi-Square value shown in Table 7.20 is not used for data interpretation (e.g. Bortz and Schuster 2010; Howell 2013).

Table 7.21 gives the 2×2 contingency table on the relationship between business process performance and strategic sourcing performance. The Phi value of .466 postulates a positive association between these concepts. A calculated Fisher's exact score of .005 identifies proposition 4a as very significant at a probability level of $1 - \propto \ \leq 99\%$ (Table 7.22).

Second, it can be expected that economic benefits positively impact business process performance. Figure 7.7 illustrates this relationship. The horizontal axis shows the level of economic sourcing performance. Rating of business process performance is given on the vertical axis. The squares refer to the empirical profiles as defined in Table 5.1.

This situation can be exemplified by ETA-MANUFACTURING. ETA-MANUFACTURING is a German-based manufacturer producing plastic components for luxury cars. The CIO reported on a reduced level of economic benefits from their on-premises ERP system.

Table 7.19 3 × 3 contingency table on proposition 4a

		Strategic sourcing performance			
		Negative	Neutral	Positive	Total
Business process performance	Positive	9	1	22	32
	Neutral	7	1	2	10
	Negative	2	0	0	2
Total		18	2	24	44

Table 7.20 Test statistics proposition 4a for 3 × 3 contingency table

	Value	df	Exact sig. (2-sided)
Chi-Square	10.404	1	
Phi	.486		
No. of valid cases	44		

Table 7.21 2 × 2 contingency table on proposition 4a

		Strategic sourcing performance		
		Not positive	Positive	Total
Business process performance	Positive	10	22	32
	Not positive	10	2	12
Total		20	24	44

Table 7.22 Test statistics proposition 4a for 2 × 2 contingency table

	Value	Exact sig. (2-sided)
Fisher's exact test	.	.005
Phi	.466	
No. of valid cases	44	

The update procedure is really complex. If we want to do an update in 2015, we have to start with project planning at least one year earlier. There are a lot of customizations within the system, so we have to analyse how the standard has changed. Which of our customizations are now part of the standard? What do we have to develop on our own? To give you an example, the last software update costed us 100,000 Euros. We had to buy more than 100 man-days from the software vendor to mitigate all our client-specific customizations to the new software version. CIO, ETA-MANUFACTURING

These costs reduce the investment value within the business processes.

So this money [for upgrading the on-premises ERP system] is lost. We cannot invest it within our production unit; we cannot invest it in research and development. CIO, ETA-MANUFACTURING

Drawing upon this finding, the following proposition on the relationship between economic sourcing performance and business process performance emerges:

Proposition 4b	Economic sourcing performance positively impacts business process performance

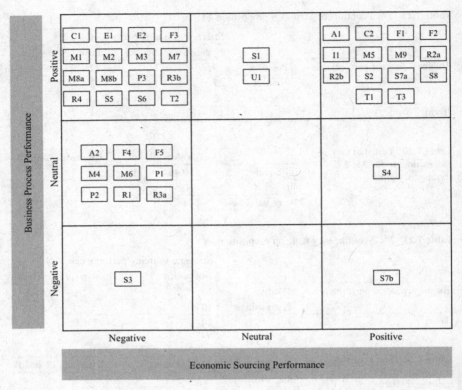

Fig. 7.7 Impact of economic sourcing performance on business process performance

Table 7.23 3 × 3 contingency table on proposition 4b

		Economic sourcing performance			
		Negative	Neutral	Positive	Total
Business process performance	Positive	16	2	14	32
	Neutral	9	0	1	10
	Negative	1	0	1	2
Total		26	2	16	44

Table 7.24 Test statistics proposition 4b for 3 × 3 contingency table

	Value	df	Exact sig. (2-sided)
Chi-Square	5.336	1	
Phi	.348		
No. of valid cases	44		

The contingency matrix for proposition 4b is presented in Table 7.23. Six cells show an expected absolute count with less than 5. The minimum expected count is .09. Consequently, the calculated Chi-Square value shown in Table 7.24 is not used for data interpretation (e.g. Bortz and Schuster 2010; Howell 2013).

Table 7.25 2 × 2 contingency table on proposition 4b

		Economic sourcing performance		Total
		Not positive	Positive	
Business process performance	Positive	18	14	32
	Not positive	10	2	12
Total		28	16	44

Table 7.26 Test statistics proposition 4b for 2 × 2 contingency table

	Value	Exact sig. (2-sided)
Fisher's exact test		.160
Phi	.251	
No. of valid cases	44	

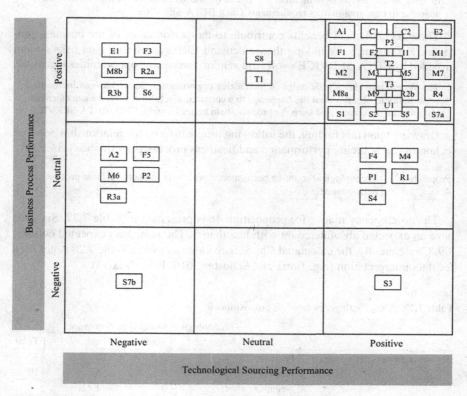

Fig. 7.8 Impact of technological sourcing performance on business process performance

Table 7.25 gives the reduced 2 × 2 contingency matrix. The calculated Fisher's exact score of .160 identifies proposition 4b as not statistically significant. In a consequence, proposition 4b has to be rejected (Table 7.26).

Finally, it can be postulated that technological benefits positively impact business process performance. Figure 7.8 illustrates this relationship. The horizontal axis shows technological sourcing performance. Rating of business process performance is given on the vertical axis. The squares refer to the empirical profiles as defined in Table 5.1 (see Chap. 5).

This situation is illustrated by BETA-SERVICE, a service provider offering IT consulting and software implementation. The interviewee reported on technological benefits from their on-demand ERP system that increases IT flexibility and offered a new technological agenda.

> We think that it is very good that we get innovations by the software. The evolution of the standard is very nice (...) we just implemented [a new data base system offered by the software vendor] and moved all our data to it. We are now able to handle a larger amounts of data in shorter periods of time. (...) clearly, the dynamic software supports us in adapting to changing market requirements CEO; BETA-SERVICE

These technological benefits contribute to the performance of the business processes. For instance, by linking the on-demand ERP system to a data base system provided by BETA-SERVICE's software vendor, forecasting opportunities increased.

> The system provides a wide range of forecasting opportunities. So we have an increasing opportunity to observe what has happened to a certain project. Moreover, we can calculate orders more accurately and keep the process chain better in mind. CEO; BETA-SERVICE

Drawing upon this finding, the following proposition on the relationship between technological sourcing performance and business process performance arises:

Proposition 4c	Technological sourcing performance positively impacts business process performance

The contingency matrix for proposition 4c is presented in Table 7.27. Six cells have an expected absolute count with less than 5. The minimum expected count is .09. Consequently, the calculated Chi-Square value shown in Table 7.28 is not used for data interpretation (e.g. Bortz and Schuster 2010; Howell 2013).

Table 7.27 3×3 contingency table on proposition 4c

		Technological sourcing performance			
		Negative	Neutral	Positive	Total
Business process performance	Positive	6	2	24	32
	Neutral	5	0	5	10
	Negative	1	0	1	2
Total		12	2	30	44

Table 7.28   Test statistics proposition 4c for 3×3 contingency table

	Value	df	Exact sig. (2-sided)
Chi-Square	4.675	1	
Phi	.326		
No. of valid cases	44		

Table 7.29 2×2 contingency table on proposition 4c

		Technological sourcing performance		Total
		Not positive	Positive	
Business process performance	Positive	8	24	32
	Not positive	6	6	12
Total		14	30	44

Table 7.30 Test statistics proposition 4c for 2×2 contingency table

	Value	Exact sig. (2-sided)
Fisher's exact test		.152
Phi	.239	
No. of valid cases	44	

A Fisher's exact test was conducted on the relationship between business process performance and technological benefits in a concentrated 2×2 matrix. A P-value of .152 identifies the association as not statistically significant (see Table 7.16). The related 2×2 contingency matrix is given in Table 7.29. Proposition 4c is rejected (Table 7.30).

To sum up, three additional propositions on the relationship between sourcing performance and business process performance were identifies. It was argued that strategic (proposition 4a), economic (proposition 4b), and technological (proposition 4c) benefits positively impact business processes. Looking at the test statistics, proposition 4a is very significant at a probability level of $1 - \alpha \leq 99\%$. Propositions 4b and 4c are rejected.

7.2.2 The Role of Software Sourcing Modes

Previous studies on the value of process-centric enterprise systems have not incorporated different sourcing modes (e.g. Grant 2003; Maurer et al. 2012; Ravishankar et al. 2011; Sia and Soh 2007; Soh and Sia 2004; Strong and Volkoff 2010). In a consequence, this study is the first that investigates the impact of in-house, on-premises, and on-demand sourcing on alignment and performance.

7.2.2.1 The Direct Impact of Software Sourcing Modes on Dynamic Fit

Previous studies on software alignment focused on packaged applications in general (e.g. Grant 2003; Ravishankar et al. 2011; Sia and Soh 2007; Soh and Sia 2004; Strong and Volkoff 2010). It is argued that the inherent standardization of such enterprise systems are a central source of misfit (Sia and Soh 2007; Strong and Volkoff 2010). Therefore, lower levels of ownership on physical, deep, and surface structures, which result in an increasing standardization, can have a negative impact

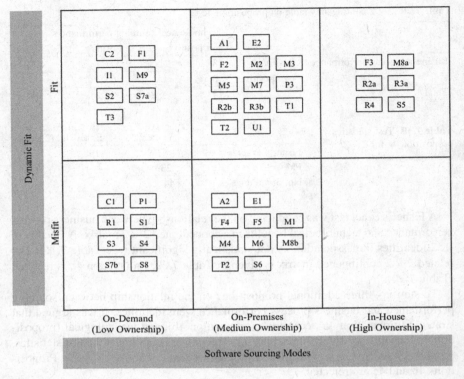

Fig. 7.9 Impact of software sourcing modes on dynamic fit

on dynamic fit. On the other hand, due to the external development of packaged applications, software providers adapt their enterprise systems on a regular basis and provide modifications to their customers based on industry best practices (Koehler et al. 2010; Sia and Soh 2007; Xin and Levina 2008; Yang and Tate 2012). Such modifications can assist companies to keep pace with changing environmental conditions (Scott 1987; Sia and Soh 2007). Therefore, it can also be proposed that lower levels of ownership on physical, deep, and surface structures, which result in an increasing provision of industry best practices, can have a positive impact on dynamic fit.

Figure 7.9 gives the relationship between software sourcing modes and dynamic fit. The horizontal axis shows the level of this ownership expressed by in-house, on-premises, and on-demand sourcing modes. Rating of dynamic fit is given on the vertical axis. The squares refer to the empirical profiles as defined in Table 5.1 (see Chap. 5).

Cross-case synthesis shows mixed results on the relationship between software sourcing modes and dynamic fit. Approximately half of the empirical profiles that were sourced on-premises (medium level of software structure ownership) and on-demand (low level of software structure ownership) were found to be in line

Table 7.31 2×3 contingency table on proposition 5

		Software sourcing modes			
		On-demand	On-premises	In-house	Total
Dynamic fit	Fit	7	13	6	26
	Misfit	8	10	0	18
Total		15	23	6	44

Table 7.32 Test statistics proposition 5 for 2×3 contingency table

	Value	df	Exact sig. (2-sided)
Chi-Square	5.174	1	
Phi	.343		
No. of valid cases	44		

Table 7.33 2×2 contingency table on proposition 5

		Software sourcing modes		
		On-demand	In-house, on-premises	Total
Dynamic fit	Fit	7	19	26
	Misfit	8	10	18
Total		15	29	44

Table 7.34 Test statistics proposition 5 for 2×2 contingency table

	Value	Exact sig. (2-sided)
Fisher's exact test		.334
Phi	−.182	
No. of valid cases	44	

with business process structure. The other half of the packaged applications suffered from dynamic misfit. In contrast to this, all enterprise systems that were sourced in-house (high level of software structure ownership) were found to be in line with business process structure.

Drawing upon this finding, the following proposition on the relationship between software structure ownership and dynamic fit emerged:

Proposition 5	Software ownership positively impacts dynamic fit

The contingency matrix for proposition 5 is presented in Table 7.31. Two cells have an expected absolute count with less than 5. The minimum expected count is 2.45. Consequently, the calculated Chi-Square value shown in Table 7.32 is not used for data interpretation (e.g. Bortz and Schuster 2010; Howell 2013).

Table 7.33 gives the 2×2 contingency table on the relationship between software sourcing modes and dynamic fit. The calculated Fisher's exact score of .334 identifies proposition 5 as not statistically significant (see Table 7.34). Consequently, proposition 5 is dropped.

7.2.2.2 The Impact of Software Sourcing Modes on Alignment Gestalts

Beside this direct impact of in-house, on-premises, and on-demand software procurement on dynamic fit, it can be argued that software sourcing modes have different relationships with patterns of the dynamic alignment process. In sum, this dynamic alignment process possesses 288 patterns that were linked to eight alignment clusters (see Chap. 3). This clustering was done with respect to governance of software structure change. Pioneer innovator gestalt and technology-push non-gestalt are clusters in which software structure change occurs under external control (Currie et al. 2004). In contrast to this, software structure change of cautious innovator gestalt, conservative gestalt, business-pull non-gestalt, and no innovation non gestalt occurs under internal control (Carmel and Sawyer 1998). Ambidextrous innovator gestalt and push-pull non-gestalt rely on a shared control of software structure change. Software structure change is partially executed internally and partially procured on a market.

Figure 7.10 gives the relationship between software sourcing modes and control of software structure change. The horizontal axis shows the sourcing mode. The control of software structure change is given on the vertical axis. The squares refer to the empirical profiles as defined in Table 5.1 (see Chap. 5). The contingency matrix presented in Table 7.35 allows to test whether a general relationship between software sourcing modes and control of software structure change exists. Five cells have an expected absolute count with less than 5. The minimum expected count is 1.50. Consequently, the calculated Chi-Square value shown in Table 7.36 is not used for data interpretation (e.g. Bortz and Schuster 2010; Howell 2013). To understand whether the three software sourcing modes under study have distinct relationships with control of software structure change, three tables are discussed subsequently.

In an on-demand setting, ownership on physical, deep, and surface structures is held outside a firm's hierarchy. Updates are constantly and automatically implemented by a software vendor (Koehler et al. 2010; Xin and Levina 2008; Yang and Tate 2012). In a consequence, technological push innovation occurs constantly (Currie et al. 2004; Currie 2004). As shown in Fig. 7.10, nine out of 15 empirical on-demand profiles rely on external control of software structure change by technological-push innovation. Five on-demand profiles combine technological-push with business-pull innovation in a shared control arrangement. Only IOTA-MANUFACTURING (M9) has internal control of software structure change. Over the years, the company was increasingly dissatisfied with the vendor-driven updates of their on-demand ERP system. Due to the fact that the company served as a key reference customer for the software vendor, the provider agreed to run a separate version of the system for this specific client in a private cloud. IOTA-MANUFACTURING benefited from adjusted inertia in the absence of software structure change. To sum up, most on-demand profiles are linked to external control of software structure change. Drawing upon this finding, the following proposition emerged:

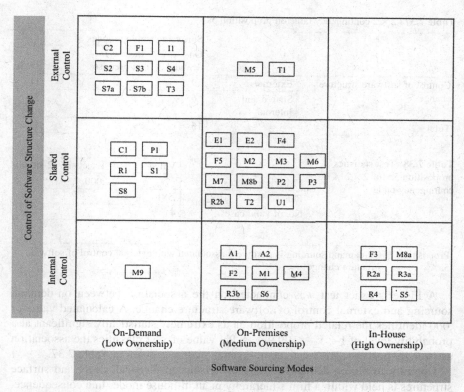

Fig. 7.10 Relationship between software sourcing modes and control of software structure change

Table 7.35 3 × 3 contingency table on software sourcing modes and control of software structure change

		Software sourcing modes			
		On-demand	On-premises	In-house	Total
Control of software structure change	External	9	2	0	11
	Shared	5	14	0	19
	Internal	1	7	6	14
Total		15	23	6	44

Table 7.36 Test statistics software sourcing modes and control of software structure change for 3 × 3 contingency table

	Value	df	Exact sig. (2-sided)
Chi-Square	4.675	1	
Phi	.326		
No. of valid cases	44		

Table 7.37 2×2 contingency table on proposition 5a

| | | Software sourcing modes | | Total |
		On-demand	In-house, on-premises	
Control of software structure change	External	9	2	11
	Shared and Internal	6	27	33
Total		15	29	44

Table 7.38 Test statistics proposition 5a for 2×2 contingency table

	Value	Exact sig. (2-sided)
Fisher's exact test		.000
Phi	.581	
No. of valid cases	44	

Proposition 5a	On-demand sourcing is positively associated with external control of software structure change

A Fisher's exact test was conducted on the association between on-demand sourcing and external control of software structure change. A calculated value of .000 identifies the related proposition 5a as extremely statistically significant at a probability level of $1 - \propto \; \leq 99.9\%$. A Phi value of .581 classifies the association as strongly positive. The related contingency matrix is given in Table 7.37.

Contrary to the on-demand setting, ownership on physical, deep, and surface structures is held within a firm's hierarchy in an in-house mode. In a consequence, the software artefact is not developed by an external vendor, which leads to the absence of technological push innovation (Carmel and Sawyer 1998; Currie et al. 2004; Currie 2004). As shown in Fig. 7.10, all in-house profiles has internal control of software structure change. While five of these companies established dynamic fit in terms of adjusted expansion, BETA-RETAIL benefited from adjusted inertia of their CRM system (R2a) (Table 7.38).

In summary, all empirical in-house profiles were linked to the internal control of software structure change. Drawing upon this finding, the following proposition emerged:

Proposition 5c	In-house sourcing is positively associated with internal control of software structure change

The related contingency matrix is given in Table 7.39. A Fisher's exact score of .000 determines proposition 5c as extremely statistically significant at a probability level of $1 - \propto \; \leq 99.9\%$. A Phi value of .582 identifies a strong positive association between internal control of software structure change and in-house software sourcing (Table 7.40).

Finally, in an on-premises mode, ownership on deep and surface structures is held outside a firm's hierarchy, while physical structures are provided internally. In

Table 7.39 2×2 contingency table on proposition 5c

		Software sourcing modes		
		In-house	On-demand, on-premises	Total
Control of software structure change	Internal	6	8	14
	Shared and External	0	30	30
Total		6	38	44

Table 7.40 Test statistics proposition 5c for 2×2 contingency table

	Value	Exact sig. (2-sided)
Fisher's exact test		.000
Phi	.582	
No. of valid cases	44	

a consequence, on-premises sourcing is related to push-pull innovation by combining technological push with business pull (Carmel and Sawyer 1998). Fourteen out of 23 empirical profiles have shared control of software structure change (see Fig. 7.10). Two companies relied on pure technological push and a market governance. In addition, seven empirical profiles were found within the hierarchical mode.

To sum up, most on-premises profiles are positioned within the shared control of software structure change. Drawing upon this finding, the following proposition emerged:

Proposition 5b	On-premises sourcing is positively associated with shared control of software structure change

Table 7.41 gives the contingency table on the relationship between on-premises sourcing and shared control. The calculated Chi-Square statistic identifies proposition 5b as significant at a probability level of $1 - \alpha \leq 95\%$. In addition, the association between these two variables is moderately positive with a Phi value of .374 (Table 7.42).

It can be concluded that on-demand sourcing is related to external control (pioneer innovator gestalt and technology push non-gestalt), on-premises to shared control (ambidextrous innovator gestalt and push-pull non-gestalt), and in-house to internal control (cautious innovator gestalt, conservative gestalt, business pull non-gestalt, and no innovation non-gestalt) on software structure change.

Table 7.41 2 × 2 contingency table on proposition 5b

		Software sourcing modes		
		On-premises	In-house, on-demand	Total
Control of software structure change	Shared	14	5	19
	External and Internal	9	16	25
Total		23	21	44

Table 7.42 Test statistics proposition 5b for 2 × 2 contingency table

	Value	Exact sig. (2-sided)
Fisher's exact test		.017
Phi	.374	
No. of valid cases	44	

7.2.3   Moderating Effects of Control on Software Structure Change

Two moderating effects of software structure change governance were identified by the cross-cases synthesis. First, it was found that external control on software structure change positively moderates the relationship between dynamic fit and economic sourcing performance. This connection is discussed in Sect. 7.2.3.1. Second, shared control on software structure change serves as moderator between dynamic fit and technological sourcing performance. This link is outlined in Sect. 7.2.3.2.

As outlined in Chap. 4, moderating effects of categorical variables are analyzed in three-way contingency tables (e.g. Azen and Walker 2011; Howell 2013; Powers and Xie 2008). Like above, the strength of relationships are evaluated by Phi tests (Azen and Walker 2011). To assess the significance of associations between moderated categorical variables, Sect. 7.2.3 relies on Mantes-Haenszel statistics (Azen and Walker 2011; Howell 2013). To compute this test, all tables has to be concentrated to $2 \times 2 \times K$ matrixes (Azen and Walker 2011; Howell 2013). An application of traditional Chi-Square statistics to $M \times N \times K$ three-way contingency tables would only allow for testing conditional relationships for each of the K partial tables independently from the remaining ones (Janssen and Laatz 2003). Test statistics for the $M \times N \times K$ matrixes are given in Appendix G.

7.2.3.1   External Control in Relation to Dynamic Fit and Economic Benefits

Findings from data triangulation (Eisenhardt 1989; Myers 2009; Yin 2009) indicate a moderating effect of external control on software structure change in the relationship between dynamic fit and economic sourcing performance. This relationship can be exemplified by looking at GAMMA-FINANCE. GAMMA-FINANCE is a social project funding organization with more than four million supporters. Despite the fact that its in-house CRM system was in line with business process structure, negative economic outcomes were reported by the interviewee:

> I assume that there are lower cost alternatives available; especially when it comes to maintenance and operating costs. One key reason for that is that packaged software provides some inherent standards that we have to develop ourselves. For instance, if there is a legislative amendment, we have to invest in reprogramming of our in-house system. CIO, GAMMA-FINANCE

A similar example can be given by ETA-MANUFACTURING. While the company's on-premises ERP system was aligned with business process structure, economic sourcing performance was found to be negative.

> The update procedure is really complex. If we want to do an update in 2015, we have to start with project planning at least one year earlier. There are a lot of customizations within the system, so we have to analyse how the standard has changed. Which of our customizations are now part of the standard? What do we have to develop on our own? To give you an example, the last software update costed us 100,000 Euros. We had to buy more than 100 man-days from the software vendor to mitigate all our client-specific customizations to the new software version. CIO, ETA-MANUFACTURING

It can be concluded that relying on a internal or shared control of software structure change increases the financial effort to adapt and modify the software artefact. Corporations have to invest more in updating procedures, which reduced economic sourcing performance. In contrast to this, relying on external control simplifies software structure change. The CEO at BETA-SERVICE reported on positive economic outcomes.

> All updates are already included in this fee. I do not need any servers. I do not need to install any updates. I do not need to make data backups. See, even if you only need one employee for all of these things, it costs a lot of money. (...) One employee costs at least between 40,000 and 50,000 Euros. CEO; BETA-SERVICE

Figure 7.11 gives the moderating role of external control on software structure change. The horizontal axis shows dynamic fit. Economic sourcing performance is given on the vertical axis. Figure 7.11a illustrate empirical profiles relying on external control on software structure change, while the remaining software artefacts are shown in Fig. 7.11b. The squares refer to the empirical profiles as defined in Table 5.1 (see Chap. 5).

Cross-case synthesis supports this finding. As shown in Fig. 7.11a, all of the eight empirical profiles benefiting from dynamic fit while relying on external control of software structure change realized positive economic outcomes. Contrary to this, software artefacts in a shared or internal control setting most frequently suffered from negative economic outcomes (see Fig. 7.11b). Among them, only five out of 18 software artefacts that established dynamic fit realized positive economic outcomes.

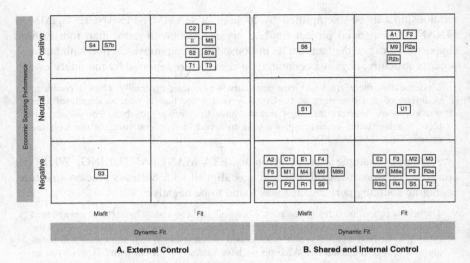

Fig. 7.11 Moderating effect of external control on software structure change. (**a**) External control. (**b**) Shared and internal control

Drawing upon this finding, the following proposition on the moderating effect of control on software structure change in the relationship between dynamic fit and economic sourcing performance emerges:

Proposition 6a	External control of software structure change positively moderates the relationship between dynamic fit and economic sourcing performance

The three-way contingency table on proposition 6a is given in Table 7.43. The calculated Phi values identifies a stronger positive association between dynamic fit and economic sourcing performance in the presence of external control (.516) than in its absence (.273). However, a Mantel-Haenszel score of 2.628 identifies an error probability of $\alpha = 10.5\%$. Consequently, proposition 6a is not significant at $1 - \alpha \leq 90\%$ and can thus not be supported by the Mantel-Haenszel test (Table 7.44).

7.2.3.2 Shared Control in Relation to Dynamic Fit and Technological Benefits

In addition to an impact of external control, findings also reveal a moderating effect of shared control on software structure change in the relationship between dynamic fit and technological sourcing performance. This relationship can be exemplified by looking at BETA-RETAIL, a wholesale distributor of car equipment and automotive parts. BETA-RETAIL reported on an increasing opportunity to link their on-premises ERP system (R2b) with other software artefacts of the company:

Table 7.43 Three-way contingency table on proposition 6a

Control of software structure change			Dynamic fit		
			Misfit	Fit	Total
External control	Economic sourcing performance	Positive	2	8	10
		Not positive	1	0	1
	Total		3	8	11
Shared and Internal control	Economic sourcing performance	Positive	1	5	6
		Not positive	14	13	27
	Total		15	18	33
Total	Economic sourcing performance	Positive	3	13	16
		Not positive	15	13	28
	Total		18	26	44

Table 7.44 Test statistics proposition 6a

	Value	df	Asymptotic sig. (2-sided)
Mantel-Haenszel	2.628	1	.105
Phi (external control)	.516		
Phi (shared and internal control)	.273		
Phi (total)	.341		
No. of valid cases	44		

It is an integrative system, which provides information at a central point. That makes the system structure efficient and effective. CIO, BETA-RETAIL

A similar example can be given by ALPHA-SERVICE. ALPHA-SERVICE is a sanitary service provider employing more than 3000 people throughout Europe. While BETA-RETAIL's ERP system was in line with business process structure, ALPHA-SERVICE's enterprise software was in a misaligned situation. However, by combining business pull and technological push innovation, the company was able to integrate their on-demand CRM system with other internal applications and establish the CRM system as core software within their IT landscape.

Now that we completed phase 2 [custom-build add-on], we get much more information on our customers. (...) Customer-Self-Service will be an important topic in phase 4 [custom-build add-on]. I know that our competitors are thinking in the same direction, but we will be faster with [the CRM software]. (...) Advantages are clearly related to the on-demand nature. We get everything via the Internet. We do not need to take care on server any more. And that is something that we realize every day. If you have any issues with some databases, with servers and so forth, the systems stop. This is something we do not have to take care on with respect to our CRM application. (...) The second thing is, when we look at our SAP landscape, it is hard to implement an update. With [the CRM system], we get new functionalities several times a year without doing anything for it. This is very important for us CIO, ALPHA-SERVICE

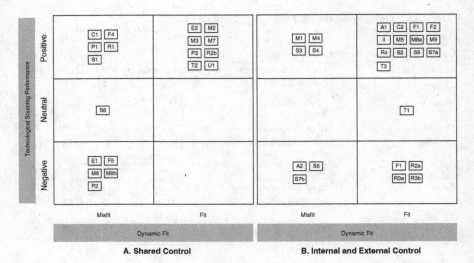

Fig. 7.12 Moderating effect of hybrid governance of software structure change. (**a**) Shared control. (**b**) Internal and external control

Contrary to this, the CEO at ETA-SERVICE reported on negative technological outcomes in terms of software structure obsolescence of their ERP system. The company relies on external control on software structure change.

> Recently, [the software vendor] announced that he stopped development of their [on-demand ERP system]. (...) It would have been great if we would get a HTML 5.0 surface or something else that would make the software run faster and thereby increase its performance. This will not be the case within the next years. (...) It is sad. We really backed the wrong horse. CEO, ETA-SERVICE

It can be concluded that relying on a shared control on software structure change increases the ability to integrate a software artefact within the company and consolidate internal IT structures as a consequence of business pull innovation. In addition, technological push helps these companies to reduce the risk of software structure obsolescence.

Figure 7.12 gives the moderating role of shared control on software structure change. The horizontal axis shows dynamic fit. Technological sourcing performance is given on the vertical axis. Figure 7.12a illustrates empirical profiles relying on a shared control on software structure change, while the remaining software artefacts are shown in Fig. 7.12b. The squares refer to the empirical profiles as defined in Table 5.1 (see Chap. 5).

Cross-case synthesis supports this finding. As shown in Fig. 7.11a, all of the eight empirical profiles benefiting from dynamic fit while relying on shared control of software structure change realized positive technological outcomes. Contrary to this, only 13 out of 18 software artefacts realizing dynamic fit in an external or internal control setting realized positive technological outcomes (see Fig. 7.11b).

Table 7.45 Three-way contingency table on proposition 6b

Control of software structure change			Dynamic fit		Total
			Misfit	Fit	
Shared control	Technological sourcing performance	Positive	5	8	13
		Not positive	6	0	6
	Total		11	8	19
External and Internal Control	Technological sourcing performance	Positive	4	13	17
		Not positive	3	5	8
	Total		7	18	25
Total	Technological sourcing performance	Positive	9	21	30
		Not positive	9	5	14
	Total		18	26	44

Table 7.46 Test statistics proposition 6b

	Value	df	Asymptotic sig. (2-sided)
Mantel-Haenszel	3.531	1	.060
Phi (shared control)	.579		
Phi (external and internal control)	.145		
Phi (total)	.325		
No. of valid cases	44		

Drawing upon this finding, the following proposition on the moderating effect of shared control in the relationship between software alignment and technological sourcing performance emerges:

Proposition 6b	Shared control of software structure change positively moderates the relationship between dynamic fit and technological sourcing performance

The three-way contingency table on proposition 6b is given in Table 7.45. The calculated Phi values identifies a stronger positive relationship between dynamic fit and technological sourcing performance in the presence of shared control (.579) than in its absence (.145). A Mantel-Haenszel value of 3.531 detects proposition 6b as significant at $1- \propto \ \leq 90\%$ (Table 7.46).

7.2.4 Summary

"The key to good cross-case comparison is (...) looking at the data in many divergent ways." (Eisenhardt 1989: 540). Therefore, researchers must to search for intragroup similarities and intergroup differences (Eisenhardt 1989; Yin 2009).

This section outlined the findings from the inductive data interpretation (Eisenhardt 1989; Myers 2009; Ravishankar et al. 2011). The relationship between sourcing performance and business process performance is discussed in Sect. 7.2.1. Findings from cross-case synthesis indicate a positive impact of strategic, economic, and technological benefits on performance outcomes in business units. In Sect. 7.2.2, the role of software sourcing modes is discussed. Data triangulations revealed a positive influence of ownership on dynamic fit. In addition, it was found that the three software sourcing modes possess different associations with control of software structure change.

In particular, it was exposed that on-demand sourcing is related to external control (pioneer innovator gestalt and technology push non-gestalt), on-premises to shared control (ambidextrous innovator gestalt and push-pull non-gestalt), and in-house to internal control (cautious innovator gestalt, conservative gestalt, business pull non-gestalt, and no innovation non-gestalt). Finally, Sect. 7.2.3 identifies a moderating effect of market governance in the relationship between dynamic fit and economic benefits as well as a moderating effect of hybrid governance in the impact of dynamic fit on technological sourcing performance. Section 7.3 continues with a statistical test of propositions. The significance of the five initially proposed associations as well as the significance of the nine emerging propositions was evaluated. A summary on test statistics is given in Table 7.47.

Table 7.47 Overview on test statistics

Proposition		Applied tests	Test values	Interpretation
P1	Alignment gestalts positively impact dynamic fit	Fisher's exact test	.000	Significant at $1-\alpha \leq 99.9\%$
		Phi test	.760	Very strong positive association
P2	Dynamic fit positively impacts business process performance	Fisher's exact test	.000	Significant at $1-\alpha \leq 99.9\%$
		Phi test	.632	Strong positive association
P3a	Dynamic fit positively impacts strategic sourcing performance	Fisher's exact test	.031	Significant at $1-\alpha \leq 95\%$
		Phi test	.354	Moderate positive association
P3b	Dynamic fit positively impacts economic sourcing performance	Fisher's exact test	.030	Significant at $1-\alpha \leq 95\%$
		Phi test	.341	Moderate positive association

(continued)

Table 7.47 (continued)

Proposition		Applied tests	Test values	Interpretation
P3c	Dynamic fit positively impacts technological sourcing performance	Fisher's exact test	.049	Significant at $1 - \alpha \leq 95\ \%$
		Phi test	.325	Moderate positive association
P4a	Strategic sourcing performance positively impacts business·process performance	Fisher's exact test	.005	Significant at $1 - \alpha \leq 99\ \%$
		Phi test	.466	Moderate positive association
P4b	Economic sourcing performance positively impacts business process performance	Fisher's exact test	.160	Not statistically significant
		Phi test	.251	Moderate positive association
P4c	Technological sourcing performance positively impacts business process performance	Fisher's exact test	.152	Not statistically significant
		Phi test	.239	Moderate positive association
P5	Software ownership positively impacts dynamic fit	Fisher's exact test	.334	Not statistically significant
		Phi test	−.182	No/weak negative association
P5a	On-demand sourcing is positively associated with external control of software structure change	Fisher's exact test	.000	Significant at $1 - \alpha \leq 99.9\ \%$
		Phi test	.581	Strong positive association
P5b	On-premises sourcing is positively associated with shared control of software structure change	Fisher's exact test	.017	Significant at $1 - \alpha \leq 95\ \%$
		Phi test	.374	Moderate positive association
P5c	In-house sourcing is positively associated with internal control of software structure change	Fisher's exact test	.000	Significant at $1 - \alpha \leq 99.9\ \%$
		Phi test	.582	Strong positive association

(continued)

Table 7.47 (continued)

Proposition		Applied tests	Test values	Interpretation
P6a	External control of software structure change positively moderates the relationship between dynamic fit and economic sourcing performance	Mantel-Haenszel test	2.628	Not statistically significant
		Phi test	.516 (External)	Strong positive association
		Phi test	.273 (Shared & Internal)	Moderate positive association
P6b	Shared control of software structure change positively moderates the relationship between dynamic fit and technological sourcing performance	Mantel-Haenszel test	3.531	Significant at $1 - \alpha \leq 90$ %
		Phi test	.579 (Shared)	Strong positive association
		Phi test	.145 (External & Internal)	Weak/no positive association

7.3   Summary

Supplementary to the single-case investigation in Chap. 6, this chapter offers an aggregated analysis of the 44 empirical profiles under study. The goal of the presented cross-case synthesis was to explore, validate, and test associations among concepts. As a result of the aggregated analysis, the initial research model is refined and extended.

Section 7.1 focused on an investigation of the five propositions in the initial research model. Thereby, the initial propositions helps "*to focus attention on certain data and to ignore other data*" (Yin 2009: 130). Proposition 1 postulates a positive relationship between dynamic fit and pioneer innovator, cautious innovator, ambidextrous innovator, and conservative gestalts. Cross-case analysis supports this relationship. It was found that proposition 1 is extremely significant.

Looking at the impact of dynamic fit on performance outcomes, all four propositions in the initial research model were supported. It was postulated that dynamic fit positively impacts business process performance. Cross-case analysis corroborates this relationship. Proposition 2 was identified to be extremely significant. In addition, cross-case synthesis support this positive association between dynamic fit and sourcing performance in terms of strategic, economic, and technological outcomes. The related propositions 3a, 3b, and 3c were found to be significant.

While Sect. 7.1 focused on an investigation of the five propositions in the initial research, Sect. 7.2 continued with an inductive data interpretation (Eisenhardt and Graebner 2007). Therefore, all 44 empirical profiles were reinvestigated and explanations that arise out of the data were included (Eisenhardt 1989; Ravishankar et al. 2011). New insights emerge on the relationship between sourcing performance and business process performance. Findings from cross-case synthesis indicate a positive impact of strategic (proposition 4a), economic (proposition 4b), and technological benefits (proposition 4c) on performance outcomes in business units. While proposition 4a was found to be extremely significant, propositions 4b and 4c were rejected by the statistical test. As a consequence, propositions 4b and 4c are dropped, while the former proposition 4a is renamed towards proposition 4.

The role of software sourcing modes was derived from cross-case synthesis. Data triangulations revealed a positive impact of software ownership on dynamic fit. The related proposition 5 was not supported by the statistical test and is dropped. In a consequence, software sourcing modes are not directly related to higher or lower levels of dynamic fit. However, it was found that the three software sourcing modes possess different associations with control of software structure change. First, it was recognised that on-demand sourcing impacts external control (pioneer innovator gestalt and technology push non-gestalt). The related proposition 5a was found to be extremely significant. Second, on-premises sourcing influences shared control (ambidextrous innovator gestalt and push-pull non-gestalt). The related proposition 5b was found to be extremely significant. Third, in-house sourcing effects internal control (cautious innovator gestalt, conservative gestalt, business pull non-gestalt, and no innovation non-gestalt). The related proposition 5c was found to be extremely significant.

Finally, two moderating effects of control of software structure change emerged from data triangulation. First, external control positively moderates the relationship between dynamic fit and economic sourcing performance. The related proposition 6a was not supported by Mantel-Haenszel test. Second, a positive moderating effect of shared control in the relationship between dynamic fit and technological sourcing performance was identified. The related proposition 6b was found to be significant.

In summary, the statistical tests in Sect. 7.3 support ten out of 14 propositions. Four relationships are not statistically significant and are dropped. The final research model as well as a discussion of the presented study is given in Chap. 8.

Chapter 8
Summary and Discussion

Following the single-case analysis in Chap. 6 and the cross-case synthesis combined with a statistical test of associations in Chap. 7, this chapter presents a summary and discussion of key findings. The final explanatory research model is presented in Sect. 8.1. Section 8.2 continues with an outline of central theoretical contributions of this study. Managerial implications are provided in Sect. 8.3. Subsequently, limitations and future research are summarized in Sect. 8.4.

8.1 Explanatory Research Model on Software Sourcing Value

The aim of the presented study is to contribute to theory in the area of software sourcing, software-business process fit, and their relationship to business process performance of a firm. "*A theory is a statement of relations among concepts within a set of boundary assumptions and constraints*" (Bacharach 1989: 496). Each theoretical argument consists of the three building blocks, "what?", "how?", and "why?" (Heinrich et al. 2011). The "what?"-questions refers to the objects of a theory in terms of its constructs (Bacharach 1989; Gregor 2006; Heinrich et al. 2011). The constructs of this study were identified *a priori* following the recommendations by Eisenhardt (1989) and are discussed in Chaps. 2 and 3. The "how?"-question refers to the relationship among constructs (Heinrich et al. 2011). Fourteen propositions were discussed in the presented study. Five of these propositions were identified *a priori* while nine relationships were derived from an aggregated cross-case and single-case analysis. Out of the nine inductively developed associations, four were not supported by the statistical tests in Chap. 7. These propositions were dropped. Finally, the "why?"-question focuses on the cause of the association among constructs (Heinrich et al. 2011). Causal relationships are discussed from an inductive and deductive point of view in this study. The five

© Springer International Publishing Switzerland 2016
M. Nöhren, *Enterprise Software Sourcing Performance*, Progress in IS,
DOI 10.1007/978-3-319-23926-2_8

propositions of the initial research model (see Chap. 3) are derived from previous literature in conjunction with the applied reference theories. A single-case analysis provided in Chap. 6 substantiates the causality. The inductively developed propositions were derived from a qualitative reasoning. Individual as well as cross-case evidences support these relationships.

Figure 8.1 presents the final explanatory research model. Looking at software sourcing value, it was found that dynamic fit positively impacts business process performance. The related proposition 2 was extremely significant at $1 - \alpha \leq 99.9\%$. In addition, the analysis shows that dynamic fit positively impacts strategic, economic, and technological sourcing performance. The related propositions 3a, 3b, and 3c were significant at $1 - \alpha \leq 95\%$. In can therefore be concluded that dynamic fit is beneficial for companies. It leads to higher levels of business process performance as well as sourcing performance. The aggregated cross-case and single-case analysis indicates a relationship between the dependent constructs under study. In particular, a positive impact of strategic sourcing performance on business process performance was identified. The related proposition 4 was very significant at $1 - \alpha \leq 99\%$. A similar impact of economic and technological sourcing performance was not supported by the statistical tests.

Drawing upon Sabherwal and Robey (1995), process and variance logic are combined in this study. In particular, the dynamic fit process is transferred into clusters. Clustering was done with respect to the type of software structure change, due to the fact that the presented study focuses on an investigation of the value of enterprise software. For each type of software structure change, ideal patterns of environmental change, business process structure change, software customizability, and business process adaptability were derived. These patterns were grouped into eight clusters in Chap. 3. Four of these clusters were referred to as gestalts, while the remaining four were labelled non-gestalts (Lee et al. 2004; Venkatraman 1989). Gestalts are further grouped into external control gestalts, shared control gestalts, and internal control gestalts. Shared control gestalts refers to clusters that provide software structure change outside a firm's hierarchy. It includes the pioneer innovator gestalt and the related technology push non-gestalt. Internal control gestalts refers to clusters in which software structure change is executed internally. It encompasses the cautious innovator gestalt and the related business pull non-gestalt as well as the conservative gestalt and the linked no innovation non-gestalt. Shared control gestalts refers to clusters in which software structure change is partially executed internally and partially procured on a market. It encompasses the ambidextrous innovator gestalt and the related push-pull non-gestalt. It was found that gestalts positively impact dynamic fit. The related proposition 1 was extremely significant at $1 - \alpha \leq 99.9\%$. In addition, two moderating effects emerged from data triangulation. First, external control gestalts positively moderates the relationship between dynamic fit and economic sourcing performance. The related proposition 6a was not statistically significant. Second, a positive moderating effect of shared control gestalts in the relationship between dynamic fit and technological sourcing performance was identified. The related proposition 6b was found to be significant at $1 - \alpha \leq 90\%$.

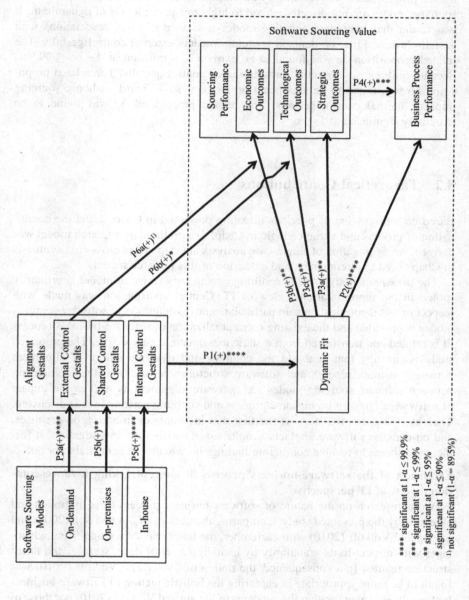

Fig. 8.1 Final explanatory research model

The role of software sourcing modes was derived inductively from the aggregated cross-case and single-case analysis. Despite the fact that data triangulations revealed a slight positive impact of software structure ownership on dynamic fit, the related proposition 5 was rejected by the statistical test. In a consequence, software sourcing modes are not directly related to higher or lower levels of dynamic fit. It was found that individual sourcing modes possess distinctive associations with gestalt clusters. First, on-demand sourcing impacts external control gestalts. The related proposition 5a was found to be extremely significant at $1- \propto \; \leq 99.9\%$. Second, on-premises sourcing impacts shared control gestalts. The related proposition 5b was found to be significant at $1- \propto \; \leq 95\%$. Third, in-house sourcing impacts internal control gestalts. The related proposition 5c was found to be extremely significant at $1- \propto \; \leq 99.9\%$.

8.2   Theoretical Contributions

Based on a discussion of previous literature presented in Chap. 2 and the combination of process and variance logic in Chap. 3, a preliminary research model was derived. An aggregation of single-case analysis in Chap. 6 and cross-case synthesis in Chap. 7 led to a refinement and extension of this research model.

The presented study and the resulting explanatory research model is primarily rooted in the representational view of IT. Central contribution was made with respect to this theoretical lens. In particular, a novel definition of software sourcing modes is provided and the existing conceptualization of software-business process fit is refined and transferred from a static to a dynamic perspective. The presented study is the first that analysed the complex and dynamic nature of alignment between business process and software structures. In addition, the relationship between software sourcing modes and software alignment as well as the impact of software alignment on business process and sourcing performance is discussed. Thereby, the presented study is the first that incorporates in-house, on-premises, and on-demand software artefacts simultaneously within the investigation. It further contributes to resolve conflicting findings on whether fit is desirable or not.

Extension of the software-business process fit concept taking a representational view of IT perspective
Previous research on the nature of software-business process fit is discussed and extended by the presented study. Comparing the notions of Sia and Soh (2007) and Strong and Volkoff (2010) with each other, the latter one shows significant advantages with respect to its granularity by including a set of deep, surface, and latent structure misfits. In a consequence, the notion of Strong and Volkoff (2010) was found to be more appropriate in capturing the holistic picture of software-business process fit. However, neither the concepts of Strong and Volkoff (2010) nor those of Sia and Soh (2007) take changing business process or software structures into account. This shortcoming was addressed by the concept of dynamic fit (Nöhren

et al. 2014). If a company suffers from dynamic misfit in terms of excessive or insufficient software change, software and business process structures are drifting apart (Nöhren et al. 2014). In this situation, an organization experiences deficiencies by the means of functionality, data, usability, role or control misfits (Strong and Volkoff 2010). In contrast to this, if company realizes dynamic fit by the means of adjusted expansion or inertia, business process and software structures coevolve with each other (Nöhren et al. 2014). In such conditions, organizations benefit from coverage fit (Strong and Volkoff 2010). Consequently, dynamic fit extends the IT artefact of Strong and Volkoff (2010) from static software structures to dynamic ones.

Understanding the dynamic nature of alignment between business process and software structures and its impact on software-business process fit
By combining process and variance logic, the presented study makes a significant contribution to our understanding of the essence of software-business process fit. Based on a literature review and selected reference theories, it was found that software-business process fit is dynamic in nature (Benbya and McKelvey 2006; Nöhren et al. 2014). Dynamic fit of an enterprise system depends on the coevolution between business process and software structures (Nöhren et al. 2014; Sabherwal et al. 2001). If software structure change is greater than business process structure change or vice versa, a company will suffer from dynamic misfit. Both, business process and software structures depend on their environments. Particular shifts in an organization's macro or micro environment cause changes in the structures of institutions and software artefacts (Scott 1987; Sia and Soh 2007). This process was found to be supported by the flexibility of business processes—referred to as business process adaptability (Tatikonda and Montoya-Weiss 2001; Yang and Papazoglou 2000)—and flexibility of the software artefact—referred to as software customizability (Benlian et al. 2009; Winkler and Brown 2014).

The dynamic alignment process consists of five concepts with different values attached. Based on Sabherwal and Robey (1995), specifications of these five concepts were transferred into alignment clusters. Due to the fact that the presented study investigates software artefacts, dynamic fit process patterns are clustered with respect to the type of software structure change. For each of the four types of software structure change, ideal patterns of environmental change, business process structure change, software customizability, and business process adaptability were derived and transferred into gestalt clusters (Lee et al. 2004; Sabherwal and Robey 1995). The remaining patterns are labelled non-gestalts (Lee et al. 2004; Venkatraman 1989).

The aggregated cross-case and single-case analysis shows great support for the existence of the superior gestalt clusters. In particular, all 20 empirical profiles linked to one of the four gestalt clusters established dynamic fit. Only six enterprise systems that were linked to one of the four non-gestalt clusters benefited from a constant coevolution between business process and software structures. It has to be noted that with business process structure change possessing two specifications (yes and no), environmental change (macro, micro, macro and micro, and stable) and

software structure change (technology push, push-pull, business pull, and no innovation) taking four specifications each, and business process adaptability as well as
software customizability holding three values (high, medium, and low), the total
number of possible patterns amounts to 288. Out of these, only 19 combinations
($\approx$7 %) are linked to the four gestalt clusters while the remaining 269 patters
($\approx$93 %) are non-gestalts. In a consequence, 7 % of the dynamic fit process patterns
outperform all other combinations of the related constructs with respect to
dynamic fit.

Contribution to research on the value of process-centric enterprise software
As outlined in Chap. 2, the notion of value is rather vague in nature. It was found
that this is particularly true for research in the area of enterprise software performance. No strong concepts for capturing the impact of the software artefacts were
identified by the literature review. Previous studies either assessed outcomes on an
organizational level (e.g. Cotteleer and Bendoly 2006; Houdeshel and Watson
1987) or relied on mixed concepts that capture performance on multiple levels
simultaneously (e.g. Grant 2003; Shang and Seddon 2002). The presented study
contributes to research on software value in two ways. First, it was found that
enterprise software generates a certain intermediary outcome. This outcome is
directly related to the artefact under investigation and can be measured in terms
of dynamic fit. Second, previous research on software-business process fit has not
investigated its impact on performance outcomes (e.g. Maurer et al. 2012; Sia and
Soh 2007; Strong and Volkoff 2010). An extremely significant positive relationship
between dynamic fit and business process performance was identified (see proposition 2). In addition, the positive impacts of dynamic fit on strategic (see proposition 3a), economic (see proposition 3b), and technological sourcing performance
(see proposition 3c) were found to be significant as well. In a consequence, an
appropriate investigation of software value implies both, measuring the intermediary outcome in terms of dynamic fit as well as an analysing performance outcomes
in terms of business process and sourcing performance.

Provision of a novel and holistic understanding of software sourcing modes
Looking at literature in the area of software sourcing, a precise and strong definition
of the phenomenon does not exist (e.g. Banker and Kemerer 1992; Choudhary
2007a; Kern et al. 2002a, b; Schwarz et al. 2009; Walden 2005; Wang 2002). With
reference to representational view of IT, software sourcing modes are classified
according to their ownership on physical, deep, and surface structures and are
categorized into in-house, on-premises, and on-demand settings in the presented
study. In-house sourcing refers to applications that hold physical, deep, and surface
structures of the software artefact within a firm's hierarchy. In this sourcing
arrangement, an application is custom-developed for a specific company (Schwarz
et al. 2009). The development is either performed by an internal IT department or a
subcontracted software vendor under control of the client (e.g. Nidumolu 1995;
Sawyer 2000; Schwarz et al. 2009; Wang 2002). The enterprise system is installed
on a corporate's IT infrastructure representing an internal allocation of physical
structures. In contrast to this, the ownership on deep and surface structures of

packaged applications is held outside a firm's hierarchy by a specialised software vendor. Packaged applications differ with respect to their deployment. Whereas on-premises applications are installed on a firm's own IT infrastructure, representing an internal ownership on physical structures, on-demand applications are hosted at a software vendor and are accessed via the Internet, expressing an external ownership on physical structures (Winkler et al. 2011).

This novel definition of software sourcing modes possesses two central advantages for future research. First, by defining the phenomenon taking a representational view of IT perspective, every existing and emerging software procurement arrangements can be linked to in-house, on-premises, or on-demand settings. Second, this novel definition allows not only for treating the software sourcing concept as pure categorical variable—nominal scale of measurement—but also to understand it in a discrete linear fashion—ordinal scale of measurement (Bortz and Schuster 2010; Racine and Li 2004). In particular, software sourcing can also be understood as a discrete linear variable by expressing the degree of software structure ownership. The extent of ownership on physical, deep, and surface structures decreases from in-house through on-premises to on-demand sourcing.

Understanding and explaining the role of software sourcing modes in value generation

Previous studies on the value of process-centric enterprise systems have not incorporated software sourcing modes (e.g. Grant 2003; Maurer et al. 2012; Ravishankar et al. 2011; Sia and Soh 2007; Soh and Sia 2004; Strong and Volkoff 2010). In a consequence, this study is the first that investigates the impact of in-house, on-premises, and on-demand sourcing on alignment and performance.

Previous studies on software alignment focused on packaged applications in general (e.g. Grant 2003; Ravishankar et al. 2011; Sia and Soh 2007; Soh and Sia 2004; Strong and Volkoff 2010). It is debated that the inherent standardization of such software artefacts forms a central source of misfit (Sia and Soh 2007; Strong and Volkoff 2010). Therefore, lower levels of ownership on physical, deep, and surface structures, which result in an increasing standardization of the software artefact, can have a negative impact on dynamic fit. However, due to the external development of packaged applications, software providers adapt their enterprise systems on a regular basis and provide modifications to their customers based on existing and emerging industry best practices (Koehler et al. 2010; Sia and Soh 2007; Xin and Levina 2008; Yang and Tate 2012). Such modifications can assist companies to keep pace with changing environmental conditions (Scott 1987; Sia and Soh 2007). Therefore, lower levels of ownership on physical, deep, and surface structures, which result in an increasing provision of such industry best practices, can have a positive impact on dynamic fit. The aggregated cross-case and single-case analysis in combination with a statistical test of association neither supports a positive nor a negative impact of software ownership on dynamic fit. In a consequence, all three sourcing modes under study can be beneficial as well as harmful for a company. The relationship between software sourcing modes and dynamic fit is established via the alignment gestalts. In particular, it was found that on-demand sourcing is related to external control gestalts (pioneer innovator gestalt and technology push non-gestalt), on-premises to shared control gestalts (ambidextrous innovator gestalt and push-pull non-gestalt), and in-house to internal control gestalts (cautious innovator gestalt, conservative gestalt, business pull non-gestalt, and no innovation non-gestalt).

8.3 Managerial Implications

The findings of the presented study provide valuable insights for IT decision makers and practitioners in client companies. The role of software sourcing modes in a post-implementation phase is discussed. By linking software sourcing modes to the dynamic alignment process, findings assist practitioners in making the "right" sourcing decision and in continuously aligning business process and software structures. In addition, the complexity of software sourcing value is outlined by discussing relationship between dynamic fit, business process performance, and sourcing performance. Key contributions to practice are introduced subsequently.

Understanding the role of software sourcing modes and their relationship to the dynamic alignment process
Enterprise software, such as ERP and CRM systems, are deployed to support central business processes within an organization (Grant 2003; Shang and Seddon 2002; Strong and Volkoff 2010). The average lifetime of such systems ranges from 10 to 20 years (Shang and Seddon 2000, 2003). Consequently, making the right software sourcing decision and managing the application in a post-implementation phase is essential for IT decision makers.

The presented study indicates that software sourcing modes are not directly related to software-business process fit. However, it was found that software sourcing modes possess individual associations with alignment gestalt clusters. On-demand sourcing is related to external control gestalts. Companies that source their enterprise systems in such a setting establish dynamic fit by relying on a pioneer innovator gestalt. This was found to be beneficial if the company is primarily driven by macro environmental changes and if corporate's business processes possess a high adaptability. On-premises sourcing is related to shared control gestalts. Companies that source their enterprise systems in such a setting realize dynamic fit by following an ambidextrous innovator gestalt. Therefore, both, software as well as business processes must be flexible in nature in order to address macro and micro environmental changes. Finally, in-house sourcing is related to internal control gestalts. Companies that source their enterprise systems internally establish dynamic fit either by relying on a cautious innovator or a conservative gestalt. The first one was found to be beneficial if the company is primarily driven by micro environmental changes and if the software artefact is highly customizable. Conservative gestalt is valuable for companies within a stable market and the absence of environmental changes. As a consequence, the presented

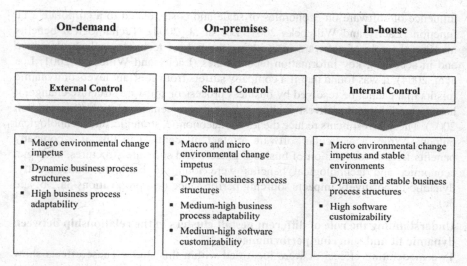

Fig. 8.2 Managerial implications for sourcing and managing process enterprise software

study supports practitioners in making the "right" sourcing decision and in how to align enterprise software in a post-implementation phase. Figure 8.2 summarizes these implications.

Understanding and measuring the impact of software-business process misfit on business process and sourcing performance
This study includes two outcome concepts in terms of business process performance (Grant 2003; Shang and Seddon 2002) and sourcing performance (Lacity and Willcocks 2001; Lee et al. 2004). The former one captures the impact of enterprise software on those business processes that were directly supported by this particular application. Dynamic fit expresses the coevolution between business process and software structure (Benbya and McKelvey 2006; Nöhren et al. 2014; Sia and Soh 2007; Strong and Volkoff 2010). A company suffers from dynamic misfit if it experiences an insufficient or excessive software structure change (Nöhren et al. 2014). Misfits are instances, where the structures embedded within the system conflicts with an organizational reality (Sia and Soh 2007; Strong and Volkoff 2010). Such a drifting apart between business process and software structures is destructive for a company (Wand and Weber 1990). In contrast to this, dynamic fit between business process and software structures contributes to efficiency and effectiveness of business processes (Sia and Soh 2007; Strong and Volkoff 2010). As a consequence, dynamic fit positively impacts business process performance (see proposition 2).

Sourcing performance captures software's contribution to strategic, economic, and technological benefits. The former one assesses software's contribution to increase IT competence and IT function's ability to refocus on its core competencies (Lacity and Willcocks 2001; Lee et al. 2004). Economic benefits reveal the influence of software on economies of scale and costs related to a corporate's IT function (Lacity and Willcocks 2001; Lee et al. 2004). Technological benefits measure the role of software in reducing the risk of technological obsolescence and in accessing key information technologies (Lacity and Willcocks 2001; Lee et al. 2004). It was found that if a company suffers from constant levels of dynamic misfits that cannot be resolved by business process or software structure change, it has to search for and to invest in alternative software-centric solutions (Sia and Soh 2007). These investments reduce the level of economic, strategic, and technological outcomes from a particular software artefact. In contrast to this, if a company benefits from a coevolution of business process and software structures, strategic, economic, and technological benefits were found to be high. Consequently, dynamic fit positively impacts sourcing performance (see propositions 3a, 3b, and 3c).

Understanding the role of different gestalt clusters in the relationship between dynamic fit and sourcing performance
Two moderating effects of were identified within this study. These effects show valuable insights for practitioners sourcing packaged applications. First, external control gestalts positively moderates the relationship between dynamic fit and economic sourcing performance. The absence of business pull innovation reduces efforts for managing and updating the software artefact. It can be concluded that while having a software structure that is in line with business process structure, pure technology push innovation increases the economic gains. It has to be noted that while this relationship is not statistically significant. Second, shared control gestalts positively moderates the relationship between dynamic fit and technological sourcing performance. Such a hybrid governance enhances the ability to integrate and transform the software artefact within a company's IT landscape. It was found that while having a software structure that is in line with business process structure, a combination between business pull and technological push innovation increases technological outcomes.

8.4 Limitations and Future Research

In studying enterprise software performance and the role of in-house, on-premises, and on-demand software, several limitations were taken into account. These limitations and required future research in order to overcome these constraints are discussed below.

Boundary assumptions of the explanatory research model
Each theoretical argument implies certain restrictions with respect to its temporal and spatial boundaries (Bacharach 1989). The presented findings on software and sourcing performance were captured in post-implementation phase (Swanson and Ramiller 2004). Software structure misfits and performance implications that only occur during software implementation were not investigated. Second, a specific

type of enterprise software was observed. The presented study focuses on process-centric enterprise software—such as ERP or CRM systems—having their primary impact within business units (Swanson 1994).

Limited number of empirical profiles
The presented study builds upon the qualitative field study design of Guillemette and Paré (2012). Consequently, the minimum number of empirical profiles was set to 33 (Guillemette and Paré 2012). The final sample of this study encompassed 44 profiles in terms of process-centric enterprise systems. Thereby, the proposed sample size of Guillemette and Paré (2012) was extended considerably. However, two limitations were taken into account. First, this study incorporated three software sourcing modes. While the data set includes 23 systems that were sourced on-premises and 15 applications that were provided on-demand, only six in-house software artefacts were included. The minor presence of in-house applications mirrors market reality and a decreasing diffusion of custom-built applications in the market (Sawyer 2000). Future research may address this limitation by focusing on in-house systems. Building own large-scale ERP systems is very cost intensive while packaged applications matured and nowadays serve clients in various industrial sectors. Due to a limited number of companies that still rely on such internally developed ERP systems, in-depth case studies within the identified companies might be appropriate to study enterprise software's impact on value in the absence of an external best practice standard. Second, eight alignment clusters were identified in this study. In order to extend the discussion of the related gestalts and non-gestalts, future research may either increase their generalizability by the means of a quantitative confirmatory factor analysis or test and refine these clusters by conducting an exploratory factor analysis.

Aggregation of $M \times N \times K$ contingency tables to $2 \times 2 \times K$ matrixes
Categorical data in this study was analysed in two-way and three-way contingency tables. Chi-Square test was applied to evaluate associations in non-dichotomous $M \times N$ contingency tables (Azen and Walker 2011; Bortz and Schuster 2010). In settings, were the expected absolute frequencies were less than 5, $M \times N$ contingency tables were aggregated to 2×2 matrixes to run Fisher's exact tests (Camilli 1995; Howell 2013). In addition, both $2 \times 3 \times 2$ three-way tables were aggregated to $2 \times 2 \times 2$ matrixes to apply Mantel-Haenszel test (Azen and Walker 2011; Janssen and Laatz 2003). Test statistics for original $2 \times 3 \times 2$ tables are given in Appendix G.

A certain loss of information was incorporated by this interpretive reduction of categories. Key reason why tests in this study required aggregations is the small sample size (Bortz and Schuster 2010; Camilli 1995; Howell 2013). To overcome this limitation, future research should focus on increasing the number of empirical profiles under investigation.

Single-level observation of dynamic fit
This study relies on a single-level observation of dynamic fit. Thereby, the overall alignment between business process and software structures was captured in order

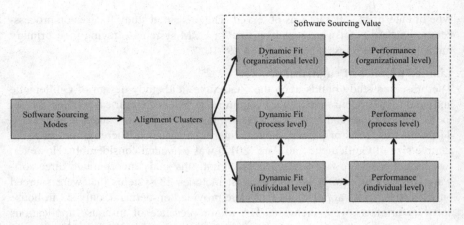

Fig. 8.3 Multilevel research agenda for future research

to analyse the impact on business process and sourcing performance. As outlined in previous research, software structure fit is an emerging concept (Strong and Volkoff 2010). In particular, while software structure fit might be present on a process level, misfit on an individual level may occur (Maurer et al. 2012). Dissatisfaction of users could result in lower levels of perceived usefulness or perceived enjoyment of usage, which in return reduces employee's individual performance (van der Heijden 2004b). Lower levels of individual performance could have a negative impact on business process and organizational outcomes (DeLone and McLean 1992). As shown in Fig. 8.3, future research may investigate the relationship between individual and process level fit as well as between individual and process level performance outcomes by means of a multilevel data analysis (Klein et al. 1994, 1999).

Sourcing outcomes in terms of SET satisfaction
In IT outsourcing research, the notion of outcome is used in a vague and inconsistent way (e.g. DeLone and McLean 1992; Dibbern et al. 2004; Schryen 2010). Most frequently, previous studies relied on perceptual measures in terms of (out)sourcing success (Dibbern et al. 2004; Lacity et al. 2010), assessing performance in terms of economic, technological, and strategic benefits (e.g. Goo et al. 2008; Grover et al. 1996; Lee and Kim 1999; Lee et al. 2004; Saunders et al. 1997). Economic benefits refer to the *"(. . .) efficiency of the outsourcing arrangement and the extent to which it helped the company avoid a major capital expenditure (. . .)"* (Saunders et al. 1997: 71). It evaluates the perceived financial value of a particular sourcing arrangement. Technological benefits refer to *"(. . .) new skills and new technologies afforded as a result of outsourcing (. . .)"* (Saunders et al. 1997: 71). It serves as a measure of the ability to acquire, secure, and control IT potentials via outsourcing (Goo et al. 2008). Strategic benefits refer to *"(. . .) the strategic advantage, insourcing capability, and changed focus on strategic activities derived from the outsourcing arrangement (. . .)"* (Saunders et al. 1997: 71). It describes the

contribution to realize business goals and/or execute corporates' strategies (Goo et al. 2008).

Despite the fact that SET satisfaction emerged to a preferred construct for evaluating (out)sourcing performance (e.g. Goo et al. 2008; Grover et al. 1996; Lee and Kim 1999; Lee et al. 2004; Saunders et al. 1997), one major questions revolve around this concept. While economic benefits serve as measure of efficiency, technological and strategic outcomes are concerned with evaluating effectivity of sourcing arrangements. It remains uncertain whether the technological and the strategic dimension of SET satisfaction are independent from each other or whether technological outcomes impact the level of perceived strategic performance. In addition, higher levels of technological performance might also impact economic value derived from IT outsourcing. Future research should focus on testing this relationship in order to improve the construct.

Self-reported statements of key informants

In interorganizational research relying on statements of interviewees, information bias in terms of tainted reports may occur (Kumar et al. 1993). This study relies on reports of executives responsible for management of a particular process-centric enterprise system under study. In order to reduce the likelihood of subjectively biased answers, questions were asked from different angle of views during the interviews (Yin 2009). In addition, all empirical profiles and key informants were anonymised. However, there is always a certain risk of political answers (Kumar et al. 1993), especially when it comes to alignment and performance of such enterprise systems provided under key informant's internal governance. Consequently, future research could conduct in-depth case studies with multiple informants within a smaller number of companies (Yin 2009).

Single-case versus cross-case design

According to Yin (2009), qualitative research can be classified into single-case and multiple-case designs with different preconditions and advantages attached (see Fig. 8.4). Single-case approaches are a common design in case study research (Yin 2009). They either focus on studying a single unit or multiple units within a one case company (Yin 2009). Such single case approaches are used to investigate critical cases, unique cases, representative cases, revelatory cases, or longitudinal cases (Yin 2009). An in-depth single-case analysis and detailed description of individual case findings form the basis of data interpretation (Yin 2009). For instance, Strong and Volkoff (2010) investigate alignment of an ERP system within a single organization. Ravishankar et al. (2011) study alignment cultures of introducing a novel knowledge management system in three business units of a case company.

In contrast to this, a multiple-case design follows replication logic, in which each case is comparable to a new experiment (Dibbern et al. 2008; Yin 2009). Cases have to be selected that they either predicts similar results (literal replication logic) or that they predicts contrasting findings for anticipated reasons (theoretical replication logic) (Yin 2009). In a consequence, theory development rather follows a cross-case comparison than a single-case investigation in theory development

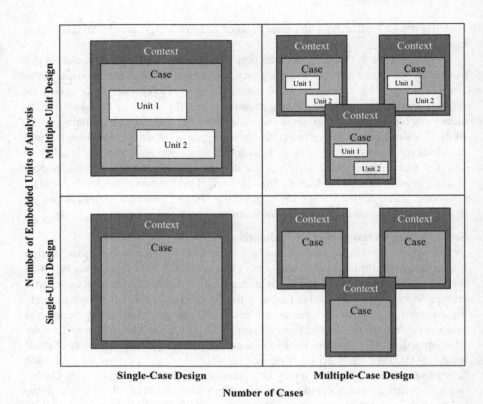

Fig. 8.4 Case study focus in qualitative research based on Yin (2009)

(Dibbern et al. 2008; Guillemette and Paré 2012). This is particularly true for a qualitative field study (Guillemette and Paré 2012).

The presented study follows a multiple-case design. Eight empirical profiles are selected to discuss single-case evidence in Chap. 6. Thereby, the discussion of these findings follows replication logic. Unique cases were not discussed in greater detail following the guidelines of a qualitative field study design (Guillemette and Paré 2012). However, it can not be precluded that very few empirical profiles may conflict with the developed research mode (e.g. Fig. 7.1). Future research should take the challenge to investigate such cases in greater detail by the means of a single-case analysis. One potential explanation of conflicting findings is discussed in the next paragraph.

The role of relational characteristics in the dynamic alignment process
Studying software-business process fit, this study includes contextual factors related to the software artefact—in terms of software customizability—and to the business process—in terms of business process adaptability. The role of relational characteristics between vendor and client was not explicitly investigated. However, distinctive distributions of power between client organizations were found within

the data set. For instance, ALPHA-INNOVATION, a huge life sciences company employing more than 80,000 people around the globe, was found to be a technology push non-gestalt. However, the company established dynamic fit as well as positive business process and sourcing performance. In contrast to other companies within the data set, ALPHA-INNOVATION's power in the relationship to their on-demand software vendor was high.

> I should mention that we are a premium customer of [the software vendor]. (...) If we experience any shortcomings with respect to the CRM system, I directly talk to a first tier executive of [the software vendor] in the US. CIO; ALPHA-INNOVATION

The same on-demand CRM system was sourced by ALPHA-SERVICE. ALPHA-SERVICE was a sanitary service provider employing more than 3000 people throughout Europe. The company was not satisfied with the technology push of its CRM system, which resulted in dynamic misfit. The CIO reported that he has limited influence on the development of the standard.

> In view of the flexibility of our provider with respect to change requests, I can only say: There is considerable potential for improvement. (...) On a global scale, we are just one client. Sometimes we have the feeling that [the software vendor] has other priorities with respect to software development. The US market mainly drives these priorities. (...) There is a good exchange between provider's management staff in Germany and ourselves. However, I often get the impression that it is difficult for them [German management staff of provider] to enforce change requests of their European clients within their organization. CIO; ALPHA-SERVICE

Future research may analyse the influence of power distribution as additional contextual factor within the dynamic alignment process. It can be proposed that the greater client's relational power, the greater the likelihood that technology push innovation will be beneficial for a company. Pioneer innovator and ambidextrous innovator gestalts can be extended if future research support this finding.

Chapter 9
Conclusion

"Information technology and business are becoming inextricably interwoven. I don't think anybody can talk meaningfully about one without the talking about the other." (Gates 1999: 6). In a consequence, enterprise systems can be both, vulture and value for organizations depending on how their evolution is managed and executed in a post-implementation phase. Performance of process-centric software is highly discussed but has remained little understood. Despite the fact that large and small companies around the globe increasingly depend on sophisticated and reliable enterprise resource planning or customer relationship management systems, the process of how such systems generate value for organizations remained a "black box".

This study aims at opening this "black box" and at increasing our understanding of what software sourcing value is, how dynamic software alignment impacts performance on a process-level, and how software sourcing modes impact value generation in a post-implementation phase. Drawing upon an extended literature review combined with reference theories, a preliminary research model was developed. This research model combines process and variance logic in order to study software-business process fit taking a dynamic perspective. The preliminary research model was extended and refined based on a qualitative field study within 40 case companies.

In this study, software value is understood as a mediated process. Drawing upon the representational view of information technology, software-business process fit was identified as an intermediate outcome, which is directly linked to an enterprise system. Findings indicate that this intermediate outcome impacts the dependent performance concepts under study. These concepts differentiate between business process performance and sourcing performance. It was found that software-business process fit results in positive outcomes for those business processes that were directly supported by a particular software artefact as well as in higher levels of strategic, economic, and technological benefits related to a corporate's information technology function.

© Springer International Publishing Switzerland 2016
M. Nöhren, *Enterprise Software Sourcing Performance*, Progress in IS,
DOI 10.1007/978-3-319-23926-2_9

Large scale process-centric enterprise systems are typically implemented and used over long periods of time. In the light of changing macro and micro environmental conditions that result in shifting structures of corporate's business processes, software-business process fit must be understood as a non-deterministic and vigorous process. In order to capture the continuous coevolution between software and business process structures, the concept of dynamic fit was introduced. This dynamic fit extends the static view of structural software alignment in previous research by expressing the constant coevolution between software and organization.

In recent years, the corporate software ecosystem has been subject to tremendous changes. Cloud computing is on the rise. In Germany, every fourth IT executive has already done significant investments in cloud services (CIO 2014). Vendors are increasingly offering enterprise systems in an "as-a-service"-setting. Market leader SAP expects that on-demand services will account for 10 % of their target turnover in 2015 (Bayer 2014). For most of their applications, client companies can now choose between developing software in-house (make) or sourcing packaged systems in an on-premises (buy) or an on-demand (lease) mode. However, no attempt has been made so far to explicitly compare these three sourcing arrangements with each other in terms of alignment and performance. The presented study makes a contribution to fill this research gap. Drawing upon the representational view of information technology, a novel understanding of software sourcing modes from a degree of software structure ownership is developed and applied.

All three modes of software sourcing can be beneficial as well as harmful for companies. It was found that in-house, on-premises, and on-demand sourcing impact the dynamic alignment process of enterprise software in a post-implementation phase. Four superior alignment clusters linked to in-house, on-premises, and on-demand software were identified. These alignment clusters impact the intermediate value in terms of dynamic fit.

To the best of the author's knowledge, this study is the first that opens the software sourcing value "black box" by explaining how dynamic fit impacts performance outcomes and how software sourcing modes are related to value generation in a post-implementation phase. Thereby, this study shows researchers and business experts *the impact logic of on-demand, on-premises, and in-house software on dynamic fit and process-level performance outcomes in client organizations*.

Appendix A: Literature Search Strategy

Table A.1 Keywords on software sourcing outcomes

Keyword 1: Software artefact	Keyword 2: Value
Application	Asset
Software	Benefit
Enterprise System	Competitive Advantage
Enterprise Systems	Effectiveness
Cloud	Efficiency
Software-as-a-Service	Impact
On-Demand	Outcome
Off the Shelf	Payoff
Shrink Wrap	Performance
On-Premises	Productivity
Customized	Quality
Custom-build	Success
In-house	Value

The first step of the conducted literature review was a keyword search (Kitchenham et al. 2009; Webster and Watson 2002). Keywords related to the software artefact were combined with keywords related to its value (Webster and Watson 2002). Table 7.17 gives the list of keywords. Consequently, 169 keyword combinations were searched in 14 journals and conference proceedings (see Table 7.18).

© Springer International Publishing Switzerland 2016
M. Nöhren, *Enterprise Software Sourcing Performance*, Progress in IS,
DOI 10.1007/978-3-319-23926-2

Table A.2 List of top IS journals and conferences

IS journals	IS conferences
European Journal of Information Systems	International Conference on Information Systems (ICIS)
Information Systems Journal	European Conference on Information Systems (ECIS)
Information Systems Research	Americas Conference on Information Systems (AMCIS)
Journal of Association for Information Systems	Pacific Asia Conference on Information Systems (PACIS)
Journal of Information Technology	Hawaii International Conference on Information Systems (HICSS)
Journal of Management Information Systems	
Journal of Strategic Information Systems	
MIS Quarterly	
Business & Information Systems Engineering	

Appendix B: Exemplified Items Related to the Dependent Constructs

Sourcing performance is based on a definition provided by Lacity and Willcocks (2001), which was later transferred applied in quantitative performance measurement (e.g. Goo et al. 2008; Grover et al. 1996; Lee et al. 2004; Saunders et al. 1997). A list of exemplified items related to this construct is given in Table 7.19. Business process performance is based on a lists of key performance indicators identified by Grant (2003) as well as Shang and Seddon (2002). A list of indicators related to business process level outcomes is provided in Table 7.20.

Table B.1 Exemplified items related to sourcing performance

Construct	Items	Source
Strategic benefits	Redirecting IT into core competencies Freed-up capacities Enhanced IT function's competence	Based on e.g. Grover et al. (1996), Lacity and Willcocks (2001), Lee et al. (2004), Saunders et al. (1997)
Economic benefits	Enhanced economies of scale in human resources and technological resources Increased control of IT expenses	
Technological benefits	Reduced risk of technological obsolescence Access to key information technologies New technological agenda	

Table B.2 Exemplified items related to business process performance

Construct	Items	Source
Business process performance	Create a platform for business process re-engineering Support the introduction of best practices in business processes Improve communication and coordination between and across business units Support the rationalization ('right sizing') of organizational infrastructures Cost reduction Cycle time reduction Productivity improvement Quality improvement Customer service improvement Better resource management Improved decision making and planning Performance improvement	Based on Grant (2003), Shang and Seddon (2002)

Appendix C: Properties of Qualitative Study Based on Dubé and Paré (2003)

Table C.1 Properties of research design

Attributes of research design	
Clear research question	Provided in Chap. 1
A priori definition of constructs	All constructs were defined *a priori*
Clear theoretical slate	Provided in Chap. 2
Theory of interest	Primarily representational view of IT and institutional theory on software sourcing modes, software-business process fit and software sourcing value. Resource-based view of the firm and transaction cost economics inform on the dynamic alignment process
Rival theories	Impact of software sourcing modes was developed inductively. Drawing upon previous literature, rival explanations of software sourcing's impact on value are discussed in Chap. 3
Multiple-case design	An exploratory field study of 44 applications within 40 case companies was conducted
Replication logic	Theoretical and literal replication logic
Unit of analysis	Unit of analysis is the IT function in terms of outsourcing on a system level
Pilot case	Not relevant for field studies based on Guillemette and Paré (2012)
Team-based research	Different people involved in research design

Table C.2 Properties of research context

Attributes of research context	
Detailed side description	Descriptive data on field study companies is provided in Chap. 5. Findings from single-case analysis are presented in Chap. 6. Eight empirical profiles are discussed in-depth. Due to page limitations, a detailed single-case description for each of the 44 empirical profiles is not presented in this study
Case period	Data had been collected over a period of 28 months
Longitudinal design	No

(continued)

© Springer International Publishing Switzerland 2016
M. Nöhren, *Enterprise Software Sourcing Performance*, Progress in IS,
DOI 10.1007/978-3-319-23926-2

Table C.2 (continued)

Attributes of research context	
Time spend onsite by the researchers	Some interviews had been conducted onsite, others via telephone meetings, depending on interviewees' preferences
Nature of data collection	Retroperspective and ongoing

Table C.3 Properties of data collection process

Attributes of data collection process	
Multiple data collection methods	Primarily based on expert interviews and secondary material, whenever available
Qualitative and quantitative data	Qualitative data only
Case study protocol	Yes
Case study database	Yes, using software package NVivo, Microsoft Excel, and Microsoft Access

Table C.4 Properties of data collection methods

Attributes of data collection methods	
Interviews	Yes
Documentations	When available
Observation	No
Questionnaires	Yes, in terms of interview guidelines (see Appendix D)
Artefacts	No
Time series	No
Sampling strategy	Described in Chap. 4.

Table C.5 Properties of data analysis process

Attributes of data analysis process	
Field notes	Yes
Coding	Yes
Visual data displays	Yes
Flexible and opportunistic process	Yes
Logical chain of evidence	Yes
Empirical testing	Qualitative reasoning plus test for significance among the proposed relationships (see Chap. 7)
Explanation building	Yes
Time series analysis	No
Searching for cross-case patterns	Yes
Use of natural controls	No
Quotes (evidence)	Yes
Project reviews	No
Comparison with extend literature	Yes

Appendix D: High-Level Interview Guideline

- Information on field study participant

  - Information on field study company (business area, size, revenues, etc.)
  - Information on interviewee (role, responsibilities, background, etc.)

- Market and competitive environment

  - Please describe your market environment! Please describe your competitive environment! Please describe your internal environment!
  - How often do you have to adapt to changing external/internal conditions? What are changes you (constantly) have to adapt to? How do these changes impact your organization? How do these changes impact your IT? How do these changes impact your enterprise software?

- Software sourcing

  - How is the software sourced? Hosting? Responsibilities?
  - Please describe the implementation process in detail! Implementation time? Duration? Software adaptation? Process adaptation? Responsibilities?
  - Please describe adaptability of software/processes!
  - Please describe internal deployment of software! Scope of usage? Supported processes?
  - Please describe the legacy system!

- Software fit

  - Please describe advantages/disadvantages of software!
  - How does the software fits with corporate processes? How does the software fits with requirements of the firm?
  - Please describe software fit! Functionalities? Data? Usability? Role? Control? Organizational culture? Which features are missing?

© Springer International Publishing Switzerland 2016
M. Nöhren, *Enterprise Software Sourcing Performance*, Progress in IS,
DOI 10.1007/978-3-319-23926-2

- Software dynamic

  - Please describe software change since its implementation! (frequency, magnitude, direction, timing)
  - How is software changed? (Client-driven? Vendor-driven?)
  - Do you need frequent software changes to cope with internal/external contingencies?
  - Does software change fits with corporate requirements?

- Outcomes

  - Please describe the relevance of the software for your company!
  - Please describe key performance indicators for software!
  - Please describe your satisfaction with software/software change!
  - Please describe the contribution of the investigated software to business process performance! (Efficiency? Effectiveness?)
  - Please describe economic/technological/strategic advantages of software!

Appendix E: List of Exemplified Evidence Based on Dibbern et al. (2008)

The specification of constructs under study is illustrated in this appendix. The tables below provide exemplified evidence on each constructs value.

Table E.1 Exemplified evidence on business process performance

Specification	Evidence
Positive	"[The ERP system] supports the efficiency and effectiveness of our processes. Efficiency is always influenced by software. In our case, the influence is very strong. There are two key aspects when talking about efficiency: First, the agent who works with this software. How efficiently can he or she navigate through the software and how fast does he or she gets the information he or she needs. How intuitive is the software? How many steps does he or she needs to do a certain task. A second point of efficiency is: How much—we call it bad processing—can the software prevent? How good are the plausibility checks, etc. (...) That is what we get from the software. So that is why this software is essential for us." Key User; ALPHA-FINANCE
	"Bottom line is: Less people are needed to execute the same processes." IT Manager; ALPHA-FINANCE
	"The important thing is that the employees are happy and productive. And this seems to be the case. The users confirm it. Whether productivity actually increased is—of course—an entirely different question. But to feel productive is very positive. Employees feel relieved so processes run better." CIO; ALPHA-INNOVATION
Neutral	"Both cases. Efficiency increased in those areas where the old system had its shortcomings. Of course, we work much more efficiently in these areas now (...) But when it comes to very simple processes the former system was much more efficient than [the ERP system]. People did their work much faster with the old system." CIO; DELTA-FINANCE
	"On the one hand, [the ERP system] supports our core processes quite good. It helps us in terms of effectiveness and 'doing the things right'. We have to follow a certain procedure in a particular order. And thereby, the system makes sure that we are not forgetting anything. However, whether this is always efficient or not remains questionable. Like I said, the system is not really flexible and it lacks a lot of features that would be helpful in executing our processes. As a

(continued)

© Springer International Publishing Switzerland 2016
M. Nöhren, *Enterprise Software Sourcing Performance*, Progress in IS,
DOI 10.1007/978-3-319-23926-2

Table E.1 (continued)

Specification	Evidence
	consequence, we often need workarounds and this is neither efficient nor effective." Key-User, ZETA-MANUFACTURING
Negative	"We were not able to reduce staff costs. The reason for that is the system itself. It is too slow. (...) We need workarounds in many areas, which is very time consuming and especially it is inefficient." CEO; GAMMA-SERVICE

Table E.2 Exemplified evidence on strategic sourcing performance

Specification	Evidence
Positive	"It [the CRM system] is way more flexible and it is easy to adapt if things change. The software is in the cloud, so we do not have to maintain it. It is quite easy to adapt. The users can do this on their owns. It is like a Bloomberg Terminal: You do not have it own your computer. You simply log in and you can change things quite easy." CIO; ALPHA-INNOVATION
	"The university grew significantly within the last two years. It would had been very difficult for us [IT department] to keep up with this growth without having this system." CIO; ALPHA-UNIVERSITY
Negative	"A great weakness of our system is that it is not as parameterizable and modular as we want to have it. This in turns leads to the typical consequences: Small changes often require a reprogramming at multiple areas. There is no opportunity to make a change somewhere in the system and roll it out through the entire application. That is a great weakness of our system. The interfaces are custom build and our satellite systems linked to it are also not standardized. So it is always a huge effort for us [IT department]. (...) We implemented a lot of user requests within the system. The more requests you implement and the bigger the system gets, the more challenging it becomes to make even small changes to it. (...) From an IT perspective, we are not really satisfied with the system." CIO; GAMMA-FINANCE
Negative	"We invest a lot of time and effort in software customization. External consultants frequently support us. (...) An example: One of the most complex things within a firm is time management. An employee may work a maximum of ten hours a day. How do we capture this time within the system? How do we control that nobody exceeds his or her ten hours maximum? What happens to the overtime? How is overtime cut back?" Key User; ZETA-MANUFACTURING

Table E.3 Exemplified evidence on economic sourcing performance

Specification	Evidence
Positive	"We have outsourced the ERP system. Therefore, no one needs to take care of hardware and other technical things anymore, which used to be extremely expensive in the past. I almost fell off the chair when I heard what we paid for it. With the on-demand system, we are paying 133 Euros per month per user now. All updates are already included in this fee. I do not need any servers. I do not need to install any updates. I do not need to make data backups. See, even if you only need one employee for all of these things, it costs a lot of money. You also need special rooms with special air conditioning systems for hardware. This is also very expensive. Electricity is expensive. (...) One employee costs at least between 40,000 and 50,000 Euros." CEO; BETA-SERVICE

(continued)

Table E.3 (continued)

Specification	Evidence
Positive	"From an economic point of view, we are highly satisfied with the system. We have been using this system for more than ten years now. We made several large adaptations to it without having any costs for external programmers and without having high development costs. This is just great." CIO, BETA-FINANCE
Neutral	"We were able to shout down several of our IT systems. Thus we have reduced costs. However, we did not do a calculation how this looks in five years. So, at first yes, but now we have to take into account how costs develop over time. So, I am not suggesting that [our CRM system] is a cost reduction program per se. I would say that the costs are about the same as before." CIO; ALPHA-SERVICE
Negative	"A lot of additional costs came up. We waste a lot of money. (...) The implementation cost a lot of money and time. We saved money in the area of hardware, but other costs increased significantly. To sum up, costs did not decrease. They just moved to other areas. (...) Several additional cost came up." CEO; GAMMA-SERVICE
	"I assume that there are lower cost alternatives available; especially when it comes to maintenance and operating costs. One key reason for that is that packaged software provides some inherent standards that we have to develop ourselves. For instance, if there is a legislative amendment, we have to invest in reprogramming of our in-house system." CIO; GAMMA-FINANCE

Table E.4 Exemplified evidence on technological sourcing performance

Specification	Evidence
Positive	"Each of our [software update] activities is on improving things. It is always about being faster (...) or including new technologies. (...) Recently, we implemented [a new database system] provided by [the software vendor]. That is—of course—just a middleware but it was a quantum leap for us. It improved our IT flexibility significantly." CIO, DELTA-MANUFACTURNG
	"The advantage is: The software is always developed proactively by the vendor. So we do not have to worry about it." Key-User, ALPHA-FINANCE
Neutral	"Whether we have a technological advantage or not remains questionable. On the one hand, we strongly combined our business processes with each other. Fact is: If I have such integrated business processes, it becomes significantly more difficult to innovate in one particular area without impacting all other areas. (...) Therefore, a highly integrated ERP system—like ours—makes it difficult to stay innovative from a technological point of view." IT Manager; ALPHA-TRANSPORTATION
Negative	"[The software vendor] focuses on hot topics and trend themes. In a consequence, the ERP system started a journey towards an increasing standardization with decreasing opportunities for us." IT Manager, ZETA- MANUFACTURING
	"Recently, [the software vendor] announced that he stopped development of their [on-demand ERP system]. (...) It would have been great if we would get a HTML 5.0 surface or something else that would make the software run faster and thereby increase its performance. This will not be the case within the next years. (...) It is sad. We really backed the wrong horse." CEO, ETA-SERVICE

Table E.5 Exemplified evidence on dynamic fit

Specification	Evidence
Fit	"The releases [provided by the vendor] are necessary to ensure our ability to act in conformance with the law. (. . .) We get those releases on the first of January and the first of July each year because—in general—these are the dates when new laws for health insurance companies come into force." IT Manager, ALPHA-FINANCE
	"So, every regulatory change, finds a complete echo within the system. From a system's side, changing competition and the regulatory environment influence us intensively. (. . .) Timeliness is the most important thing for us. So, these changes often occur very short-dated. Due to the fact that all of these changes impact our funding concepts, it has to be implemented within a few days. As you have already heard, it is simply not acceptable that we cannot get a fund on the market on time due to technical reasons. That is an absolute 'no go'" CIO, BETA-FINANCE
Misfit	"Business often complains about missing features. They would like to get new features projects-driven. That is how it was used to be in the past: There was a project and we [IT department] directly implemented the required features within the system." CIO, DELTA-MANUFACTURNG
	"It is getting problematic, each time, we require a certain software change. This is nothing we can do right away because we have to send change requests to the software vendor. Then, it takes some time and we get a service offering. Typically, these adaptations are very costly. A simple interface costs between 20,000 and 30,000 Euros, which is a lot of money for a company of our size. (. . .) In most cases we decide not to make these adaptations." CIO, BETA-ASSOCIATION

Table E.6 Exemplified evidence on business process structure change

Specification	Evidence
Yes	"We are highly dynamic. (. . .) We do not have annual goals or something like that. Our goals change quarterly. We constantly bring new innovations on the way and we have to adapt our processes to it. When we launch a new product, we do know nothing about its value. We can hardly forecast such things. We have to verify its value on the market. (. . .) So if we experience that something changes on the market, we have to change as well. So we are highly dynamic." CEO, ETA-SERVICE
	"We have to adapt ourselves to changing requirements quite often. Such changes occur more frequently nowadays and it is even getting worse. (. . .) It is getting more complex. Often, when an automotive company demands for a particular adaptation to our [ERP system], our business units have to work differently because they have to provide other data or something like that." CIO, BETA-MANUFACTURING
No	"We do not have to adapt to any market changes." CIO, ALPHA-ASSOCIATION

Table E.7 Exemplified evidence on software structure change by technology push

Specification	Evidence
Yes	"We are running the latest version of [the ERP system]. We implement all those updates available on a regular basis." IT Manager, ZETA-MANUFACTURING "We implement smaller support packages every month. In addition, we have these huge 'Christmas Packages' with lots of adaptations adding legal changes. These adaptations have to be implemented right away and must be launched until the end of January." Key-User, ZETA-MANUFACTURING
	"[The provider] is responsible for all updates. It is standard software. (...) We get new releases two times a year with new features and functionalities. (...) Those updates are very extensive ones. (...)" IT Manager, ALPHA-FINANCE
No	"Of course there is this entirely new version of the system available on the market, but we are not going to implement it; at least not before 2015. That would then be the first major disruption of the package. In fact, it would be like implementing a whole new system. You can certainly take over some of the things we have, but it would be the first upgrade in eleven or twelve years." CIO, BETA-FINANCE
	"We often decide not to implement release changes provided by [the software vendor] (...) There is an entirely new version of the ERP system available, but we are not going to implement it. (...) Our last software update was in 2009." CIO, BETA-ASSOCIATION

Table E.8 Exemplified evidence on software structure change by business pull

Specification	Evidence
Yes	"I have more than 180 employees in my department who's key responsibility is to constantly adapt the system to our business needs." CIO, DELTA-MANUFACTURNG
	"We conduct all adjustment of the CRM-system ourselves. That is the most important thing for us (...) You simply have to know the system well." CIO, BETA-FINANCE
No	"We do not adapt the software. (...) Sometimes, we change a mask or adjust a parameter, but this is not a really customization. It is rather on a 'secretary level' of software adaptation." CEO, ETA-SERVICE
	"It is standard software. We do not adapt it." IT Manager, ALPHA-FINANCE

Table E.9 Exemplified evidence on environmental change

Specification	Evidence
Macro environmental change	"Health insurance companies depend on the legislator and there are several changes per year. Of course the extend of these changes varies from year to year. Typically we see two regulatory changes within a one years time frame. Take SEPA as an example. (...) Health insurance is a financial service, so SEPA impacts our cash flows. We need SEPA functionalities within the system and we need to provide information on our customers bank accounts." IT Manager, ALPHA-FINANCE
	"Legislation and regulation continue to change. Especially in the area of human resources, constant changing legal requirements—take SEPA as an example; take ELENA as an example—impose a permanent need to transform our processes." Key-User, ZETA-MANUFACTURING

(continued)

Table E.9 (continued)

Specification	Evidence
Micro environmental change	"Our market segment is quite challenging. We are a supplier within the automotive industry. Automotive companies are very huge organizations. (...) Automotive companies have very high and complex requirements with respect to quality, documentation, and several other things. (...) Nowadays, we do not only deliver products, we also deliver information to Daimler, BMW, and all the other companies. (...) We have to keep pace with changing electronic data transfer requirements of the automotive companies. In recent years, this is getting more and more challenging. For instance, in 1988, Daimler asked whether we could deliver some information electronically. Back in the days, electronic data transfer was a foreign word for us, so we told them: 'Yes, we take care of it and we will get back to you in one and a half years.' Today, they say we need this or that change and you have fourteen days to get your system ready." CIO, BETA-MANUFACTURING
	"We grow at an annual rate of approximately 50 % to 80 % each year. (...) I would say that our goals change frequently and that is why we have to react to changing situations quite often. (...) Every time we see a change on the market we have to react to it by changing our goals. We launch a new product and we acquire new customers in new industries. (...) We compete with large international companies, so we constantly have to keep pace with market changes and technological revolutions." CEO, ETA-SERVICE
Stable environment	"We are in a very stable and static market. (...) We do not have any competitors in our domestic market." CIO, ALPHA-ASSOCIATION
	"We are market leader in this segment. There are only few competitors, which is quite comfortable for us." IOTA-MANUFACTURING

Table E.10 Exemplified evidence on software customizability

Specification	Evidence
High	"This is why we have decided in favour of this system. It is completely parameterizable without traditional programming or development activities. That means that I can control workflows, extensions, and the entire business logic of it with a simple parameterizing tool. This is manageable with simple technical IT know-how. (...) That—ultimately—is the crucial strength of our CRM-system." CIO, BETA-FINANCE
	"On the one hand, it is a standardized system that represents some of our process requirements. On the other hand—and this is the important thing—it is also kind of a developer platform that provides clients with the opportunity to integrate your on processes." CIO, ALPHA-SERVICE
Medium	"The enhancement concept of [the ERP system] is quite good. We have several opportunities to adapt and modify the system. (...) We use these opportunities quite a lot. We have several add-ons and we do a lot of additional programming to the system." IT Manager, ZETA-MANUFACTURING
	"Last year, we learned that we had too little knowledge to make all those modifications to [the ERP system] that we would require. So we hired an additional [ERP system] programmer, who had several years of experience with the software. Since then, we have been able to make lots of adaptations on our own." CIO, BETA-MANUFACTURING

(continued)

Table E.10 (continued)

Specification	Evidence
Low	"They [software vendor] has a development department and also a very professional services department that make all those customer-specific adjustments. We do not perform programming tasks by ourselves. There is nobody here within our firm, who could change the source code. We do not do such things. We do not even have the source code. So, we cannot not change the system, not even if I wanted to." CIO, ETA-MANUFACTURING
	"We cannot adapt the system. All modifications and all updates must be executed by the software vendor." BETA-ASSOCIATION

Table E.11 Exemplified evidence on business process adaptability

Specification	Evidence
High	"Our philosophy is to stick as close as possible to the standard. We rather adapt ourselves than [the ERP system]. (...) We use a lot of the standard functionalities. (...)" CIO, BETA-MANUFACTURING
	"With (the packaged software), we are highly restricted to what the software offers (...) When software change takes place, we get the opportunity to reassess our processes. (...) Frequently, this leads to process adaptations." Key-User, ALPHA-FINANCE
	"Software drives our processes more than our processes drive software. (...) Our standard software offers certain processes and it is in our interest to adapt to these processes." IT Manager, ALPHA-FINANCE
Medium	"That is always this balancing act between being system-oriented and being process-oriented. If a company is system-oriented, then I [CIO] can say: 'Dear colleague, this is [software] standard. You have to push these five keys now, whether you like it or not'. That is good for us [IT department] but it is not always beneficial for the business units. If we insist on such a system-orientation, we cannot model it in another way in the system and people have to adapt to it. In contrast to this, if my company is process-oriented, I frequently got told by the business units that 'This is completely crap. I now need three, four, five, or even ten more minutes for handling my processes. It would help me, if I could do these or those things first.', then I have to customize it for each user individually. So it is always a matter of negotiation between us [IT department] and the business units." CIO, ETA-MANUFACTURING
Medium	"We use a lot of the standard functionalities offered by [the application]. However, we have a very idiosyncratic business. Therefore, we work with system integrator that constantly implements new add-ons. (...) Our system integrator needed one month to build the first template and to link the CRM system with our SAP ERP system. (...) In phase 2, we focused on customer service (...) we build an own add-on for our customer service centre for managing more than 60,000 customer requests per month. (...). Phase 3 and phase 4 are about to start." CIO; ALPHA-SERVICE
Low	"There is the software and there is the process. Software offers a basic structure. In general, this structure is valuable to ensure integrity and regulatory compliance. (...) On the other hand, if the software processes conflict with how we do processes, it hampers our flexibility and we have to work around the system." Key-User, ZETA-MANUFACTURING

(continued)

Table E.11   (continued)

Specification	Evidence
	"We adapt the software towards our processes. For instance, we have enhanced our CRM system quite a lot. Beside the classical business partner management and business partner administration including such things as contact management or customer segmentation, we added some own functionality. Nice examples are contract agreements and investor services. All of this is captured within the CRM system. (...) Also, we included our own business logic within such things as contingent management by adding guarantee acceptance, swellings, reservations, etc. (...) We implemented these things within our CRM system as distinct modules. Another big field that we have included is contract administration. (...)" CIO, BETA-FINANCE

Appendix F: Chi-Square Distribution Table

Table F.1 Chi-square distribution

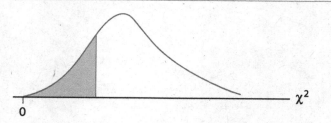

df	Probability level $1-\alpha$			
	90 %	95 %	99 %	99.9 %
1	2.70554	3.84146	6.63490	10.828
2	4.60517	5.99147	9.21034	13.816

Source: Bortz and Schuster (2010: 588–589)

© Springer International Publishing Switzerland 2016
M. Nöhren, *Enterprise Software Sourcing Performance*, Progress in IS,
DOI 10.1007/978-3-319-23926-2

Appendix G: 2 × 3 × 2 Three-Way Contingency Tables for Propositions 6a and 6b

Table G.1 2 × 3 × 2 contingency table on proposition 6a

Control of software structure change			Dynamic Fit		
			Fit	Misfit	Total
External control	Economic sourcing performance	Positive	8	2	10
		Negative	0	1	1
	Total		8	3	11
Shared and internal control	Economic sourcing performance	Positive	5	1	6
		Neutral	1	1	2
		Negative	12	13	25
	Total		18	15	33
Total	Economic sourcing performance	Positive	13	3	16
		Neutral	1	1	2
		Negative	12	14	26
	Total		26	18	44

Table G.2 Test statistics for partial tables of proposition 6a

Control of software structure change		Value	df	Exact Sig. (2-sided)
External control	Chi-square	2.933[a]	1	
	Fisher's exact test			.273
	No. of valid cases	11		
Shared and internal control	Chi-square	2.454[b]	2	
	No. of valid cases	33		
Total	Chi-square	5.119[c]	2	
	No. of valid cases	44		

[a]2 cells (33.3 %) have expected count less than 5. The minimum expected count is .82
[b]4 cells (66.7 %) have expected count less than 5. The minimum expected count is .91
[c]3 cells (75.0 %) have expected count less than 5. The minimum expected count is .27

© Springer International Publishing Switzerland 2016
M. Nöhren, *Enterprise Software Sourcing Performance*, Progress in IS,
DOI 10.1007/978-3-319-23926-2

Table G.3 2 × 3 × 2 contingency table on proposition 6b

| Control of software structure change | | | Dynamic fit | | - |
			Fit	Misfit	Total
Shared control	Technological sourcing performance	Positive	8	5	13
		Neutral	0	1	1
		Negative	0	5	5
	Total		8	11	19
External and internal control	Technological sourcing performance	Positive	13	4	17
		Neutral	1	0	1
		Negative	4	3	7
	Total		18	7	25
Total	Technological sourcing performance	Positive	21	9	30
		Neutral	1	1	2
		Negative	4	8	12
	Total		26	18	44

Table G.4 Test statistics for partial tables of proposition 6b

Control of software structure change		Value	df	Exact sig. (2-sided)
External control	Chi-square	6.378^a	1	
	No. of valid cases	11		
Shared and internal control	Chi-square	1.324^b	2	
	No. of valid cases	33		
Total	Chi-square	4.839^c	2	
	No. of valid cases	44		

[a] 4 cells (66.7 %) have expected count less than 5. The minimum expected count is .42
[b] 4 cells (66.7 %) have expected count less than 5. The minimum expected count is .28
[c] 3 cells (50.0 %) have expected count less than 5. The minimum expected count is .82

References

Abokhodair, N., Taylor, H., Mowery, S. J., & Hasegawa, J. (2012). 'Heading for the clouds?' Implications for cloud computing adopters. In *Americas Conference on Information Systems (AMCIS)*.

Adomavicius, G., Bockstedt, J. C., Gupta, A., & Kauffmann, R. J. (2008). Making sense of technology trends in the information technology landscape: A design science approach. *MIS Quarterly, 32*(4), 779–809.

Agarwal, M., Kishore, R., & Rao, H. R. (2006). Market reactions to E-business outsourcing announcements: An event study. *Information & Management, 43*(7), 861–873.

Agarwal, R., & Sambamurthy, V. (2002). Principles and models for organizing the IT function. *MIS Quarterly Executive, 1*(1), 158–162.

Aier, S., & Winter, R. (2009). Virtual decoupling for IT/business alignment—Conceptual foundations, architecture design and implementation example. *Business & Information Systems Engineering, 1*(2), 150–163.

Alpar, P., Porembski, M., & Pickerodt, S. (2001). Measuring the efficiency of web site traffic generation. *International Journal of Electronic Commerce, 6*(1), 53–74.

Andersen, E. B. (1997). *Introduction to the statistical analysis of categorical data.* Berlin: Springer.

Anderson, J. C., & Narus, J. A. (1984). A model of the distributor's perspective of distributor-manufacturer working relationship. *The Journal of Marketing, 48*(4), 62–74.

Anderson, E., & Parker, G. G. (2002). The effect of learning on the make/buy decision. *Production and Operations Management, 11*(3), 313–339.

Ang, S., & Inkpen, A. C. (2008). Cultural intelligence and offshore outsourcing success: A framework of firm-level intercultural capability. *Decision Sciences, 39*(3), 337–358.

Apte, U. M., Sobol, M. G., Hanaoka, S., Shimada, T., Saarinen, T., Salmela, T., et al. (1997). IS outsourcing practices in the USA, Japan and Finland: A comparative study. *Journal of Information Technology, 12*(4), 289–304.

Au, N., Ngai, E. W. T., & Cheng, T. C. E. (2008). Extending the understanding of end user information systems satisfaction formation: An equitable needs fulfillment model approach. *MIS Quarterly, 32*(1), 43–66.

Azen, R., & Walker, C. M. (2011). *Categorical data analysis for the behavioral and social sciences.* New York: Routledge.

Bacharach, S. B. (1989). Organizational theories: Some criteria for evaluation. *Academy of Management Review, 14*(4), 496–515.

Bahli, B., & Rivard, S. (2003). The information technology outsourcing risk: A transaction cost and agency theory-based perspective. *Journal of Information Technology, 18*(3), 211–221.

Banker, R. D., Kauffman, R. J., & Morey, R. C. (1990). Measuring gains in operational efficiency from information technology: A study of the positran deployment at Hardee's Inc. *Journal of Management Information Systems, 7*(2), 29–54.

Banker, R. D., & Kemerer, C. F. (1992). Performance evaluation metrics for information systems development: A principal-agent model. *Information Systems Research, 3*(4), 379–400.

Barney, J. B. (1991). Firm resources and sustained competitive advantage. *Journal of Management, 17*(1), 99–120.

Barney, J. B., Ketchen, D. J., & Wright, M. (2011). The future of resource-based theory: Revitalization or decline? *Journal of Management, 37*(5), 1299–1315.

Baron, R. M., & Kenny, D. A. (1986). The moderator-mediator variable distinction in social psychological research: Conceptual, strategic and statistical considerations. *Journal of Personality and Social Psychology, 51*, 1173–1182.

Bartels, A., Mines, C., & Muteba, C. (2010). US and global IT market outlook: Q2 2010. Forrester Research.

Barua, A., Kriebel, C. H., & Mukhopadhyay, T. (1995). Information technology and business value: An analytic and empirical investigation. *Communications of the ACM, 6*(1), 3–23.

Bayer, M. (2014). Bill McDermotts Botschaft an SAP Und Kunden: Alles Muss Einfacher Werden. *Computerwoche, 25*, 8–9.

Bélissent, J., Shey, H., Daley. E., & Reiss-Davis, Z. (2010). The state of global enterprise IT budgets: 2009 to 2010. Forrester Research.

Benbya, H., & McKelvey, B. (2006). Using coevolutionary and complexity theories to improve IS alignment: A multi-level approach. *Journal of Information Technology, 21*(4), 284–298.

Benlian, A., Hess, T., & Buxmann, P. (2009). Drivers of SaaS-adoption—An empirical study of different application types. *Business & Information Systems Engineering, 1*(5), 357–369.

Berente, N., & Yoo, Y. (2012). Institutional contradictions and loose coupling: Postimplementation of NASA's enterprise information system. *Information Systems Research, 23*(2), 376–396.

Bergeron, F., Raymond, L., & Rivard, S. (2001). Fit in strategic information technology management research: An empirical comparison of perspectives. *Omega, 29*(2), 125–142.

Bergeron, F., Raymond, L., & Rivard, S. (2004). Ideal patterns of strategic alignment and business performance. *Information & Management, 41*(8), 1003–1020.

Bernstein, D. (2015). *Psychology—Foundations and frontiers*. Boston: Wadsworth.

Berry, K. J., Johnston, J. E., & Mielke, P. W. (2011). Permutation methods. *Wiley Interdisciplinary Reviews: Computational Statistics, 3*(6), 527–542.

Bertschek, I., Niebel, T., Ohnemus, J., Rasel, F., Saam, M., Schulte, P., et al. (2014). *Produktivität IT-Basierter Dienstleistungen—Wie Kann Man Sie Messen Und Steuern?* Zentrum für Europäische Wirtschaftsforschung, Dokumentation Nummer 14-02, Mannheim.

Bharadwaj, A. S. (2000). A resource-based perspective on information technology capability and firm performance: An empirical investigation. *MIS Quarterly, 24*(4), 169–196.

Bharadwaj, A. S., Bharadwaj, S. G., & Konsynski, B. R. (1999). Information technology effects on firm performance as measured by Tobin's q. *Management Science, 45*(7), 1008–1024.

Blum, H. S. (2006). *Logistik-Contolling. Kontext, Ausgestaltung Und Erfolgswirkungen*. Wiesbaden: Deutscher Universitätsverlag.

Bolton, R. N. (1998). A dynamic model of the duration of the customer's relationship with a continuous service provider: The role of satisfaction. *Marketing Science, 17*(1), 45–65.

Borman, M. (2006). Applying multiple perspectives to the BPO decision: A case study of call centres in Australia. *Journal of Information Technology, 21*(2), 99–115.

Bortz, J., & Schuster, C. (2010). *Statistik Für Human- Und Sozialwissenschaftler* (7th ed.). Berlin: Springer.

Boyd, B. K., Takacs Haynes, K., Hitt, M. A., Bergh, D. D., & Ketchen, D. J. (2012). Contingency hypotheses in strategic management research: Use, disuse, or misuse? *Journal of Management, 38*(1), 278–313.

Brown, C. V., & Magill, S. L. (1994). Alignment of the IS functions with the enterprise: Toward a model of antecedents. *MIS Quarterly, 18*(4), 371–403.

Brynjolfsson, E. (1993). The productivity paradox of information technology. *Communications of the ACM, 36*(12), 67–77.

Brynjolfsson, E., & Hitt, L. M. (1998). Beyond the productivity paradox. *Communications of the ACM, 41*(8), 49–55.

Brynjolfsson, E., & Hitt, L. M. (2000). Beyond computation: Information technology, organizational transformation and business performance. *The Journal of Economic Perspectives, 14*(4), 23–48.

Bunge, M. (1993). Realism and antirealism in social science. *Theory and Decision, 35*(3), 207–235.

Burn, J. M. (1993). Information systems strategies and the management of organizational change—A strategic alignment model. *Journal of Information Technology, 8*(4), 205–216.

Byrd, A., Lewis, B. R., & Bryan, R. W. (2006). The leveraging influence of strategic alignment on IT investment: An empirical examination. *Information & Management, 43*(3), 308–321.

Camilli, G. (1995). The relationship between Fisher's exact test and Pearson's chi-square test: A Bayesian perspective. *Psychometrika, 60*(2), 305–312.

Cao, L. (2010). The misalignment between packaged enterprise systems and Chinese context: A context study of packaged ES adoption in China. In *Pacific Conference on Information Systems (PACIS)* (pp. 1596–1603).

Carmel, E., & Sawyer, S. (1998). Packaged software development teams: What makes them different? *Information Technology & People, 11*(1), 7–19.

Cha, H. S., Pingry, D. E., & Thatcher, M. E. (2009). A learning model of information technology outsourcing: Normative implications. *Journal of Management Information Systems, 26*(2), 147–176.

Chai, S., Das, S., & Rao, H. R. (2011). Factors affecting bloggers' knowledge sharing: An investigation across gender. *Journal of Management Information Systems, 28*(3), 309–342.

Chakraborty, S., Sarker, S., & Valacich, J. S. (2007). Understanding analyst effectiveness in requirements elicitation: A gestalt fit perspective. In *European Conference on Information Systems (ECIS)*.

Chalmers, A. (1999). *What is this thing called science?* (3rd ed.). Maidenhead: McGraw-Hill Education.

Chan, Y. E. (2000). IT value: The great divide between qualitative and quantitative and individual and organizational measures. *Journal of Management Information Systems, 16*(4), 225–261.

Chan, Y. E. (2002). Why haven't we mastered alignment? The importance of the informal organization structure. *MIS Quarterly Executive, 1*(2), 97–112.

Chan, Y. E., & Reich, B. H. (2007). IT alignment: What have we learned? *Journal of Information Technology, 22*(4), 297–315.

Chen, D. Q., Mocker, M., Preston, D. S., & Teubner, A. (2010). Information systems strategy: Reconceptualization, measurement, and implications. *MIS Quarterly, 34*(2), 233–259.

Chiasson, M. W., & Green, L. W. (2007). Questioning the IT artefact: User practices that can, could, and cannot be supported in packaged-software designs. *European Journal of Information Systems, 16*(5), 542–554.

Choe, J. (2003). The effect of environmental uncertainty and strategic applications of IS on a firm's performance. *Information & Management, 40*(4), 257–268.

Choudhary, V. (2007a). Comparison of software quality under perpetual licensing and software as a service. *Journal of Management Information Systems, 24*(2), 141–165.

Choudhary, V. (2007b). Software as a service: Implications for investment in software development. In *Hawaii International Conference on System Sciences (HICSS)*.

CIO. (2014). Cloud Im Kommen. *CIO—IT-Strategie für Manager, 14*(07–08).

Coase, R. H. (1937). The nature of the firm. *Economica, 4*(16), 386–405.

Cotteleer, M. J., & Bendoly, E. (2006). Order lead-time improvement following enterprise information technology implementation: An empirical study. *MIS Quarterly, 30*(3), 643–660.

Creswell, J. W. (2009). *Research design—Qualitative, quantitative, and mixed methods approaches* (3rd ed.). Thousand Oaks, CA: Sage.

Currie, W. L. (2004). The organizing vision of application service provision: A process-oriented analysis. *Information and Organization, 14*(4), 237–267.

Currie, W. L., Desai, B., & Khan, N. (2004). Customer evaluation of application services provisioning in five vertical sectors. *Journal of Information Technology, 19*(1), 39–58.

Currie, W. L., & Willcocks, L. P. (1998). Analyzing four types of IT sourcing decisions in the context of scale, client/supplier interdependency and risk mitigation. *Information Systems Journal, 8*(2), 119–143.

Davenport, T. H., & Short, J. E. (1990). The new industrial engineering: Information technology and business process redesign. *Sloan Management Review, 31*(4), 11–27.

Davern, M. J., & Kauffman, R. J. (2000). Discovering potential and realizing value from information technology investments. *Journal of Management Information Systems, 16*(4), 121–143.

Davis, G. B., Ein-Dor, P., King, W. R., & Torkzadeh, R. (2006). IT offshoring: History, prospects and challenges. *Journal of the Association for Information Systems, 7*(11), 770–95. Retrieved August 19, 2014, from http://aisel.aisnet.org/jais/vol7/iss1/32/.

Dehning, B., & Richardson, V. J. (2002). Returns on investments in information technology: A research synthesis. *Journal of Information Systems, 16*(1), 7–30.

DeLone, W. H., & McLean, E. R. (1992). Information systems success: The quest for the dependent variable. *Information Systems Research, 3*(1), 60–95.

DeLone, W. H., & McLean, E. R. (2003). The DeLone and McLean model of information systems success: A ten-year update. *Journal of Management Information Systems, 19*(4), 9–30.

Dibbern, J. (2004). *Sourcing of application software services: Empirical evidence of cultural, industry and functional differences.* Heidelberg: Physica Verlag.

Dibbern, J., Goles, T., Hirschheim, R., & Jayatilaka, B. (2004). Information systems outsourcing: A survey and analysis of the literature. *ACM SIGMIS Database, 35*(4), 6–102.

Dibbern, J., & Heinzl, A. (2009). Outsourcing of information systems functions in small and medium sized enterprises: A test of a multi-theoretical model. *Business & Information Systems Engineering, 1*(1), 101–110.

Dibbern, J., Winkler, J., & Heinzl, A. (2008). Explaining variations in client extra costs between software projects offshored to India. *MIS Quarterly, 32*(2), 333–366.

DiMaggio, P. J., & Powell, W. W. (1983). The iron cage revisited: Institutional isomorphism and collective rationality in organizational fields. *American Sociological Review, 48*(2), 147–160.

Dohmen, A., Leyer, M., & Patas, J. (2010). Towards a methodology to assess changes in IT business value in terms of business process performance. In *Americas Conference on Information Systems (AMCIS)*.

Domberger, S., Fernandez, P., & Fiebig, D. G. (2000). Modelling the price, performance and contract characteristics of IT outsourcing. *Journal of Information Technology, 15*(2), 107–118.

Downing, C. E., Field, M., & Ritzman, L. P. (2003). The value of outsourcing: A field study. *Information Systems Management, 20*(1), 86–92.

Du, J., Lu, Y., & Tao, Z. (2009). Bi-sourcing in the global economy. *Journal of International Economics, 77*(2), 215–222.

Dubé, L., & Paré, G. (2003). Rigor in information systems positivist case research: Current practices, trends, and recommendations. *MIS Quarterly, 27*(4), 597–635.

Eisenhardt, K. M. (1989). Building theories from case study research. *Academy of Management Review, 14*(4), 532–550.

Eisenhardt, K. M., & Graebner, M. E. (2007). Theory building from cases: Opportunities and challenges. *Academy of Management Journal, 50*(1), 25–32.

Elliott, A. C., & Woodward, W. A. (2007). *Statistical analysis quick reference guidebook: With SPSS examples.* Thousand Oaks, CA: Sage.

Ellis, V. D. (1938). *A source book of gestalt psychology.* New York: Harcourt, Brace & World.

Floyd, S. W., & Woolridge, B. (1990). Path analysis of the relationship between competitive strategy, information technology, and financial performance. *Journal of Management Information Systems, 7*(1), 47–64.

Forbes. (2013). *2013 ERP market share update: SAP solidifies market leadership*. Retrieved September 20, 2014, from http://www.forbes.com/sites/louiscolumbus/2013/05/12/2013-erp-market-share-update-sap-solidifies-market-leadership/.

Gates, B. (1999). *Business @ the speed of thought: Using a digital nervous system*. New York: Warner Books.

Gefen, D., Wyss, S., & Lichtenstein, Y. (2008). Business familiarities as risk mitigation in software development outsourcing contracts. *MIS Quarterly, 32*(3), 531–551.

Gemino, A., Reich, B. H., & Sauer, C. (2007). A temporal model of information technology project performance. *Journal of Management Information Systems, 24*(3), 9–44.

Gewald, H., & Gellrich, T. (2007). The impact of perceived risk on the capital market's reaction to outsourcing announcements. *Information Technology and Management, 8*(4), 279–296.

Gilley, K. M., Greer, C. R., & Rasheed, A. (2004). Human resource outsourcing and organizational performance in manufacturing firms. *Journal of Business Research, 57*(3), 232–240.

Goo, J., Huang, C. D., & Hart, P. (2008). A path to successful it outsourcing: Interaction between service-level agreements and commitment. *Decision Sciences, 39*(3), 469–506.

Goodhue, D. L., & Thompson, R. L. (1995). Task-technology fit and individual performance. *MIS Quarterly, 19*(2), 213–236.

Gopal, A., Mukhopadhyay, T., & Krishnan, M. S. (2002). The role of software processes and communication in offshore software development. *Communications of the ACM, 45*(4), 193.

Grant, R. M. (1991). The resource-based theory of competitive advantage: Implications for strategy formulation. *California Management Review, 33*(3), 114–135.

Grant, R. M. (1996). Toward a knowledge-based theory of the firm. *Strategic Management Journal, 17*(Winter Special Issue), 375–88.

Grant, G. G. (2003). Strategic alignment and enterprise systems implementation: The case of Metalco. *Journal of Information Technology, 18*(3), 159–175.

Gregor, S. (2006). The nature of theories in information systems. *MIS Quarterly, 30*(3), 611–642.

Grover, V., Cheon, M. J., & Teng, J. T. C. (1996). The effect of service quality and partnership on the outsourcing of information systems functions. *Journal of Management Information Systems, 12*(4), 89–116.

Guba, E. G., & Lincoln, Y. S. (1994). Competing paradigms in qualitative research. In N. K. Denzin & Y. S. Lincoln (Eds.), *Handbook of qualitative research* (pp. 105–117). Thousand Oaks, CA: Sage.

Guillemette, M. G., & Paré, G. (2012). Towards a new theory of the contribution of the IT function in organizations. *MIS Quarterly, 36*(2), 529–551.

Hahn, C., Repschläger, J., Erek, K., & Zarnekow, R. (2013). An exploratory study on cloud strategies. In *Americas Conference on Information Systems (AMCIS)*, Vol. 19.

Heinrich, L. J., Heinzl, A., & Riedl, R. (2011). *Wirtschaftsinformatik: Einführung Und Grundlegung* (4th ed.). Berlin: Springer.

Heinzl, A. (1993). *Die Ausgliederung Der Betrieblichen Datenverarbeitung* (2nd ed.). Stuttgart: Schäffer-Poeschel Verlag.

Helfat, C. E., & Peteraf, M. A. (2003). The dynamic resource-based view: Capability lifecycles. *Strategic Management Journal, 24*(10), 997–1010.

Henderson, J. C., & Venkatraman, N. (1993). Strategic alignment: Leveraging information technology for transforming organizations. *IBM Systems Journal, 32*(1), 472–484.

Herath, T., & Kishore, R. (2009). Offshore outsourcing: Risks, challenges, and potential solutions. *Information Systems Management, 26*(4), 312–326.

Horbach, J., Rammer, C., & Rennings, K. (2012). Determinants of eco-innovations by type of environmental impact—The role of regulatory push/pull, technology push and market pull. *Ecological Economics, 78*, 112–122.

Houdeshel, G., & Watson, H. J. (1987). The management information and decision support (MIDS) system at Lockheed-Georgia. *MIS Quarterly, 11*(1), 127–141.

Howell, D. C. (2013). *Statistical methods for psychology* (8th ed.). Belmont: Wadsworth.

Hsieh, P. H., & Huang, C. L. (2012). A study of effectiveness and satisfaction of cloud CRM users in Taiwan's enterprises. In *International Conference on Information Systems (ICIS)*.

Hustad, E., & Olsen, D. H. (2011). Exploring the ERP pre-implementation process in a small-and-medium-sized enterprise: A case study of a Norwegian retail company. In *European Conference on Information Systems (ECIS)*.

Janssen, J., & Laatz, W. (2003). *Statistische Datenanalyse Mit SPSS Für Windows* (4th ed.). Berlin: Springer.

Jayatilaka, B., Schwarz, A., & Hirschheim, R. (2003). Determinants of ASP choice: An integrated perspective. *European Journal of Information Systems, 12*(3), 210–224.

Johnson, E. M. (1972). The Fisher-Yates exact test and unequal sample sizes. *Psychometrika, 37*(1), 103–106.

Jones, M. R., & Karsten, H. (2008). Giddens's structuration theory and information systems research. *MIS Quarterly, 32*(1), 127–157.

Kateri, M. (2010). *Contingency table analysis: Methods and implementation using R*. New York, NY: Springer Science + Business Media.

Kearns, G. S., & Lederer, A. L. (2003). A resource-based view of strategic IT alignment: How knowledge sharing creates competitive advantage. *Decision Sciences, 34*(1), 1–29.

Keil, M., & Tiwana, A. (2006). Relative importance of evaluation criteria for enterprise systems: A conjoint study. *Information Systems Journal, 16*(3), 237–262.

Kern, T. (1997). The gestalt of an information technology outsourcing relationship: An exploratory analysis. In *International Conference on Information Systems (ICIS)*.

Kern, T., Kreijger, J., & Willcocks, L. (2002a). Exploring ASP as sourcing strategy: Theoretical perspectives, propositions for practice. *The Journal of Strategic Information Systems, 11*(2), 153–177.

Kern, T., Willcocks, L. P., & Lacity, M. C. (2002b). Application service provisioning: Risk assessment and mitigation. *MIS Quarterly Executive, 1*(2), 113–126.

Kim, J. W., & Park, S. C. (2010). Outsourcing strategy in two-stage call centers. *Computers & Operations Research, 37*(4), 790–805.

Kim, D. J., Yue, K. B., Hall, S. P., & Gates, T. (2009). Global diffusion of the internet XV: Web 2.0 technologies, principles, and applications: A conceptual framework from technology push and demand pull perspective. *Communications of the Association for Information Systems, 24*, 657–672.

Kirsch, L. J. (2004). Deploying common systems globally: The dynamics of control. *Information Systems Research, 15*(4), 374–395.

Kishore, R., Agrawal, M., & Rao, H. R. (2004). Determinants of sourcing during technology growth and maturity: An empirical study of E-commerce sourcing. *Journal of Management Information Systems, 21*(3), 47–82.

Kitchenham, B., Brereton, O. P., Budgen, D., Turner, M., Bailey, J., & Linkman, S. (2009). Systematic literature reviews in software engineering—A systematic literature review. *Information and Software Technology, 51*(1), 7–15.

Klein, K. J., Dansereau, F., & Hall, R. J. (1994). Levels issues in theory development, data collection, and analysis. *Academy of Management Review, 19*(2), 195–229.

Klein, K. J., Tosi, H., & Cannella, A. A. (1999). Multilevel theory building: Benefits, barriers, and new developments. *Academy of Management Review, 24*(2), 248–253.

Koehler, P., Anandasivam, A., Dan, M. A., & Weinhardt, C. (2010). Customer heterogeneity and tariff biases in cloud computing. In *International Conference on Information Systems (ICIS)*.

Koh, C., Ang, S., & Straub, D. W. (2004). IT outsourcing success: A psychological contract perspective. *Information Systems Research, 15*(4), 356–373.

Kohli, R., & Devaraj, S. (2003). Measuring information technology payoff: A meta-analysis of structural variables in firm-level empirical research. *Information Systems Research, 14*(2), 127–145.

Koslowski, T., & Strüker, J. (2011). ERP-on-demand-plattform: Komplementäreffekte Am Beispiel Eines Nachhaltigkeits-Benchmarking-Dienstes. *Wirtschaftsinformatik, 53*(6), 347–356.

Kumar, N., Stern, L. W., & Anderson, J. C. (1993). Conducting interorganizational research using key informants. *Academy of Management Journal, 36*(6), 1633–1651.

Lacity, M. C., Khan, S., & Willcocks, L. P. (2009). A review of the it outsourcing literature: Insights for practice. *The Journal of Strategic Information Systems, 18*(3), 130–146.

Lacity, M. C., Khan, S., Yan, A., & Willcocks, L. P. (2010). A review of the it outsourcing empirical literature and future research directions. *Journal of Information Technology, 25*(4), 395–433.

Lacity, M. C., Reynolds, P., Khan, S., & Willcocks, L. P. (2013). Outsourcing cloud services: The great equalizer for SMEs? In *Forth international conference on the outsourcing of information systems (ICOIS)*.

Lacity, M. C., Solomon, S., Yan, A., & Willcocks, L. P. (2011). Business process outsourcing studies: A critical review and research directions. *Journal of Information Technology, 26*(4), 221–258.

Lacity, M. C., & Willcocks, L. P. (1998). An empirical investigation of information technology sourcing practices: Lessons from experience. *MIS Quarterly, 22*(3), 363–408.

Lacity, M. C., & Willcocks, L. P. (2001). *Global information technology outsourcing: In search of business advantage*. New York: Wiley.

Lacity, M. C., & Willcocks, L. P. (2013). Strange bedfellows no more: Researching business process outsourcing and dynamic innovation. In *Forth international conference on the outsourcing of information systems (ICOIS)*.

Langley, A. (1999). Strategies for theorizing from process data. *Academy of Management Review, 24*(4), 691.

Lee, J., & Kim, Y. G. (1999). Effect of partnership quality on IS outsourcing success: Conceptual framework and empirical validation. *Journal of Management Information Systems, 15*(4), 29–61.

Lee, J., Miranda, S. M., & Kim, Y. M. (2004). IT outsourcing strategies: Universalistic, contingency, and configurational explanations of success. *Information Systems Research, 15*(2), 110–131.

Lehmann, S., & Buxmann, P. (2009). Pricing strategies of software vendors. *Business & Information Systems Engineering, 1*(6), 452–462.

Lin, A. C. (1998). Bridging positivist and interpretivist approaches to qualitative methods. *Policy Studies Journal, 26*(1), 162–180.

Lin, A., & Chen, N. C. (2012). Cloud computing as an innovation: Percepetion, attitude, and adoption. *International Journal of Information Management, 32*(2012), 533–540.

Lo, H., Bartels, A., Daley, E., & Muteba, C. (2009). The state of enterprise IT budgets: 2009. Forrester Research.

Lu, Y., & Ramamurthy, K. (2010). Proactive or reactive IT leaders? A test of two competing hypotheses of IT innovation and environment alignment. *European Journal of Information Systems, 19*(5), 601–618.

Luftman, J., & Ben-Zvi, T. (2010). Key issues for IT executives 2009: Difficult economy's impact on IT. *MIS Quarterly Executive, 9*(1), 49–59.

Luftman, J. N., Zadeh, H. S., Derksen, B., Santana, M., Rigoni, E. H., & (David) Huang, Z. (2013). Key information technology and management issues 2012–2013: An international study. *Journal of Information Technology, 28*(4), 354–366.

Luo, W., & Strong, D. (2004). A framework for evaluating ERP implementation choices. *IEEE Transactions on Engineering Management, 51*(3), 322–333.

Madill, A., Jordan, A., & Shirley, C. (2000). Objectivity and reliability in qualitative analysis: Realist, contextualist and radical constructionist epistemologies. *British Journal of Psychology, 91*(1), 1–20.

Mahnke, V., Overby, M. L., & Vang, J. (2005). Strategic outsourcing of IT services: Theoretical stocktaking and empirical challenges. *Industry and Innovation, 12*(2), 205–253.

Malladi, S., & Krishnan, M. (2012a). Cloud computing adoption and its implications for CIO focus—An empirical analysis. In *International conference on information systems (ICIS)* (pp. 1–19).

Malladi, S., & Krishnan, M. (2012b). Does software-as-a-service (SaaS) has a role in IT-enabled innovation? An empirical analysis. In *Americas Conference on Information Systems (AMCIS)*. Retrieved February 28, 2014, from http://aisel.aisnet.org/amcis2012/proceedings/EnterpriseSystems/17/.

Maltz, E., & Kohli, A. K. (1996). Market intelligence dissemination across functional boundaries. *Journal of Marketing Research, 33*(1), 47–61.

Markus, M. L., & Robey, D. (1988). Information technology and organizational change: Causal structure in theory and research. *Management Science, 34*(5), 583–599.

Mata, F. J., Fuerst, W. L., & Barney, J. B. (1995). Information technology and sustained competitive advantage: A resource-based analysis. *MIS Quarterly, 19*(4), 487–506.

Matzke, P., McCarthy, J. C., Daley, E., Radcliffe, E., & Muteba, C. (2009). The state of enterprise IT services: 2009. Forrester Research.

Maurer, C., Berente, N., & Goodhue, D. (2012). Are enterprise system related misfits always a bad thing? In *Hawaii International Conference on System Sciences (HICSS)* (pp. 4652–4661).

McKeen, J. D., & Smith, H. (2006). *Making IT happen: Critical issues in IT management.* Chichester: Wiley.

McLaren, T. S., Head, M. M., Yuan, Y., & Chan, Y. E. (2011). A multilevel model for measuring fit between a firm's competitive strategies and information system capabilities. *MIS Quarterly, 35*(4), 371–403.

Melville, N., Kraemer, K., & Gurbaxani, V. (2004). Review: Information technology and organizational performance: An integrated model of IT business value. *MIS Quarterly, 28*(2), 283–322.

Merz, S., Eschinger, C., Eid, T., Pang, C., & Wurster, L. (2011). Forecast: Software as a service, worldwide, 2010–2015, 1h11 update. Gartner Research.

Miles, M. B., & Huberman, M. A. (1994). *Qualitative data analysis: An expanded sourcebook.* Thousand Oaks, CA: Sage.

Mingers, J., Mutch, A., & Willcocks, L. (2013). Critical realism in information systems research. *MIS Quarterly, 37*(3), 795–802.

Mintzberg, H. (1987). The strategy concept I: Five Ps for strategy. *California Management Review, 30*(1), 11–24.

Mithas, S., Ramasubbu, N., & Sambamurthy, V. (2011). How information management capability influences firm performance. *MIS Quarterly, 35*(1), 237–256.

Mittal, N., & Nault, B. R. (2009). Research note—Investments in information technology: Indirect effects and information technology intensity. *Information Systems Research, 20*(1), 140–154.

Mohr, L. B. (1982). *Explaining organizational behavior.* San Francisco: Jossey-Bass.

Mojsilović, A., Ray, B., Lawrence, R., & Takriti, S. (2007). A logistic regression framework for information technology outsourcing lifecycle management. *Computers & Operations Research, 34*(12), 3609–3627.

Mooney, J. G., Gurbaxani, V., & Kraemer, K. L. (1996). A process oriented framework for assessing the business value of information technology. *ACM SIGMIS Database, 27*(2), 68–81.

Murphy, N. (1990). Scientific realism and postmodern philosophy. *The British Journal for the Philosophy of Science, 41*(3), 291–303.

Murray, J. Y., Kotabe, M., & Westjohn, S. A. (2009). Global sourcing strategy and performance of knowledge-intensive business services: A two-stage strategic fit model. *Journal of International Marketing, 17*(4), 90–105.

Myers, M. D. (2009). *Qualitative research in business & management* (1st ed.). London: Sage.

Nidumolu, S. (1995). The effect of coordination and uncertainty on software project performance: Residual performance risk as an intervening variable. *Information Systems Research, 6*(3), 191–219.

Niemann, F. (2013). ERP Aus Der Cloud Kommt Langsam in Fahrt. *Computerwoche* (51–52), 14–15.

Nissen, M. E., & Burton, R. M. (2011). Designing organizations for dynamic fit: System stability, maneuverability, and opportunity loss. *IEEE Transactions on Systems, Man, and Cybernetics Part A: Systems and Humans, 41*(3), 418–433.

Nöhren, M., & Heinzl, A. (2012). Relative efficiency of IT outsourcing global delivery models: A resource-based perspective. In *European Conference on Information Systems (ECIS)*.

Nöhren, M., Heinzl, A., Kramer, T., Kude, T., & Kurasov, P. (2013). IT global delivery model efficiency: An exploratory case study to identify input and output factors. In J. Kotlarsky, I. Oshri, & L. Willcocks (Eds.), *Advances in global sourcing: Models, governance and relationships* (pp. 1–17). Berlin: Springer.

Nöhren, M., Heinzl, A., & Kude, T. (2014). Structural and behavioral fit in software sourcing alignment. In *47th Hawaii Conference on System Sciences (HICSS)* (pp. 3949–3958).

Orlikowski, W. J. (1993). CASE tools as organizational change: Investigating incremental and radical changes in systems development. *MIS Quarterly, 17*(3), 309–340.

Orlikowski, W. J., & Baroudi, J. J. (1991). Studying information technology in organizations: Research approaches and assumptions. *Information Systems Research, 2*(1), 1–28.

Oxford Dictionaries. (2014a). Cluster. Retrieved December 26, 2014, from http://www.oxforddictionaries.com/definition/english/cluster.

Oxford Dictionaries. (2014b). Process. Retrieved September 24, 2014, from http://www.oxforddictionaries.com/definition/english/process.

Oxford Dictionaries. (2014c). Value. Retrieved September 24, 2014, from http://www.oxforddictionaries.com/definition/english/value.

Parameswaran, M., & Whinston, A. B. (2007). Research issues in social computing. *Journal of the Association for Information Systems, 8*(6), 336–350.

Patton, M. Q. (2002). *Qualitative research and evaluation methods* (3rd ed.). Thousand Oaks, CA: Sage.

Pentland, B. T. (1999). Building process theory with narrative: From description to explanation. *Academy of Management Review, 24*(4), 711.

Pfeffer, J., & Salancik, G. R. (1978). *The external control of organizations: A resource dependence perspective*. New York: Harper & Row.

Poole, M. S., Van de Ven, A. H., Dooley, K., & Holmes, M. E. (2000). *Organizational change and innovation processes*. New York: Oxford University Press.

Powell, T. C. (1992). Organizational alignment as competitive advantage. *Strategic Management Journal, 13*(2), 119–134.

Powers, D. A., & Xie, Y. (2008). *Statistical methods for categorical data analysis* (2nd ed.). Bingley: Emerald Group.

Preston, D. S., & Karahanna, E. (2008). Antecedents of IS strategic alignment: A nomological network. *Information Systems Research, 20*(2), 159–179.

Racine, J., & Li, Q. (2004). Nonparametric estimation of regression functions with both categorical and continuous data. *Journal of Econometrics, 119*(1), 99–130.

Rammer, C., & Köhler, C. (2012). Innovationsverhalten Der Unternehmen in Deutschland 2010. Mannheim.

Rammer, C., & Ohnemus, J. (2011). *Innovationsleistung Und Innovationsbeiträge Der Telekommunikation in Deutschland*.

Ranganathan, C., & Brown, C. V. (2006). ERP investments and the market value of firms: Toward an understanding of influential ERP project variables. *Information Systems Research, 17*(2), 145–161.

Ravishankar, M. N., Pan, S. L., & Leidner, D. E. (2011). Examining the strategic alignment and implementation success of a KMS: A subculture-based multilevel analysis. *Information Systems Research, 22*(1), 39–59.

Reich, B. H., & Benbasat, I. (2000). Factors that influence the social dimension of alignment between business and information technology objectives. *MIS Quarterly, 24*(1), 81–113.

Reitzig, M., & Wagner, S. (2010). The hidden costs of outsourcing: Evidence from patent data. *Strategic Management Journal, 1201*(February), 1183–1201.

Robey, D., & Farrow, D. (1982). User involvement in information system development: A conflict model and empirical test. *Management Science, 28*(1), 73–85.

Roeder, F. C., & Labrie, Y. (2012). *The private sector within a public health care system: The German example.* Retrieved August 25, 2014, from http://www.researchgate.net/publication/230710592_The_private_sector_within_a_public_health_care_system_the_German_example/file/79e41503548c25c406.pdf.

Sabherwal, R., Hirschheim, R., & Goles, T. (2001). The dynamics of alignment: Insights from a punctuated equilibrium model. *Organization Science, 12*(2), 179–197.

Sabherwal, R., & Robey, D. (1995). Reconciling variance and process strategies for studying information system development. *Information Systems Research, 6*(4), 303–327.

Sarker, S., Sahaym, A., & Bjørn-Andersen, N. (2012). Exploring value cocreation in relationships between an ERP vendor and its partners: A revelatory case study. *MIS Quarterly, 36*(1), 317–338.

Saunders, C., Gebelt, M., & Hu, Q. (1997). Achieving success in information systems outsourcing. *California Management Review, 39*(2), 63–80.

Sawyer, S. (2000). Packaged software: Implications of the differences from custom approaches to software development. *European Journal of Information Systems, 9*(1), 47–58.

Schryen, G. (2010). Preserving knowledge on is business value—What literature reviews have done. *Business & Information Systems Engineering, 2*(4), 233–244.

Schumacher, M., & Schulgen-Kristiansen, G. (2002). *Methoden Klinischer Studien: Methodische Grundlagen Der Planung, Durchführung Und Auswertung.* Heidelberg: Springer.

Schwarz, A., Jayatilaka, B., Hischheim, R., & Goles, T. (2009). A conjoint approach to understanding IT application services outsourcing. *Journal of the Association for Information Systems, 10*(10), 748–781.

Scott, W. R. (1987). The adolescence of institutional theory. *Administrative Science Quarterly, 32*(4), 493–511.

Scott, J. E. (1999). The FoxMeyer drugs' bankruptcy: Was it a failure of ERP? In *Americas Conference on Information Systems (AMCIS)* (pp. 223–225).

Shang, S., & Seddon, P. B. (2000). A comprehensive framework for classifying the benefits of ERP systems. In *Americas Conference on Information Systems (AMCIS)*.

Shang, S., & Seddon, P. B. (2002). Assessing and managing the benefits of enterprise systems: The business manager's perspective. *Information Systems Journal, 12*(4), 271–299.

Shang, S., & Seddon, P. B. (2003). A comprehensive framework for assessing and managing the benefits of enterprise systems: The business manager's perspective. In G. Shanks, P. B. Seddon, & L. P. Willcocks (Eds.), *Second-wave enterprise resource planning systems—Implementing for effectiveness* (pp. 74–101). New York: Cambridge University Press.

Shepherd, D. A., & Sutcliffe, K. M. (2011). Inductive top-down theorizing: A source of new theories of organization. *Academy of Management Review, 36*(2), 361–380.

Sia, S., Koh, C., & Tan, C. X. (2008). Strategic maneuvers for outsourcing flexibility: An empirical assessment. *Decision Sciences, 39*(3), 407–443.

Sia, S., & Soh, C. (2002). Severity assessment of ERP-organization misalignment: Honing in on ontological structure and context specificity. *International Conference on Information Systems (ICIS), 23*, 723–29.

Sia, S., & Soh, C. (2007). An assessment of package–organisation misalignment: Institutional and ontological structures. *European Journal of Information Systems, 16*(5), 568–583.

Simonoff, J. S. (2003). *Analyzing categorical data*. New York: Springer Science + Business Media.

Slaughter, S. A., & Levine, L. (2006). Aligning software processes with strategy. *MIS Quarterly, 30*(4), 891–918.

Soh, C., & Markus, M. L. (1995). How IT creates business value: A process theory synthesis. In *International Conference on Information Systems (ICIS)*.

Soh, C., & Sia, S. (2004). An institutional perspective on sources of ERP package–organisation misalignments. *The Journal of Strategic Information Systems, 13*(4), 375–397.

Son, J., & Benbasat, I. (2007). Organizational buyers' adoption and use of B2B electronic marketplaces: Efficiency- and legitimacy-oriented perspectives. *Journal of Management Information Systems, 24*(1), 55–99.

Strong, D. M., & Volkoff, O. (2010). Understanding organization-enterprise system fit: A path to theorizing the information technology artifact. *MIS Quarterly, 34*(4), 731–756.

Stuckenberg, S., Fielt, E., & Loser, T. (2011). The impact of software-as-a-service on business models of leading software vendors: Experiences from three exploratory case studies. In *Pacific-Asia Conference on Information Systems (PACIS)*.

Suh, A., Shin, K., Ahuja, M., & Kim, M. S. (2011). The influence of virtuality on social networks within and across work groups: A multilevel approach. *Journal of Management Information Systems, 28*(1), 351–386.

Susarla, A., Barua, A., & Whinston, A. B. (2003). Understanding the service component of application service provision: Empirical analysis of satisfaction with ASP services. *MIS Quarterly, 27*(1), 91–123.

Susarla, A., Barua, A., & Whinston, A. B. (2009). A transaction cost perspective of the 'software as a service' business model. *Journal of Management Information Systems, 26*(2), 205–240.

Susarla, A., Barua, A., & Whinston, A. B. (2010). Multitask agency, modular architecture, and task disaggregation in SaaS. *Journal of Management Information Systems, 26*(4), 87–118.

Swanson, E. B. (1994). Information systems innovation among organizations. *Management Science, 40*(9), 1069–1092.

Swanson, E. B., & Ramiller, N. C. (2004). Innovating mindfully with information technology. *MIS Quarterly, 28*(4), 553–583.

Takane, Y., & Zhou, L. (2013). Anatomy of Pearson's chi-square statistic in three-way contingency tables. In R. E. Millsap, L. A. van der Ark, D. M. Bolt, & C. M. Woods (Eds.), *New developments in quantitative psychology: Springer proceedings in mathematics & statistics* (Vol. 66, pp. 41–57). New York: Springer.

Tallon, P. (2007). A process-oriented perspective on the alignment of information technology and business strategy. *Journal of Management Information Systems, 24*(3), 227–268.

Tallon, P., Kraemer, K. L., & Gurbaxani, V. (2000). Executives' perceptions of the business value of information technology: A process-oriented approach. *Journal of Management Information Systems, 16*(4), 145–173.

Tallon, P., & Pinsonneault, A. (2011). Competing perspectives on the link between strategic information technology alignment and organizational agility: Insights from a mediation model. *MIS Quarterly, 35*(2), 463–486.

Tan, F. B., & Gallupe, R. B. (2006). Aligning business and information systems thinking: A cognitive approach. *IEEE Transactions on Engineering Management, 53*(2), 223–237.

Tanriverdi, H., Konana, P., & Ge, L. (2007). The choice of sourcing mechanisms for business processes. *Information Systems Research, 18*(3), 280–299.

Tatikonda, M. V., & Montoya-Weiss, M. M. (2001). Integrating operations and marketing perspectives of product innovation: The influence of organizational process factors and capabilities on development performance. *Management Science, 47*(1), 151–172.

Teece, D. J. (1986). Profiting from technological innovation: Implications for integration, collaboration, licensing and public policy. *Research Policy, 15*(February), 285–305.

Tiwana, A., & Keil, M. (2009). Control in internal and outsourced software projects. *Journal of Management Information Systems, 26*(3), 9–44.

Tsuang, M. T., Tohen, M., & Jones, P. (2011). *Textbook of psychiatric epidemiology* (3rd ed.). Chichester: Wiley-Blackwell.

Van der Heijden, H. (2004a). Measuring IT core capabilities for electronic commerce: Results from a confirmatory factor analysis. *MIS Quarterly, 28*(4), 695–704.

Van der Heijden, H. (2004b). User acceptance of hedonic information systems. *MIS Quarterly, 28* (4), 695–704.

Van de Ven, A. H., & Huber, G. P. (1990). Longitudinal field research methods for studying processes of organizational change. *Organization Science, 1*(3), 213–219.

Venkatraman, N. (1989). The concept of fit in strategy research: Toward verbal and statistical correspondence. *Academy of Management Review, 14*(3), 423–444. Retrieved March 6, 2014, from http://amr.aom.org/content/14/3/423.short.

Venters, W., & Whitley, E. (2012). A critical review of cloud computing: Researching desires and realities. *Journal of Information Technology, 27*(3), 179–197.

Verma, J. P. (2013). *Data analysis in management with SPSS software*. New Delhi: Springer.

Vessey, I., & Ward, K. (2013). The dynamics of sustainable IS alignment: The case for IS adaptivity. *Journal of the Association for Information Systems, 14*(6), 283–311.

Volkoff, O., & Strong, D. M. (2013). Critical realism and affordances: Theorizing IT-associated organizational change processes. *MIS Quarterly, 37*(3), 819–834.

Wade, M., & Hulland, J. (2004). Review: The resource-based view and information systems research: Review, extension, and suggestions for future research. *MIS Quarterly, 28*(1), 107–142.

Walden, E. A. (2005). Intellectual property rights and cannibalization in information technology outsourcing contracts. *MIS Quarterly, 29*(4), 699–720.

Walther, S., Plank, A., Eymann, T., Singh, N., & Phadke, G. (2012). Success factors and value propositions of software as a service providers—A literature review and classification. In *Americas Conference on Information Systems (AMCIS)*.

Wand, Y., & Weber, R. (1990). Toward a theory of the deep structure of information systems. In *International Conference on Information Systems (ICIS)* (pp. 61–71).

Wand, Y., & Weber, R. (1995). On the deep structure of information systems. *Information Systems Journal, 5*(3), 203–233.

Wand, Y., & Weber, R. (2002). Research commentary: Information systems and conceptual modeling—A research agenda. *Information Systems Research, 13*(4), 363–376.

Wang, E. (2002). Transaction attributes and software outsourcing success: An empirical investigation of transaction cost theory. *Information Systems Journal, 12*(2), 153–181.

Wang, L., Gwebu, K. L., Wang, J., & Zhu, D. X. (2008a). The aftermath of information technology outsourcing: An empirical study of firm performance following outsourcing decisions. *Journal of Information Systems, 22*(1), 125–159.

Wang, E., Ju, P., Jiang, J. J., & Klein, G. (2008b). The effects of change control and management review on software flexibility and project performance. *Information & Management, 45*(7), 438–443.

Wang, E., Tai, J., & Wei, H. (2006). A virtual integration theory of improved supply-chain performance. *Journal of Management Information Systems, 23*(2), 41–64.

Weber, R. (2012). Evaluating and developing theories in the information systems discipline. *Journal of the Association for Information Systems, 13*(1), 1–30.

Webster, J., & Watson, R. T. (2002). Analyzing the past to prepare for the future: Writing a literature review. *MIS Quarterly, 26*(2), xiii–xxiii.

Weisberg, R. W., & Reeves, L. M. (2013). *Cognition—From memory to creativity*. Hoboken, NJ: Wiley.

Wertheimer, M. (1923). Laws of organization in perceptual forms. Edited by W. Ellis (1938) A source book of gestalt psychology (pp. 71–88). First published as Untersuchungen zur Lehre von der Gestalt II, in Psycologische Forschung, 4, 301–350. Translation published in Ellis. London: Routledge & Kegan Paul.

Willcocks, L. P., Kern, T., & van Heck, E. (2002). The winner's curse in IT outsourcing: Strategies for avoiding relational trauma. *California Management Review, 44*(2), 47–70.

Williamson, O. E. (1973). Markets and hierarchies: Some elementary considerations. *The American Economic Review, 5*(61), 316–325.

Williamson, O. E. (1979). Transaction-cost economics: The governance of contractual relations. *Journal of Law and Economics, 22*(2), 233–261.

Williamson, O. E. (1998). Transaction cost economics: How it works; where it is headed. *De Economist, 146*(1), 23–58.

Winkler, J. (2009). *International entry mode choices of software firms: An analysis of product-specific determinants*. Frankfurt: Peter Lang Verlag.

Winkler, T., & Benlian, A. (2012). The dual role of IS specificity in governing software as a service. In *International conference on information systems (ICIS)*.

Winkler, T., & Brown, C. (2014). Horizontal allocation of decision rights for on-premise applications and software-as-a-service. *Journal of Management Information Systems, 30*(3), 13–48.

Winkler, T., Goebel, C., Benlian, A., Bidault, F., & Günther, O. (2011). The impact of software as a service on IS authority—A contingency perspective. In *Thirty second international conference on information systems (ICIS)*.

Xin, M., & Levina, N. (2008). Software-as-a service model: Elaborating client-side adoption factors. In *International conference on information systems (ICIS)*.

Yang, J., & Papazoglou, M. P. (2000). Interoperation support for electronic business. *Communications of the ACM, 43*(6), 39–47.

Yang, H., & Tate, M. (2012). A descriptive literature review and classification of cloud computing research. *Communications of the Association for Information Systems, 31*(2), 35–60.

Yin, R. K. (2009). *Case study research—Design and methods* (4th ed.). Thousand Oaks, CA: Sage.

Zajac, E. J., Kraatz, M. S., & Bresser, R. K. F. (2000). Modeling the dynamics of strategic fit: A normative approach to strategic change. *Strategic Management Journal, 21*(4), 429–453.

Zar, J. H. (1987). A fast and efficient algorithm for the fisher exact test. *Behavior Research Methods, Instruments, & Computers, 19*(4), 413–414.

Zhang, J., & Seidmann, A. (2010). Perpetual versus subscription licensing under quality uncertainty and network externality effects. *Journal of Management Information Systems, 27*(1), 39–68.